Red Dust Over
SHANGHAI

A Shanghai—New Zealand Memoir 1937–1954

Red Dust Over
SHANGHAI

TYL VON RANDOW

EUNOIA
PUBLISHING

First Edition published by Eunoia Publishing (NZ) 2016.
Tyl von Randow asserts his moral right to be identified as the author of this work.

ISBN-13 978-0-9941047-7-9

A catalogue record for this book is available from the National Library of New Zealand.

Eunoia Publishing
www.eunoiapublishing.com

Eunoia Publishing Limited
PO Box 33890 Takapuna
Auckland 0740
New Zealand
Level 13, WHK Tower
51-53 Shortland St
Auckland 1140
New Zealand

Copyright © 2016 Tyl von Randow
Book design by Karl von Randow
Cover design by Matthew Buchanan
Title fonts: Domaine Display Narrow and Domaine Sans Text by Kris Sowersby, Klim Type Foundry, New Zealand

Printed in China through Asia Pacific Offset Ltd

22 21 20 19 18 17 16 APOL 10 9 8 7 6 5 4 3 2 1

For my children
Daniel
Hanna
Karl
and
Martin
whose childhoods tossed
on the ripples of my own

and
Jonas
who died after a heart operation
aged two days.

Contents

Words of thanks

Thanks, Martin, for giving me your MacBook and entering into it the reams of hand-corrected copy from my Olivetti. Thanks, Karl, for your participation and judgment and for the countless hours you put into creating my first pdf. Daniel, for your acuitous observations on reading the manuscript and Hanna for your far-reaching interventions when I was about to panic.

My thanks, no less, to you, Judith White, Fiona Farrell, Margaret Harraway and Jo Ffowcs Williams, for reading the manuscript and giving me your personal and professional feedback. Your thoughts have actively helped to shape the work.

Nor any less do I thank you, my friends, who sat still and listened when I read to you from freshly handwritten pages— and still encouraged me to go on writing.

And I thank you, Rebecca Isaac, for getting me started. You, who left school when you were fifteen and who, twenty-five years later, wheeled yourself along accessible university corridors to attend courses. You will remember interviewing me on my Shanghai childhood for an assignment on gender studies. You listened as I revisited that childhood for the first time in half a century. Your assignment got top marks. The following year I started this book.

Finally, I thank the team at Eunoia Publishing for insisting on the highest standards and inviting me to be an author under the compass of the flying giraffe.

Tyl von Randow
Bethells Beach
New Zealand

A peek behind the curtain

This book is a memoir. I have put it together from the memories of my own childhood 60-70 years ago. I have been careful of those memories, with the past still clinging to them like a fine dust. Memories of my living days and my dreams.

They have let me back in, like very old friends, so that I could see again the spiral pattern of the sea shell, hear the sound of rails, smell the freshness of Quickies, feel the storm-trooper's whistle on my lips, Wölfi's breath in my face, the pain in Amah's eyes.

They have let me into the houses I have known and into the rooms and back stairs and classrooms and gardens; and they have let me look into the eyes of all the people who were there and see the unmistakable tilt of the head when they laughed or scorned. They have let me hear again the honeydew and the chaff of their voices. And, if I have put words into people's mouths to lift them off the page, every one of those words truly speaks for them.

The purpose in exploring memories is a personal one, very old friends that they are. And they command respect. In writing them as a memoir, I am making them public and fragile. There is a purpose in that, too: to see if they've got wings. You, dear reader, will be the only judge of that. Apart from anything else, writing them down has given me the sheer enjoyment of telling what Sir Laurence Olivier, speaking about *Hamlet*, once called *a rattling good yarn*.

My heart leaps up when I behold
    A rainbow in the sky:
So was it when my life began;
So is it now I am a man;
So be it when I shall grow old,
    Or let me die!
The Child is father of the Man;
And I could wish my days to be
Bound each to each by natural piety.

William Wordsworth

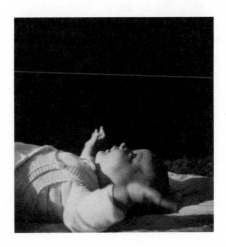

Remembering
AMAH

Red Dust Over Shanghai

The beginning more far

One by one, the lights come up behind the curtain and with each one a new shadow falls. The shape is always my mother's. There are four of them now, huddling together. They overlap in shades of grey. The huddle covers half the curtain. It shifts from one side to the other with sudden movements. Then, dead centre, yet another shadow appears, ghost-like at first, wavering, becoming still. Mami has just lit the *Lebenskerze*, the candle for the whole of life. She pulls back the curtain. It stands alight, tall and waxy, in the hole in the centre of the *Marmorkuchen*, my birthday cake. Four smaller candles burn in a diamond around its base.

"Didi, come." Amah holds my hand and I take the two steps up onto the stage. Hasi crosses to where Mami stands and the three of them watch as I gaze at the presents. The candlelight closes them in for me. This is *my* day.

The scissors with the rounded tips had been first on my wish list. I burned my arm and knocked over a candle as I reached for them. A spatter of red candlewax indelibly marked the tablecloth for every birthday to come. But it missed the pad of coloured paper with its glossy leaves of purple, green and gold. Mami re-lit the candle. Amah blew on my arm. An amber glint outlined the bottle of gum Arabic with its fleshy pink snout, the slit not yet cut. Hasi wanted to pierce it with the scissors and I had to snatch them from him. Hasi was my big brother. That was his nickname. I was the little brother and everyone called me Didi. The girl between us died the day she was born and I inherited her baby clothes. "Pink suits you," Mami often told me. "I think you should have been a girl."

The wooden box with the shiny metal handle was from Daddi. He wasn't there. He worked. On the lid was a picture of Minnie Mouse. I would recognise her some years later when the American comics came. Mami thought it was a silly picture. She also thought it spoiled the natural beauty of the wood. The box had compartments inside. I placed the scissors into one of the compartments and ran upstairs to get my coloured pencils and my rubber to go in the other compartments. The paper pad wouldn't fit and I closed the lid and placed the pad on top of Minnie Mouse and the gum Arabic on top of that.

Amah stood beside me. She was beaming. Her white teeth matched her cotton smock. I looked up into her face. Very brown it was, for a Chinese, with full lips. "Happy birthday, Didi," she said and held up a pair of slippers, new-smelling, with flat leather soles and purple caps for the toes. They were embroidered with a bird and blossoms and shiny green leaves. I remembered Amah tracing the outlines of my feet and I had wondered about it but said nothing. I pulled off my shoes and socks and slid my feet into my new slippers. Amah watched.

"Can I have some cake now?" I said.

"You'll have to blow out the candles first," Mami said.

"This is how you do it," Hasi said. He wet his fingers between his lips and pinched out the flames. I was awed. He never even got burnt.

"Thank you for all the presents," I said to no one in particular. Mami's hands squeezed my shoulders. "Now you can really get to work," she said.

The stage opened into the sitting room with its beamed ceiling. Mami always said they weren't real beams, just fake. *Unecht*, she called them. The German word bites deep. It pulls off your covers and prods at your core. I looked at the beams with a mixture of disgust and self-pity.

In an alcove to the side of the stage Daddi had his Telefunken gramophone. No one was allowed to touch it. Underneath there was a cupboard full of records. I never took them out of their sleeves, but loved the labels that showed through the hole in the middle. Some were red, with a white dog and a kind of trumpet. I liked those the best. Mami told me she'd come downstairs one night because the music was very loud. She had found Daddi standing on a chair, waving a chopstick. "He loved Tchaikowsky," she said and showed it with her arms, as if raising up a storm. I wanted to laugh and I thought she was going to laugh, too, but she didn't.

"Have I had a birthday before?" I asked Amah.

"Of course, when you belong three years old," she said. "But not in this house. In Tunsin Road."

"Tunsin Road?"

"You belong in Tunsin Road before you come to Columbia Circle," Amah said.

"You also?"

Amah laughed. "I all the time belong together you and Hasi. All the time."

She was right. She belonged with us all the time. "You can remember Unzen?" she said. "In the summer?"

There are photographs. Two naked boys, Hasi and me, in a shallow stream. But there is something else, too, behind the image. I can see steam rising from pools, Japanese men bulging over their jockstraps, fetid vapours escaping out of rocks, so clear, I want to tell Amah, but already they're gone. Not even the smell of sulphur remains. I said, "Did we go on a ship?"

"Yes, also to Seefeld and Jena, in the winter more far. You can remember?" There is a photo of Amah and me on a sledge in a snowy landscape. I said, "Did I fall off when we stopped?" Amah laughed. "You got a blood nose," she said. I see a spattering of red holes in the snow. "We don't come back in a ship," Amah said. "We come in a train. Long way. Many

4

many night." Snow-mantled forests go sliding by and wolves weave in and out of tree trunks. The image seems to linger, but in fact it has already vanished.

It was then that I realised that my life so far had left no memory. The whole four years of it. None of my own, anyway. I might as well have been born when those candles were lit, with a blank slate in my head. It was only the stories the grown-ups told that accounted for the time from the very beginning and the odd photos that showed they weren't making them up.

And that would have been all, except that they left a kind of afterimage, or even just an after*glow*, but it was enough to tell me they must have been real, because the afterimage was inside *my* head. It still happens to me. It's as if milliseconds of time got split off from the rest all those years ago and never made it into the ordered past. As if they're just idling around

in space, killing time, and my mind can race out there and tag them. And then they have the freshness of the original event, be it an image, a sound, a smell, or just a feeling.

That picture of me after falling off the sledge always makes it happen. It feels like hurt pride, but the boy's face (mine) is on the verge of capitulating into laughter. I can still feel the laughter trying to break through. I know I'm going to lose. The others are laughing at me and all I have left is to laugh at myself, too. That and my anger. A child's impotent rage.

There were lots of stories in the family archive and you could always tell when one was about to be pulled out. Let's say I'd just had a fight with Hasi and one of us got hurt. Wait for it. "You remember Neu-Galow?" Mami would say to me. "That's where you pushed Hasi off the balcony. He broke his leg. You just laughed." On one of the sea voyages he had climbed the ship's railing and stood on the outside of it, hanging on. "Your big brother has no sense of fear," she liked to say, feigning exasperation, showing pride. "He has a guardian angel." A fear grabs me that I might want to push him off again, if only to see if he really has one.

At dinner with our elderly host in Rausdorf, one story goes, I grabbed the bread she'd baked and flung it across the table. Probably I had aimed it at Hasi, but it hit the wall and tumbled to the floor. "Bread is the Body of Christ!" the woman said. I can still hear the thud of *His* body against the wall. And the ensuing silence.

Masserberg was the place I'm told I scribbled on the wallpaper in the hostel. I denied doing it, saying it was Hasi. Mami dragged me outside and shut me under the house as punishment. She came to the old wooden door from time to time for my confession, but I never weakened. At last I was let out because it was getting dark and the goat needed to be brought in. Amah couldn't have been there. I can't remember. The only thing that comes up is a terror of dungeons. And a feeling for goats.

On my fourth birthday, in the autumn of 1941, I started my own memory box in the back of my head. I have remembered everything ever since.

Skirmishes and diplomacy

There are photos of the house in Tunsin Road, where Amah said we'd lived. Mami and Daddi are smiling happily. I'm sitting astride the Pullman train, aged one, and Hasi is there with his hair in locks. A white wire-haired terrier prances around. Amah is there, too, just as she said. I can't remember the house or anything else.

At Columbia Circle, where we live now, there are three wire-haired terriers and all three of them are white. They are sunning themselves on the tiled floor. "Your father's crazy about them," Mami says as she circumnavigates them on her way to the potted cyclamens, a watering can in her hands. It puts them in their place, and Daddi, too. And me, come to think of it, since he's *my* father (though I didn't think of it at the time, just picked it up the way you pick up a cold). Mami had a way with words.

The terriers squatted by Daddi's chair at breakfast and he fed them sparrow bones from his plate. Boy, our number one servant, stood by. His face betrayed no censure. Mami's did, but she was sick of saying anything. Boy held out a steaming towel with a pair of tongs and Daddi had to juggle with it before he could bring it up to his face. He finished his coffee and rolled up his serviette in the silver ring with his initials on it. He was off to the consulate. His chauffeur would be waiting for him, the green 1937 Opel cabriolet idling outside the front porch.

I wondered about the consulate and couldn't picture it. Hasi was just starting school and I thought perhaps the consulate was something like school, only for grown-ups. So I asked him. "Oh no, no, no," he said. "The consulate is nothing like school. When you're old enough, you'll understand." "Bet you don't even know," I said and he said, "School is for writing and arithmetic; church is for Christmas and the angels; the consulate is for diplomatic negotiation and settlement between great nations." He must have got that from Daddi. So, one morning, I asked Daddi to tell me at first hand what he did at the consulate.

"I work," he said and put down the Sunday paper. Boy brought in breakfast. Mami sliced the top off my egg and I checked the runny yolk for bits of eggshell. I dunked pieces of bread into it and tried not to get egg on the tablecloth. Daddi ate his roasted sparrows in silence. Boy poured him the rest of the coffee and left, the swing door heaving to behind him. The terriers gagged on splintered bones.

"You *see*," Mami said, but Daddi was tapping a pill into his hand from a screw-top jar. "Elgar, don't," she said. *"Please."* She made a lunge for the jar, but he slapped his hand to his mouth and washed the pill down with coffee.

Mami grabbed me by the arm and told Hasi to follow. She had the open pill jar in her hand. She stopped as we crossed the sitting room and flung it at Daddi. It landed in his lap and disappeared in the folds of his dressing gown. Pills rained on the floor. Daddi pretended to go on reading the paper. The terriers scrambled after the pills, but only sniffed at them and went away. I was glad Boy had left the room and not witnessed the scene.

11

Daddi stood up and folded the paper under his arm. Hasi and I huddled up to Mami. As he came towards us, I thought there was a kind of laughter in his eyes, but the rest of his face remained stern. He didn't look at us. He simply walked past us across the floor, letting his slippers slap against the bare soles of his feet, slip-slap, slip-slap. It was a funny thing to do, but it made you feel sick, because you could tell it wasn't meant to be funny. We listened as he went upstairs and slip-slapped across the landing and then we heard the door shut.

Boy came in to clear up and called the coolie[1] to sweep the floor. He placed Mami's vase in the centre of the table. It was black all over and had square shoulders and a small neck with a chip off the rim, exuding antiquity. The straight-backed dining chairs gazed at it respectfully and gave off a faint scent of cedar oil.

*

1 Male servant for menial tasks. Labourer.

12

THERE WERE SIX OR SEVEN GERMAN FAMILIES living in Columbia Circle and our amahs decided among themselves in whose gardens we would spend the afternoons playing while they exchanged neighbourhood news. Some of the older boys wanted to play war games, but the war was far away and, for the time being, had no place in our fantasies. Instead, we played games of tag and hide-and-seek. We splashed about naked in the cool blue of the new swimming pool in our neighbour's garden. It was so new, we had watched it being built. Some twenty bare-backed coolies, trousers rolled up above their knees, had dug out the hole and its silty sides oozed wet slime. *Eh-ya-a-ho!* they chanted as they carried it out in buckets, day after day. Finally, against all odds, they had produced a hole big enough to build a whole bunker in. It was going to be an air raid shelter, Hasi said. Then they built the swimming pool on top of that. It was shaped like a giant's footprint and the grass sloped up to its rim. When it was freshly mown, the gardener had to skim away the clippings we'd trailed into the water on the soles of our feet. He'd shoo us out of the pool and not let us back in the water.

We went down into the bunker. The steps cut a gash between brick walls, getting colder under our feet. Darkness wrapped us in as we huddled together under the pool's dripping underside, our bodies soft and milky. We kicked up cold splashes off the concrete floor and planted wet hands on each other's warm skin, shrieking. Next day we talked our amahs into taking us swimming again, but we just slipped down into the bunker and stayed, more quietly this time and a little too long. We had even begun shivering a little, when the slot of sky filled with the clamour of amahs and they came tumbling down the steps to hustle us off to get dressed. After that the bunker was kept locked until the air raids began.

On Tuesday evenings, Daddi invited Hasi and me into his study. We had been washed and groomed and put into fresh pyjamas ready for bed. We would unfold the latest copy of BILDERDIENST, a weekly that Daddi brought home from the consulate. It was full of pictures of war planes and tanks and things. They were dark and deadly. But they were also heroic. Swastikas pranced on their tail fins and turrets. Bomb clusters fell from open hatches. The pictures scared me, but I couldn't take my eyes off them.

Then Daddi brought down the jar of dates from the top shelf. I sank my teeth into their resisting skins and asked for more. Sometimes, he had little gifts for us, like the whistle he gave me. It was a real storm-trooper's whistle. I loved its breathy sound and the feel on my lips as I closed them around the flared barrel. "Enough for now," Daddi said and tied it round my neck. When our time was up, he unscrewed the bottle by his desk and blew across its mouth. "The dreamboat is about to set sail," he would say and let the bottle sound with a far-away note of farewell.

The war must have been getting closer. Armed squadrons of Japanese marched up Amherst Avenue, the street off which Columbia Circle ran. The Chinese gathered their staring children from the footpaths and pulled them back into the narrow alleyways of Fahwha village on the far side of the street, to stare again from a safer distance between shuttered house fronts.

Dr Mengert, our family doctor, who did her rounds on a bicycle, brought news of English and American families being taken from their homes by Japanese soldiers and transported to camps. But we tagged along the streets with the older boys of our German neighbourhood, secure in the knowledge that the Japanese wouldn't touch us. They were our allies, however forbidding they might appear in their uniforms and absurdly high combat hats. "They need those hats to make them look taller to the Chinese, because they are really all quite short," Mami joked.

We began getting up to mischief. We gathered stones out of gutters and fired them over bamboo fences. When I heard glass shatter, I ran. The older boys didn't follow, but dispersed. Before I could round the corner into Columbia Circle, I saw I was being chased by the Chinese landlord who owned the glasshouses. I knew it was my stone that had hit. I raced upstairs. From my window I could see him coming up to the house. Between heartbeats I heard Amah's voice down in the street and, after a while, I saw him walking away. Amah had her own way of settling things. "I give him Daddi's pills," she told me later. "Coolie have got. He give to me." Then she placed her finger to her mouth and the wrinkles played around the corners of her eyes. "That man," she said, "he go away. Make no more trouble." And she laughed and shook until the tears ran down her face.

The older boys teased me for getting caught out and I accused them of deserting me. For all that, I let them set me up again when we went around the streets ringing doorbells and running away. No one would approach the house of the Japanese general in the back leg of Columbia Circle. But they dared me and I wanted to show my mettle. I tip-toed up the porch steps and pushed the button. I heard heavy footsteps inside and hid behind the cypresses by the porch. The others fled down the street. The front door opened and the general stepped out and looked left and right and saw me. He came thundering towards me, let off a wild battle cry and crushed me in his arms. He shook me up and down, bellowing at me in Japanese, his rank breath in my face, his yellowed teeth only inches from my nose. Then he shoved me backwards into the cypresses. He watched me scramble up and come to attention. I saluted him, the way I'd seen Japanese soldiers salute, elbow forward, my hand shielding my eyes from the rising sun.

"Where you live?" he barked and I told him. "German," he said. I nodded. He took a step forward and slapped me across the face. I didn't let him see how much it hurt. Then he wheeled around and marched back into the house.

I told no one what had happened and lied about the stripes his hand had left on my cheek. Some days later, however, at dinner, I came to realise that my story had already shot ahead of me and was waiting for me to catch it up. We were eating green peppers stuffed with rice and minced meat. I had learned to enjoy the bitter green taste of peppers (feeling pretty grown up about it) and wasn't at all prepared for the fire that filled my mouth on the first bite. The tears shot from my eyes. Mami passed me a glass of water. Daddi said, "Eat it and stop making a fuss." I only gaped and could say nothing. Mami took my plate and tried a pepper against her lips. She passed my plate to Daddi. He cut a large piece and made sure I was watching. Then he flicked it into his mouth. Sweat broke from his face. He pretended nothing was wrong and took another mouthful and swallowed it. Then he pushed the plate aside and reached for the water jug.

16

Somewhere inside, I had begun laughing, but it would have been undiplomatic to show it. Daddi must have noticed and I thought he was about to say something. When he did, he caught me off guard. "Next time you play tricks on people," he said, "make sure it isn't an officer of the Japanese supreme command. He laid a complaint against me. In the end it had to be referred to the ambassador in Chungking."

I nodded meekly. My mouth still burned and I felt chastened. Yet, at the same time, I was stirred by the fact that my little back-street skirmish had been negotiated and settled between two great nations at a high diplomatic level.

The promise

My start at Kindergarten was marred by the red outfit I wore. It had a short-sleeved jacket to which matching shorts were buttoned. It was made from a cotton twist, more like string, that Amah had knitted for me on a pair of thick needles. With it she earned herself the only demerit points in my otherwise untarnished estimation of her.

Not only did the coarse knit leave a pattern of painful indentations in my bottom, it also caused problems when I needed to unbutton my pants. Instead of passing cleanly through the holes provided for them, the buttons got caught up in the knit and, the more I tried to get them undone, the more entangled they became.

Bobbing up and down with my back to the toilet pan, I fought a losing battle. I conceded to my buttons and bowels with humiliation. A heap of screwed-up paper began to clog the bowl as I wiped my legs. I was on my knees, cleaning the floor, when I heard, *Whatever are you doing?* I tried a lie, but gave up.

In fresh clothes reserved for cases like mine, I was sent to stand in the corner of the classroom. *The new boy shat himself!* someone sniggered. I faced the red fabric of a flag that hung

19

from the high ceiling with the swastika somewhere above me. I had never felt such shame.

When I turned my head, I could see the others sitting in a half-circle around the teacher. They were playing at something. Only Julia wasn't playing. She sat cross-legged and looked at me with unblinking eyes. I could see the white sickle of her underpants. I dried my tears and wiped my nose on the flag.

I was sent home with a paper bag and a note for Mami. I stayed away from Kindergarten for the rest of the week and the red outfit vanished without a mention.

My return to Kindergarten was procured with a promise. "We're going to Pei-tai-ho for the holidays," Mami said. It was the first thing I told the teacher and she repeated it to the class. I made my fresh start on the upper rung.

The German ambassador had a villa by the beach at Pei-tai-ho. "We're going by train," Mami said. "Ilse Stein is coming with us." We had never been to the beach before, only seen pictures of beaches. "Promise?" Mami put an arm around me. "Promise," she said.

When the time came, Ilse Stein couldn't come. Mami had begun a weekly routine of bicycle trips to the newly established ghetto in Hongkew, at the other end of Shanghai. She didn't tell us. Amah told us. "Mami gone downtown more far, see Ilse Stein," she said. Mami had filled the bamboo carrier that hung from the handlebars with black bread, sausage, butter, tins of cocoa and powdered milk and delivered them to friends in the ghetto. The Japanese guards let her through when they saw her German diplomatic passport. "Daddi had me shadowed," she told me much later. "I recognised the diplomatic car. I was an embarrassment to your father."

THE CHAUFFEUR DROPPED US OFF at Shanghai North Railway Station and drove Daddi to the consulate. Two trains stood waiting at the station, one on the main platform, the other across on a siding. The first was red and smooth and round and the carriages were linked together with flexible connecting tunnels. Very smart. The other was green with straight up-and-down sides like my wooden train at home. It had porches with iron railings and steps and you could see the bell-shaped couplings that joined the carriages together.

A porter was trundling our trunk toward the red train. When I saw it being lifted into the luggage van, I cried out, "That's not our train. I want to go in the green one." But Mami said the red one was nicer. It was clean and new and comfortable. "That other train hasn't even got proper seats, just wooden benches...no, Didi, we're not taking that train... well, then you'll have to go without us." But she caught my arm and pulled me along. She checked the numbers on the coaches that stretched in an unbroken line. Their skirts tucked under just clear of the edge of the platform, but you could see the sharp sickle of the wheels and a glint of rails through the gap. "In you go and stop being silly," Mami said and gave me a push that sent me across the gap, clambering into the creamy belly of the coach. Through the window opposite, I could see the green train. It was empty and looked unwanted. There was rust on its undercarriage. Mami and Hasi were laughing. They would never understand. We found our seats amid the creaking of leather. I kept my hand over my face, partly because I didn't want them to see my tears, but mostly because I was afraid I would not be able to stop myself from laughing, too.

As the train pulled out, the platform slid back with only a faint metallic hum. Then came the slow, rhythmic clacking of the wheels, first up front, then behind, as they rode over the joints in the tracks. Hasi provided the technical commentary, pointing out that the clacking was getting faster. Soon it got so fast that it didn't have time to make a proper clacking sound and became nothing more than a tiny double click that flew past like a wind in the rails.

If you opened the window, which notched down on brass catches, you could see the guard's van tailing the train around the slow bend and I thought of our trunk stowed in there with all the other luggage, going where we went, but in another time, one that hadn't yet reached what we had already passed, the signal pole with the green light still a thing of the future. Far out in front, the locomotive hunted, trailing a streamer of smoke. The line of coaches flexed easily as we swung over the plains and the furrowed fields unfolded like a broad fan under the distant hills, which didn't move at all.

I watch a water buffalo plod endlessly in a circle, a pole tied to its back. The other end turns a wooden shaft and, close by, a slanting chute lifts water to irrigate the fields. I can see the water being scooped up the chute by wooden pallets on a chain. A peasant family has stepped down from the path that follows the tracks; two bare-bottomed boys and an infant bound to its mother's breast. They wave as we pass.

I got something in my eye just as I was waving back. "Shut the window," Mami said and the instant silence felt like a pressure in my ears and through it the clickety-click of the wheels whispered to me from under the floor. Telegraph lines dipped and peaked on poles that whipped past the window. A uniformed guard appeared at the door to check our tickets. They were in English, French and Chinese and had been filled out in a scrawl of Chinese characters and sealed with the official chop[1] of the Chinese National Railways and Shanghai North Station. He tore out some carbon copies and nodded and moved on. The compartment door latched shut behind him.

Fräulein Dittberner was at the station in Nanking. I spotted her waving a shawl above the heads of hawkers selling mandarins. "Unfortunately we haven't got long," she said. "Your ferry goes in half an hour. I will walk with you." Mami came up and gave her a hug. She was puffing. "Just had to check on our trunk," she said. "Good idea," said Fräulein Dittberner. "I hope you gave the porter a good cumshaw[2]. It pays."

1 stamp
2 tip

23

In the bag she thrust at me were mandarins, two bottles of green tea and a tin of Quickies. There was a picture of a dancing stick-figure on the lid. "Bon voyage," she said as I clutched the bag to my chest. The jetty emptied itself into the ferry and we were carried along with the crowd. I could feel the engine pounding under my feet. Through a gap between bodies the solitary figure of Fräulein Dittberner on the jetty receded in our wake. She was waving her shawl.

The Yangtze River swelled up the side of the ferry and every now and then washed the deck through the scupper openings. Mami was looking up at the passengers who had climbed the superstructure, where two lifeboats were fastened. "They look as if they might hold twelve people at the most," she said. An entire family had clambered up on top of the wheelhouse, where they sat and dangled their feet over the edge. The ferryman shouted at them to get down and I wondered where they would find a place to stand if they did. Mami took my hand. "Stay together," she said.

The sun was going down by the time we tied up. When we got clear of the ferry, I could barely make out the southern shore, where we had embarked. Below it, the Yangtze lay spread out in every direction as if it had been the sea. "God knows what's become of our trunk," Mami said. The Blue Train glinted under the platform lights and a guard ushered us towards our sleeper. Up front, a station attendant uncoupled a large water hose from the locomotive and let it dangle while a derrick swung it away. The engine responded with a burst of steam that engulfed him completely. Doors were slammed shut. A guard held up a green flag. Then a whistle blew and we began our long haul into the North.

That evening we opened the tin of Quickies and wiped our hands. We sniffed the cool eau-de-cologne and tossed the spent swabs into the bin. Then Mami pulled out the picnic case from under her bunk. Amah had packed black bread and hard-boiled eggs. Screw-top jars contained peanuts and raisins. We peeled the loose skins off mandarins and separated their juicy segments, contending with each other who could boast the fattest one, she who couldn't squeeze into a train. Then we wiped our hands again and Mami ran Quickies over our travel-grimy faces.

As darkness closed and I could only see my own reflection in the window, I clambered into my bunk and let myself be lulled to sleep by the train's rhythm, only to be startled awake by the sudden hollow thunder of the wheels as we went over bridges and the equally sudden return to the comfortable clickety-click of the rails on dry land. When I woke again in the dead of night, I could hear neither. The compartment was dark and the darkness was muffled and choked with heat. No light showed from the corridor, no station lights marked our arrival. We had stopped in the middle of nowhere.

"Mami?" I said into the darkness, but I could tell she wasn't there. Then I made out her shape in the corridor, leaning out of the window. She was looking toward the front of the train where lights played and I could hear voices and the striking of steel. "Something up with the railway tracks," she said and put an arm around me. "They're fixing them." It was the war again. I didn't have to ask. "They probably bombed the lines by mistake," she said, making light of it. But we had seen the blacked-out train at nightfall. Its shockwave had rocked the compartment and it had hurled its bulky load past the window, truck after truck after truck. The bomb may have missed, but it wasn't hard to make the connection.

Some Chinese were getting off the train. They helped older men down the steps. The younger ones jumped. They joined others who were already squatting together at the edge of the cornfield. The lights from up front occasionally lit up their cotton outlines and the glow of their cigarettes came and went in the dark. They talked and laughed and fanned themselves with their hats. A Japanese guard carrying a rifle walked the length of the train. We looked down on top of his head as he passed. He also smoked. No one took any notice of him.

"Go back to sleep," Mami said. "This is going to take a while." She poured me some tea. It was bitter and lukewarm. At last, she tucked the stiff cotton sheet around me in the bunk. I woke again to a sudden jarring before the train began to move forward as if feeling its way in the greying light and then I knew nothing more until the broad day and the clamour of the station and Mami herding us out for a late breakfast in the railway café.

"Tsi-nan-fu," she said. "Onkel Siegel grew up in this city. His father was a very important man. He built the railway, also the famous bridge. You will see." It began without a superstructure. The plain simply fell away below us and we seemed to be climbing into the air. A glint of water showed above a wide embankment. "Look, the Yellow River," Mami said and immediately a hollow rumble came up through the floor and the steel girders rose and the crazy zig-zag of struts danced up and down in the window. I watched the train's shadow work its way along each of the twelve wide spans across the slow water, the colour of puddles.

We changed trains at Tientsin and headed east towards the coast. Mami unfolded a map. It had been printed on flimsy paper and all the places had been marked in Chinese characters. Someone had written in the names under the characters so Mami could read them. She showed us the route of our journey and I could see that we didn't have all that far to go. At Chinwangtao we were met by the ambassador's wife, who had been waiting for us most of the day. She gave the porter a cumshaw and spoke to him in perfect Mandarin. She was pointing to a train that waited amongst some dry weeds. It looked like my toy train and ran on tracks so close together, I could have straddled them with my legs. We sat on wooden benches and jostled each other when the train leaped into motion.

"I think you are happy now," Mami said, but my nose was already glued to the window and I pretended not to hear. We wound through a landscape of low hills. So low, I imagined running over the top and still catching the end of the train around the next bend. A man led two donkeys along the tracks.

27

The whistle blew with a puff of steam and he dragged them up the slope, their necks stretched out to the reins. Women stood up to watch the train pass, sickles hanging from their hands. The window let in the sun-ripe smell of straw.

We came to the end of the line amid a cluster of mud-and-thatch houses. Chickens picked at watermelon shells on the dusty ground. "Welcome to Pei-tai-ho," the ambassador's wife said. My heart sank. Then I saw the wrinkles around her eyes give way to a smile, a wait-and-see kind of smile. A man with a mule-drawn cart appeared and, in it, ordinary and utterly familiar, our trunk. He let Hasi and me hop on for the ride. The women walked.

We entered a grove of trees in the late dappled sunlight and stopped in the forecourt where the ambassador's house stood. The trees formed a leafy canopy over the entire space, which was filled with the shrill of a thousand cicadas. Somewhere under that bright vibrancy I could hear a slower pulse that came from beyond the trees, where a band of white stretched under a blue horizon. I stopped and looked. Oh *yes!* The promise of Pei-tai-ho was about to be fulfilled.

Vanishing sands

The ambassador, in shorts and socks, strode off the verandah. "You've made it," he said and shook Mami's hand. "Too bad about Frau Stein. How is she?" They talked. I listened to the sea. "It won't be long now," I heard him say. I thought he meant going to the beach, but he added, "A year, maybe two. And Hongkew's not so bad, as ghettos go." He led her toward the house. They stopped on the verandah steps. His eyes twinkled. "I'm told you see to that," he said.

Hasi shook his hand and bowed. "My, how you've grown," the ambassador said and heard him out as he delivered a detailed account of the journey. The man with the mule cart set our trunk down on the verandah and the ambassador helped him carry it inside. His wife paid and tipped the man. I started for the beach. "Come inside now," the women chorused. "We'll go in the morning." "It's getting late," Hasi explained in his big brother voice and helped the ambassador pull the mosquito screen across behind me.

The sun was already high above the horizon when we headed out in the morning. The ambassador led the way through rough grass. His bathing outfit left only his arms and calves exposed. Grey curls sprouted around his neck. We wore

29

our new woollen bathing suits that had been specially bought for the occasion and our bamboo coolie hats. Amah had sewn a padded ring into the hats to help them stay on and make them more comfortable. Hasi's head was larger than mine and she customised the hats, sewing a red binding along the rim for him and blue for me. The hats were a success and we wore them all the time, but my bathing suit prickled against my skin and I pulled it off and never wore it again.

The sand was dry and lightly blown. We left no footprints in it as we headed for the sea, only a brushed trail in the vastness of it. Tiny eddies spun into the air. "Little devils," Mami called them. A sudden gust of wind whipped up the sand and stung my legs, then peppered my naked body. I had to crouch down and cover my eyes until it moved on. Transparent veils of sand drifted away down the beach and vanished. I shook the sand out of my coolie hat. My skin tingled. When the first cool tongue of the sea licked around my feet, the beach behind me lay unmarked in the sun. I looked for the crown of trees where the house stood. It was only just visible above the grassy rise.

Green breakers rose and fell with a thump on a sandbank some way out. Closer in, the waves splashed and frothed and, after that, they merely slid over each other and didn't break at all. Hasi ventured out and had to be called back. He told me about the jellyfish he'd seen, the size of pudding bowls. I let myself drift with each wave as it passed, tasting its salt and occasionally swallowing a mouthful when one caught me by surprise. I tried holding my breath and going under. If I kept my eyes open and pinched my nose, I could see little families of fish darting through the water.

The man with the donkeys I'd seen from the train appeared at the house in the afternoon and led us, saddled on blankets, along shady paths. He showed us how to use the reins and let us ride back on our own. Next day, he turned up on the beach and a naked Chinese boy about my age rode bareback on a third donkey. I wanted to ride bareback, too, and not have the woollen blanket against my thighs. "Better without," Mami agreed. "It's bound to harbour lice." The ambassador and his wife laughed. I mounted and rode bare-bottomed on the donkey's dorsal bones.

I turned back after a little way, but the man wanted us to go for a longer ride. He waved his arms into the distance, calling out in Chinese. Then he arranged us in a starting line. He gave a shout and slapped my donkey on the flank and it bolted. My bottom hammered into its back and I tugged at the reins, but to no avail. So I held on with my knees and leaned forward with my bottom up in the air. I didn't come off. My terror gave way to exhilaration. I wondered where the others were, but didn't dare turn round to see. We charged on, this unstoppable animal and I. And, since the beach was without end, it didn't seem to matter whether we would ever stop.

Now sand dunes rose up on my left, pile upon pile of shining sand, gathering up the beach below a background of hills. To my right, waves smashed against a rocky outcrop. The beach narrowed. The donkey came to a halt. I dug my heels into its sides, but it wouldn't take another step. "So this is as far as you'll go," I said. "Alright. But I want to come here again tomorrow and go on a bit further. Am I going to have to walk?" The donkey nodded its head and turned around.

Hasi and the Chinese boy were a long way behind and I rode towards them. The donkey had spent its fury and left me sore. I winced at every slow step it took, but was careful not to show it. I pulled my coolie hat back on my head and prepared to be greeted as a hero. The Chinese boy gave me the thumbs-up and tried a few words of German. *Sehr gut!* he said. Very good. It made us laugh, so he said it again and again.

"My father he not speak German," he told us. We were squatting together on the beach. "My father he take *me*, speak German." He tapped his finger on the end of his nose, grinning. *Eins, zwei, drei*, he said, showing off. *Sehr gut.* Again we laughed and he reached out his hand and shook mine, then Hasi's, then mine again. When he'd finished, he looked down and watched as he let a clear stream run into the sand, where a tiny crater had formed to take it in.

"Those dunes, we call them the Horsemen's Dunes, because people rode into them and never returned." The ambassador prised the lid off a tin and teased some tobacco into the hollow of his hand. He rubbed it with his palm until he had loosened all the strands. He let me smell it and it was a bit like the smell of my donkey's breath. "They sent people in to look for them, but none of them ever came back either." He plugged the tobacco into the bowl of his pipe. Hasi struck the match. "There are bandits in the hills," the ambassador went on and waved an opening in the cloud of smoke that engulfed him. "We will go to the dunes the day after tomorrow, when you can walk again." He grinned and kissed me good night with his stubble.

*

I AM PICKING UP SHELLS. They are smooth and round and perfect. The spiral pattern always turns the same way. It is pearly, with little brown lines that get closer together as they get nearer the centre. I like these shells because they are flat and don't topple over in my hand. I'm going to keep them, give them to Amah when we get back home.

I leave the rocky outcrop behind. It is strange that there is no one else around. Maybe I came alone. I don't think I rode. I can't remember how I got here. The sand dunes go on and on. I can't tell how big they are. They move away when I walk towards them. Then I am climbing the steep side. Hot sand runs under my feet. I reach the top. On the other side of a hollow the dunes are twice as high, like mountains. I climb them, too. There are more and more of them, up and down, up and down. I see the dry hills beyond. That's where the bandits roam.

I run down a slope and up the other side. From the top I can see the rocky outcrop, but it looks more like an island. There is water all round it. That was where I picked up the shells just a little while back. Is it the same rock? Was it just a little while or hours? Days even? I open my hand and it is empty. Suddenly, I feel alone.

People have got lost in these dunes. They could be here still, trying to find their way out. They would be half starved and dying of thirst. I imagine them, staggering over the dunes in the distance.

I cannot be sure if I heard voices. I stop and listen. I cannot even hear the sea. I can see it—just—skimming over the dunes, but it is silent. Then the voices return. This time I am certain.

From the top of the next crest, I see them. They are very small, smaller than ordinary people. There must be five or six of them together in the hollow, surrounded by massive walls of sand. They are very clear, their colours bright. They are sitting on straw mats. Above them is a green sun umbrella. Their voices carry, but I can't make out what they're saying. I crouch below the crest of the dune and watch them.

They are eating, passing things to each other. In their middle, I can see an open picnic case and, as I watch, a tingling feeling crawls up my neck and rises into my head. Everything becomes a blur. I close my eyes and let the tears run down my face. The lost riders and the bandits fade like a dream and memories emerge, piece themselves together.

That's Hellmuth von Ruckteschell sitting there, next to Mami. Frau Fischer is talking to the ambassador's wife. They're sitting on the straw mat Hasi and I carried between us this morning. He is kneeling in the sand, discussing something with the ambassador.

How obvious and ordinary it all was.

I didn't want to be seen. I began to skirt round behind the crest, so that I could surprise them by sliding down the sandhill at their back. But Mami was waving to me. I didn't return the wave. I had been uncovered. They watched me all the way down the face of the dune. I felt small and naked and ashamed. I covered myself with a towel when I reached them. The man called Ruckteschell was smiling at me. "Bravo the hero of the donkey race!" he said. He brought his hand up to his bald head in a salute.

Hasi frowned. He said he had been looking for me. What was I thinking of, disappearing like that? Did I not know of the dangers? Did I not listen to what the ambassador said? I just sat there. After a while, he changed his tone. "Where did you go?" he said. And I told him I'd crossed the dunes till I got to the hills. That I had climbed into the hills, looking for bandits, but found none. But what I had seen was a group of people staggering over a dune looking for a way out and they were so thin and haggard, they could hardly walk upright and some of them had to drag themselves over the sand.

*

DADDI MET US AT THE SHANGHAI NORTH RAILWAY STATION. He had grown a moustache. Mami found it distasteful and said so. He drove. "We've had a lot of air raids," he said. At the house, he had drawn the curtains and piled the easy chairs on top of the sofa that stood below the window. He had rolled up the Chinese rug and put that on top of the easy chairs. "You'll be safe here when the bombs drop," he said.

35

The door to his study was open. His desk was gone. The bookshelves were empty. Not even the date jar remained. There was a gap where his gramophone had stood in the alcove. Daddi said goodbye. The terriers followed him to the car on new red leashes.

Christmas bombs

The siren howled an air raid warning on my first day of school. Fräulein Pfeilsdorf arranged the class against the inner wall and opened the windows, even the fanlights, which she had to reach with a pole. Then she noticed Julia under her desk, her head tucked between her knees. A snigger went around and a boy called out, "Julia's hiding!" and another, "Are you hiding from the bombs?" Her voice came back, "I am only looking for something," and the whole class laughed. Fräulein Pfeilsdorf crouched down and tried to take her hand. We counted the seven waves of the siren and, as the last one wound down, we could hear the distant booming of the bombs.

The class fell silent. I crawled in beside Julia. She was crying. I held out my hand to Fräulein Pfeilsdorf and she led us away. There was a wet mark on the floor beneath Julia's desk.

The frontispiece of our workbooks showed a group of boys flying a flag. They were looking up at the swastika as it unfurled itself against the sky. In large letters above the picture it said, *YOU ARE THE LIVING GUARANTORS OF GERMANY'S FUTURE!* When I showed it to Mami she said, "As long as they live to see it." They looked exactly like the older boys at school when they paraded in the playground and the brass band played. Once Fräulein Pfeilsdorf made us sing along as they marched past. It was my favourite song and when I sang it to Mami she said it was Brahms and played me the Academic Overture on her gramophone. But the words were all about the fatherland.

> *Ich hab' mich ergeben*
> *Mit Herz und mit Hand*
> *Dir Land voll Lieb' und Leben*
> *Mein deutsches Vaterland!*

That was more for the older boys, not us. We sang songs about craftsmen and stonemasons and bakers. We filled our exercise books with the letters of the alphabet and tried to keep them upright. And then we had our story book. It was in Gothic print and the first letter of each story was very big and fancy, with little pictures weaving through it; they were pretty, but made it hard to read. Fräulein Pfeilsdorf chose a story for each of us to read for homework. Mami helped me. Next day, we had to tell the story to the class.

My story was called *A Peephole in the Window*. The windowpane was covered in ice crystals that had the shape of beautiful flowers and a boy and a girl were breathing their warm breath against it to melt the ice. They made a peephole and took turns at peering through it. What they saw in the moonlight was a bustling of little folk in red caps at the edge of the forest. They were gathering pinecones and toting them off in sacks slung over their backs. Two of the littlest ones were making a snowman and they stuck a dry twig across his shoulder and a red cap on his head.

"He wouldn't even have come up to my knee," the girl said after their mother had drawn the curtains and tucked them up in bed. But they said not a word to her about what they had seen. In the morning, they couldn't wait to get dressed and stomp through the snow to the edge of the forest. The snow lay unmarked. There was *nothing* there. "Not even the snowman's tiny red cap," the girl sobbed, but her little brother said nothing. His eyes were fixed on a dry twig that slanted out of the snow and he said nothing because he knew it had been specially left there for him to find.

When Luigi with the curly black hair told his story to the class, he had learned the whole thing by heart. He recited it word for word in his strange foreign accent. We were awed by the achievement but found it very funny and laughed at him out loud.

The sheer brick walls of the German Evangelical Church rose above the playground behind a tangle of bare branches. Christmas wasn't far off and we always went to church to see the nativity play and to sing Christmas songs. When the bells rang in the tower, they brimmed over and deafened you. You could feel the deep vibration in the stone steps of the porch as you entered.

They were still ringing when we sat in the balcony pews, staring into the brightness of the lofty interior. Angels glowed in the light of their candles. Tinsel hung from the Christmas tree as if it had been snowing in the church. "Can we have our tree like that, with lots and lots of snow?" I had to repeat it into Mami's ear. But she said, "This is a bit overdone. The tinsel should be applied sparingly, like frost." Mami must have been right, but I loved it all the same.

"Look, that angel has just flown up there!" Hasi's voice rang out over the dying bells and he pointed to the golden-winged girl in the pulpit, which jutted out from an opening high up in the wall. He didn't mind that people turned and laughed and I thought that it was unlike my elder brother to say something so naïve, but found it cute.

AMAH HELD THE CURTAINS SHUT and we stood on the stage steps and waited. It was Christmas Eve. Through a split in the curtains I could just see the treetop with its tinsel star bowed under one of the false ceiling beams. Then the lights went out and Mami rang the golden bell and said, "The Christchild has come."

The tree filled the room and the decorations reflected the solemn light of the candles. At its foot the angel hovered as always over the crib. The carved figures of Mary and Joseph and all the animals looked on in wonder at the child in the manger.

I had not expected to see Daddi. He sat there, grinning at us. Beside him sat a younger woman. "This is Tante Alix," Mami said and we shook her hand and bowed. Tante Alix picked up two presents from the foot of the tree and held them out to us, but her smile was for Daddi. "They're from us both," she said.

The furry dogs had Hasi and me laughing merrily as we

squeezed their bellies, making them bark a funny kind of bark. Later that night, Daddi and Tante Alix said good night to us in bed. As she bent over to kiss me, I smelt her sweet perfume. I thought she was very pretty. Mami didn't come to say good night to us.

I woke early on Christmas day. There was snow on the rooftops and in the gardens, on the bare branches of trees and the cross-arm of the telegraph pole. It was just like in story books. The street was a white blanket and there wasn't a mark on it. I didn't get dressed. I slipped downstairs and opened the front door. On the doorstep lay a straw bundle. A tiny head showed at one end with a crown of fine black hair. The eyes were two slits traced in black and on the brow a single snowflake clung like an ornament. There was no warmth left to melt it away.

*

"THE PEOPLE IN THE VILLAGE ARE POOR," Mami tried to explain, "and there is not enough to eat. The baby's mother must have come at night and left her at our door, hoping we would find her and take her in." "Do you think she knew about Christmas?" I asked, but Mami didn't answer. "They have no choice," she said. "The boys are the luckier ones. When they grow up they can work and earn money for the family."

Amah took charge of the matter and I didn't go out in the street. Hasi and I tried to build a snowman in the garden, but the snow had turned to slush and wouldn't hold.

We lit the Christmas tree candles again when it got dark. Mami went to get her leather-bound volume of Hans Christian

Andersen. Then she went upstairs again to get the feather quilt off her bed. She wrapped it around the three of us and it had her peculiar smell, but we pulled it tight and held it close. She read us the story of the fir tree. They had chosen it for its beauty and brought it in and decorated it and it was their Christmas tree. When it was all over, they chopped it up and burned it.

Mami came to say good night when we'd gone to bed. She talked to Hasi for a long time. They always talked about things together as if they would pass over my head. Hasi asked if Daddi was going to come back and who was Tante Alix? I picked up most of what they said, but I knew the answers already and didn't need to be told. The way Tante Alix smiled at him, I could tell that Daddi was never coming back.

Mami pulled up a chair by my bed. I asked her whether Tante Alix had any children. She said, no, she didn't. "We could have given her the baby girl," I said, "if she hadn't died." Mami remained silent. "Or we could have kept her ourselves and she could have been my sister." Still Mami said nothing. After a while I said, "She couldn't have had a guardian angel," and she said, "Every child has a guardian angel and every angel has a secret. We will never know what it is." Then she began the prayer and I brought my hands together and shut my eyes. I joined in the second verse:

> *Angels, spread your golden wings*
> *And guard me while I sleep.*

Then she kissed me. Her lips felt cold on my brow. She got halfway down the stair, to where the wall clock hung. "That's

43

funny," she said and I realised it had stopped. "I can't believe I forgot to wind it." Her whispered words came and went. "How strange." She let out her breath. "I just don't know..." I heard the key go in and the ratchet turn. The clock began to go, unevenly at first, and then settled down. I heard Mami whisper, *Oh God!*

It must have stopped again in the night. I turn my head to listen. It is dead quiet. Not a tick. Not a tock. And then it's there, faint as a whisper. It comes and goes. Then it begins to grow louder. It is getting closer. The clock is tick-tocking up the stair. I need to go to the toilet. The bathroom is just around the corner of the top landing. But the clock has come in the door and up to my bed. It hammers in my ears. It misses beats, draws out the silences between them and does a double beat, TOCK-TOCK! so loud, it makes my heart jump inside my chest. The spring tightens, the clock holds its breath, waits and lets a chime fall, a dizzy kind of chime, and then its slow decaying breath. Everything falls away. I open my eyes. There is a grey light in the window. The empty chair stands by my bed. The measured seconds sound from the landing. The wet bedclothes cling to my legs. I huddle myself into them and the secretive angels spread their wings over me.

Shrapnel

The front doorbell rang. I heard a gruff voice, followed by Boy's soft one, polite as always. Amah came upstairs. "Man want to see you," she said. "Japanese man." Her face was ashen. "Mami gone downtown. You come with me now. Is alright. Didi, come."

Amah stood beside me. Boy stood aside, but remained close. When the general saw me, he let out a cry and his face broke into a grin, showing yellow teeth packed with gold. He thrust something into my hand and jabbed the air at it, shouting at me in Japanese, over and over. When I unfurled the flag of the Rising Sun, he spread his arms and a wordless sound rumbled somewhere deep inside him. I held up the flag and he came to attention and saluted. Then he spun round and marched off to a military car, where a young officer held the door open for him. They drove off, followed by a convoy of army trucks, and I never saw him again.

"He wanted to take you with him," Mami told me when she got home. "That was two years ago, when he went to the consulate. He must have liked you." Amah laughed and held my hand. "Is alright. He gone now," she said. "Not come back."

*

SANDBAG GUN EMPLACEMENTS had been thrown up in Amherst Avenue. An anti-aircraft gun barrel appeared above the rim. Japanese sentries controlled the railway crossings into Hungjao. Mami got off her bicycle and held it by the handlebars. A guard searched the basket that hung from them. Another jabbed at the cushion on which I sat astride the back carrier. I got down and a third stuck the point of his bayonet into it. He tugged at the cotton wool filling. "What kind of behaviour is this?" Mami said in German, looking down her nose at the guards. She opened her passport and held it up, but they only laughed and flung the cushion onto the railway tracks.

When Hasi's birthday came, he got a new bicycle and I inherited his. It was black and had a horizontal bar in front, like a proper men's bike. The handlebars were a bit rusty, but Mami put a brand new bell on it for me and new wooden grips to hold on to and, with that, it became *my* bike. Soon I was flying the Rising Sun from the rear, like on a ship. If I went fast enough, I could make it flutter behind me. We went for bike rides in Hungjao and visited friends in their country gardens. With my flag, we never again had problems at the crossing.

Sirens sounded and searchlights criss-crossed the night sky. A plane's silhouette brought anti-aircraft batteries to life. Zero fighters wound upwards from Hungjao aerodrome. Bombs exploded downtown. Amah tugged us from the window and hustled us downstairs. We pushed past the bicycles and stood in the wash-house. "There is a bathroom right above us," Mami said, "and yours above that one. They are concrete, so

46

we're safe here." We waited for the steady note of the all-clear and went back to bed. We found shrapnel in the garden next day and a curled fragment of steel that had embedded itself in the stucco of the house.

Summer brought tall arches of red skies and hot northerlies. "Sand from the Gobi Desert," Mami said. "It travels for hundreds of miles." It clogged the gutters. It filtered through doorways and settled on ledges like a fine red dust. Then the wind came and sent it scurrying down the street. The willows raised their weeping boughs and lashed at the air as if enraged. Their tendrils streamed across the garden's rectangle of sky and the stripped leaves climbed and wheeled and disappeared from sight. Then it rained. Drainage lids rose up and water welled into the street. Amah walked on her heels, her tiny feet pointing skywards. As the flood deepened, a street vendor shouted the virtues of strap-on platforms that kept shoes dry. He himself had rolled up his trousers and waded barefoot through the knee-deep water, making no sales. The telegraph pole doubled its height and the power lines squiggled in the flood against a yellow monsoon sky. The bunker under the swimming pool was awash. No one had ever used it and there seemed to be no point in trying to pump it out. The pedicab arrived as usual to take us to school, but sank into a pothole and overturned. We had a three-day holiday.

My school report said I was a dreamer and needed to pay more attention. Mami had to send the report to the consulate for Daddi to sign. It also said I needed to keep my schoolwork tidy and improve my writing. Mami took no notice. She gave me paints and brushes. "Earth colours," she said. "Emma Bormann brought these for you. There are just four pots. An ochre yellow, a cobalt blue (you can mix them to make green), a red ochre and white. And she left some paper for you to paint on." I painted pictures of birthday parties and gardens with swimming pools on rough brown paper.

I was invited to Julia's birthday party. I couldn't take my eyes off the mulberries and whipped cream that topped the cake. The grown-ups got us playing blind man's buff in the garden. There were prizes of sweets in silver paper cones with pictures of flowers. We rounded the afternoon off playing hide-and-seek. Julia and I hid together behind a folded ping-pong table in the garden pavilion. It was a tight squeeze. No one found us. When the grown-ups called, we came out a little guiltily. Some of the children had gone home. Julia's mother set us looking for a bunch of keys someone had lost in the garden. I knew I would find them. I knew exactly how they would look, their bright rims glinting in the autumn leaves. I trailed the edge of the lawn under the trees until I saw them. I held the keys up in the air. I was given an extra slice of cake.

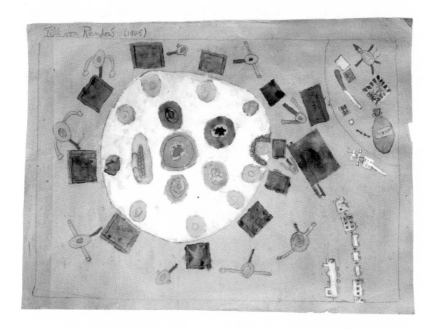

The central heating failed that winter. Water pipes froze. Life drained from the house. The dining chairs gazed at an empty table. The false beams looked down on furnishings under bulky dust covers. The chain bolt remained undrawn on the front door.

We closed our bedroom door and plugged in the three-bar heater. It was a little rusty, but one of the bars began to glow. There was a bright spot in the middle that made a ringing sound. It got brighter and then popped a spark and went out. There was a smell of ozone in the air. Amah lit the charcoal stove. It was a clay pot with a metal jacket that had a grate on top and an air hole in the front. We had to keep a window open so as not to get gassed. Mami rescued her cyclamens from downstairs and stood them on the window sill. She brought a Christmas tree home from the market, tied upright on the carrier of her bike. I said I would do the decorations. I stood the tree on a box and could still reach the top to fix the tinsel star. It was the only decoration I used. I clipped the candles on the branches and lit them. I left the angel and the carved crib in their boxes. Then I rang the golden bell.

Mami praised my work. "It's so minimal," she said, "and the symmetry is perfect." But I could see her sadness. Amah carried water upstairs in a pitcher from the only tap that still worked. She poached a carp on the charcoal stove and ate with us.

It has begun to snow. Amah is looking down at me. I am

wrapped in straw and snowflakes swirl around my head. I can't move. The straw is too tight. My sudden breath wakes me. I hear my own voice saying, "You remember that baby, last year?" "I can remember," Amah says. "That happen last Christmas. Is all finished. You go to sleep now. No more dreams."

I woke Hasi early and we took our bikes into the street. I wheeled mine past the front porch and gave it a wide berth. I saw that the snow had drifted right up to the door. It was unmarked and perfect. I came closer and my eyes fixed on a single blade of straw sticking up out of the snow.

I am flying. The air holds me up. I reach down to touch the blade of straw. I feel it between my fingertips. It is infinitely fine. Then it is gone. I turn the handlebars to go, but take one last look to make sure. The snow is unmarked. There is nothing there at all.

Our wheels made deep tracks that wobbled through the snow. I fell off my bike. Then Hasi fell off, too, and we both laughed. We pelted each other with snowballs until our hands were so cold, we had to rub them together and breathe on them to bring them back to life. If we breathed heavily enough, we could make ourselves invisible for a moment in a cloud.

That evening I sent everyone out of the bedroom. I needed to fix the Christmas tree. I cleaned out the candle holders and put in fresh candles. I opened the boxes with the decorations. I pulled out long tresses of tinsel and draped them over the branches until it looked as if it had been snowing in our bedroom. I hung the red glass balls, the green ones (that I first had to clean the candle wax off) and the big purple one with the ice crystal pattern on it. I hung all the little painted angels and the St Nicholas figure and the rocking horse. Then I placed the crib at the foot of the tree, with Mary and Joseph and all the animals standing around and the angel hovering above them and, when it was all done, I lit the candles and the room smelled of honey and the tree glowed and we sang Christmas songs and placed bets as to which flame would be the last to flicker (and yet glow secretly between the metal splines of the candle holder) before it died and left only a tiny thread of smoke hanging for a moment in the air.

*

OUR PEDICAB STOPPED across the road from school. The sirens wailed. Planes circled in the sky. Hasi and I fought our way through the rickshaws, pedicabs and cyclists all scrambling for cover. Trams stopped in the middle of the road and people swarmed off them. Cars blew their horns, but couldn't move. We got to the other side and into the building. Through the classroom window, I watched a plane corkscrew out of the sky and into the city street. Black smoke streamed from it and a parachute descended through the curling column with perfect symmetry.

My last school report from the Kaiser Wilhelm Schule is dated 23rd June, 1945. It is the end of the school year. The report says that I will move up to the third year class, but leaves the date blank. Daddi's signature doesn't appear on the report. The school never opened again.

The children of Fahwha village mobbed us as we rode our bikes down the street. Barefoot boys with shorn heads ran alongside us or held on to the carrier, shouting elaborate

52

obscenities. We didn't know what they meant (and most of the Chinese kids would have had little idea), but we shouted them back and pedalled hard to shake off the mob.

We swung into Columbia Circle and ran straight into a handful of older boys, who began pelting us with stones. They had added a new slogan to their repertoire. *Hi-te-la shi-te-la!* they cried. *Hitler is dead!* We dodged the potholes in the asphalt and got past the boys, but a stone hit me in the back of the neck and I crashed my bike. I took cover behind some bricks left over from the bunker, but now reduced to a small pile. The stones kept flying. I heaved a brick at the boys and it shattered and made some space, so I threw another one, but they picked up the shards and flung them back at me. *Hi-te-la shi-te-la!* The boys closed in, jeering, shouting, their hands slicing across their throats to simulate decapitation. The scream of an engine cut them dead. The P-51 barely skimmed the rooftops. On its tail came another, then a third, a fourth, a fifth. The boys scattered down the street, except for a tall skinny one, who stood rigid in the aftershock and then fell as if from shattered bones. No one came to his rescue.

I smelled the fighters' exhaust. There had been no sirens, no ground fire, no interceptors. I picked up my bike and stood astride the front wheel while I straightened the handlebars. We rode back to the house. Columns of dark smoke rose above Hungjao aerodrome.

The servants were huddled around a charcoal stove by the back door, drinking tea. They didn't look up or make room to let us pass. "I'm ringing the front doorbell," I protested, but Hasi caught me by the sleeve. "You can't," he said. "Mami has already told me." It was his big brother voice again. Then Boy stood up and let us through. He kept his eyes lowered. "I bring the bicycles inside," he said quietly. "You go on upstairs now." When we had reached our room, Hasi closed the door and leaned against it. "We can't afford the servants any more," he said. "Mami has told them to go, but they are waiting for the Americans to arrive."

The Americans

It was their easiness that struck me from the first. Although I couldn't understand what they were saying, I could tell they were joking a lot and their laughter rolled up the flights of stairs to the top landing where I stood listening. There were three of them and Boy, his voice quiet and polite, speaking pidgin English. The Americans were friendly with him, as if they'd known him a long time. They mimicked his pidgin and then spoke the sentence back to him their own way, slowly. I could understand them then and stored up bits for later. I would show them I was no dope.

Boy led the Americans up the stairs to the first floor. I heard him open two bedroom doors and show them in. Then he led the third man up to the top landing. The American was slim and his khaki trousers fitted tightly round his waist and hips. He moved the way a cat moves and I thought he would have taken in two steps at every stride, had not Boy gone before him at his measured pace. A large bag hung from the American's shoulder and he wore his airman's cap aslant and tilted forward on his brow.

"Hi there," he said and held out his hand. "I'm Captain Milne, 14th Air Force, pleased to meet you." "You're welcome,"

I said and bowed. Captain Milne shook my hand and smiled. Dark lashes circled his grey-blue eyes and his face was as fresh as a young boy's. He swung his bag to the floor of the pink room, in which Mami sometimes put up guests. He sat down on the bed with a thump and tried to bounce. Then he slapped it with both hands. "I thought I'd left my last army cot back in Kunming," he said. "Say, couldn't you fix me something even harder to lay on, like a couple of planks maybe?"

Boy didn't understand and I came to his help. I knew what the captain was about. We also slept on hard horsehair mattresses, because Mami said they promoted good posture. "Another bed. More soft," I said to Boy.

"You've got it," Captain Milne said. "Smart kid, eh? Come here. What's your name?"

"Till."

"Till? OK. Till we meet again, I'm gonna get me one real soft mattress, if I have to go downtown to buy it."

Boy nodded. "You go to Wing On, Master Captain. Have plenty mattress," he said.

"Wing On?" said Captain Milne. "Should've picked me one up while I was buying my pyjamas." He turned to me. "Wanna come?"

As I followed the captain down the stairs, Mami and Hasi emerged from the servants' quarters. "Hi there," I said to them, just the way he'd said it to me. "This is Captain Milne."

"How d'you do?" said Captain Milne and extended his hand. "Oh, excuse me. These are my buddies, Captain Hamilton and Captain Richardson. They'll be staying in here." He indicated their rooms. "I've landed up in the room upstairs, which is very pretty, but, no offence, I'm temporarily over sleeping in

56

an army cot." His buddies grinned. "Say, is there a bathroom anywhere?" It was my chance. "There are two bathrooms on this floor," I said and pointed them out. "Smart kid, eh?" he said again.

Mami pushed me forward and I offered my hand to Captain Richardson and gave a bow. Then to Captain Hamilton. "My son Didi," I heard Mami say. *"Till,"* I corrected her.

"Till?"

"Yeah, Till, that's his name, Till the End of Time," singing it. "Till the Clouds Roll by," swinging it. Captain Milne seemed to know a lot of songs starting with Till.

Then it was Hasi's turn. "I am called *Rabe,*" he said, not giving Mami a chance. "That is my name." He bowed as he shook Captain Milne's hand. No one knew a song that began with Rabe. As he took his last bow, Captain Hamilton spoke.

"You know, you kids want to save those bows for the Kaiser, 'cos it really does make a guy feel kind of old."

"You mean the Fuehrer, don't you?" said Captain Richardson.

"Too late for that, buddy," retorted Captain Hamilton. "Don't you listen to the radio?"

Mami seemed to have understood what they said and laughed. "No offence, Ma'am," said Captain Hamilton and gave a bow. She laughed again. "Are you the artist?" he said, pointing to a portrait on the wall. "Yes. It is him," she said and pointed at me. "I can see that," said Captain Hamilton. "Good likeness." He held out a small package in each hand, an edge of silver paper showing from under colourful wrappers. "Tutti Frutti or Dentine?" He eyed Hasi and me. I took the Tutti Frutti and unwrapped it carefully. Just the smell made my mouth water. Hasi unwrapped his and it was all sugar and spice.

"You can't eat it," Captain Hamilton said as I tried to bite off a piece. "It's chewing gum." He made chewing movements with his mouth. "You've gotta take the whole piece. That's it." After a while, my jaws began to ache and the taste had gone out of the gum, but I kept on chewing it all the same.

Captain Milne landed at the wheel of his Jeep in a single bound. "Hop in," he called to me as the engine started and I clambered in beside him. The Jeep sped forward. It had no doors and no roof and I gripped the sides of my seat so tight, it made the captain laugh. "Relax," he said. "Lean back. That's it. Sit right back and enjoy the ride."

We flew up Columbia Road into Great Western Road, but the stream of pedicabs slowed us down as we turned into Bubbling Well Road. Captain Milne tooted the horn and the Jeep pressed forward into Nanking Road. I laughed to see the traffic parting to let us through. "They don't call us the Flying Tigers for nothing!" Captain Milne shouted.

We left the Jeep standing outside the entrance to the Wing On Department Store. There was an American Air Force insignia on one side of the bonnet and the Chinese twelve-pointed sun on the other. "No one will touch it," the captain said as we went in the revolving doors.

We passed the wooden escalators, which weren't working, and headed for the lifts. The lift attendant, a diminutive Chinese in grey livery, ushered us in and slid the landing doors shut. He pulled the expanding grille across with a clatter till it latched. "Which department you like, sir?" He hopped onto his stool and pulled the control lever. I stared at the butt ends of the floors as they slid past us, each with its number stencilled on the bare concrete. Like looking at the reverse side of things, I thought, the parts you don't normally see. Like places you don't normally go, the stair through the servants' quarters at home, the bunker under the swimming pool. I would never have gone down there on my own.

"Bedroom furnishings," Captain Milne said.

I was pleased the escalators weren't working. I didn't want him to notice my terror when the slatted steps flattened out and dived under the teeth on the landing. I knew that, if those teeth caught you, they would pull you in and you'd never get back up into the world. You'd be stuck there forever in a dark place on the wrong side of everywhere.

"Bedroom furnishing," said the lift attendant.

The floor was brightly lit and full of mirrors. Quilted bed covers and dressing tables and rugs were everywhere. Captain Milne wasted no time. "Have you got a rubber latex foam mattress?" he said. "For a single bed?" "Made in United States of America," the salesman said. "One million five hundred thousand yuan." The captain fingered the Ta Chung Wah label. "United States my foot. How much for a Chinese mattress?" The salesman pretended not to understand. "It's OK, I'll take it," the captain said and they rolled it up and tied it with string.

"Aren't you going to wrap it?" the captain asked.

"Maybe you like to buy dust cover. I show you. Only one hundred thousand yuan."

They untied the mattress and slipped the dust cover around it and tied it up again. They deposited it in the back of the Jeep and Captain Milne bound it down with canvas strops. "Let's go get an ice cream soda, eh, Till the clouds roll by?"

We passed a hoarding on which workmen on extra long ladders were pasting up the poster for a new movie. I read out *Till The Clouds Roll By* and Captain Milne winked at me and sang the whole song by heart.

The place was full of American music and American airmen. They crowded the bar. "Hey, can you jitterbug?" My

American came towards me, holding two milky glasses aloft. He did some funny little dance steps to the music. "I'll have to teach you some time." The ice cream blocked my straw and splattered into my face when I blew through the straw to clear it. Captain Milne pushed a paper serviette across the table. "Thank you," I said.

I said *Thank you* again when I'd finished the glass, leaving only a tiny smear of ice cream where my straw couldn't get at it. In the street outside, two white Jeeps with the initials MP on their doors drove side by side, clearing a path through the traffic. I could see the white helmets marked MP through the windows. A column of Japanese soldiers followed, four abreast. They weren't marching. Stripped of their arms, their leather belts, even their boots, they hung their heads and shambled along in straw sandals or bare feet. They really were quite little without their combat hats, as Mami had said they were, these hapless remnants of the Imperial Army. The Chinese watched them pass with expressionless faces.

"MPs," Captain Milne said, "Military Police. They're taking them to a camp where American families spent nearly three years under the Japs. And when they've sorted them out, they're gonna send them back home to Japan." He looked down to see if I'd understood. "Look at them, poor damn kids. Some of them just a few years older than you."

We had to wait a long time for them to pass. "Let's go, or your mom's gonna start fretting."

Only as we got close to home did I notice that the gun emplacements had gone from the street corners. No more Japanese sentries, no more road barriers, even the sandbags had disappeared. Perhaps to repair houses or to construct bridges over the muddy creeks that ran through Fahwha village, or to shore up their slumping banks. *Nothing ever gets wasted*, Mami always said.

"Thank you," I said as I got out of the Jeep.

"Thanks for the company," said Captain Milne, pushing the front doorbell. He lifted the mattress from the Jeep. "Oh no, no, no," Boy said. "I go get coolie. Take mattress upstairs."

I was about to thank him again, when he stopped me on the stair and put a finger to my mouth. "No more *thankyous*," he said. "Attaboy. And for future reference, the word is *thanks*, just like that, OK?" We shook on it. Mami appeared in the doorway on the top landing. "Thanks, Captain Milne," I said and strode on up, carrying a changing world in my stride.

*

MAMI SAT BY MY BED and I told her about the ride in the Jeep and Wing On and the ice cream soda. I told her about the Japanese soldiers and that they looked like young boys. And how sad they were. "Their mothers and fathers will be there to welcome them home when they get to Japan," she said. "But will they still be alive?" I said. I had heard things about the atom bomb. "Go to sleep now. You've had a big day." She kissed me on the forehead and got up to go.

"Mami, what do you think I should do with my Japanese flag?" I had removed it from my bike and tied it to the foot of my bed. "Maybe now you should take it down. You won't need it any more." She turned to go.

"Mami," I said and she stood and waited. "Hasi says Daddi has gone to prison. I mean Rabe. Is that true?"

She sat down again. "It's a kind of prison," she said, "called Kiangwan Camp. They're keeping a number of Germans there, those who worked for the consulate and other things. They will take care of them until their repatriation."

"What's repatriation?"

"When they put them on a ship to Germany."

"Will they do it to us, too? Put us in a camp and send us back to Germany?"

"We will try to stay. Whatever happens, I don't want to go back to Germany. I don't want my sons to land in Germany. Not after all that." She took my hand. "Try not to worry, Didi," she said. "I mean Till. No one knows what's going to happen, but we three will stick together, that I promise you. Now go to sleep."

This time I didn't stop her going. I lay awake thinking of Daddi in the camp. I wondered if it was the same camp the Japanese soldiers were being taken to. I thought about Captain Milne. I really liked Captain Milne. I wondered if he had any children.

*

THE HOUSE HAD BEGUN TO COME TO LIFE AGAIN. A new gramophone appeared in the alcove downstairs, where Daddi had had his, only it was electric and the music was different. It made you want to dance. I learnt to sing the song *Tampico* which they played a lot. Captain Richardson even taught me how to put the record on. The picture on the record label had the dog and trumpet I had always loved. "It's not a trumpet," Captain Richardson said. "It's a sound horn." He explained

how it made the sound louder. Rabe seemed to understand. He hung around Captain Richardson a lot of the time. He even listened to jazz. I didn't. It made me squeamish. I don't think Mami liked jazz either. But she liked Paul Robeson. When I heard her singing *Ol' Man River*, I was happy, because it meant she was OK.

Captain Richardson acquired a dog. Mami said he was a *Wolfshund*. Captain Richardson called him an Alsation. I remember him as the first German shepherd dog in my life. He would howl when he heard the jazz trumpet and got the name *Beethoven*. Mami was appalled. They settled on *Lupo*.

Captain Richardson pulled out a photograph of his wife, Sylvia. "Would you paint me a portrait of her?" he asked Mami. It was to be the first of many such portraits and they paid well. The gold bars Daddi had left remained untouched for months. Mami showed Rabe the place where they were hidden, in case anything happened. "They're in a hole in the wall," he said to me mysteriously, "but *you'll* never be able to find it."

The easel stood in her bedroom on the first floor. Next to it, a trestle table was covered in tubes of oil paint, their silvery bodies squeezed and bent, a coloured band at the top, the labels no longer readable. Brushes sprouted from a mended china vase (there was a hawker who could fix cups and things with metal staples) and a couple of smudged pallets hung from the side. An unfinished portrait of a woman stood on the easel with a small black-and-white photograph clipped to its edge. I loved watching Mami bring its likeness into life. Against the wall, other canvasses waited their turn. Some loosely set into frames, some yet to be finished, some to be given away, some to be over-painted, but most to go on waiting for nobody-knew-what. Paintings of Chinese villages, countryside, temples, Buddhist monks. A framed watercolour of Amah knitting. Amah's daughter Bao-jin, Rabe and myself. Among them, Mami slept in a balm of linseed oil and turpentine.

Lupo is asleep on the landing outside Captain Richardson's door. I don't notice him in the dark as I creep down the stairs.

The upstairs toilet is blocked and I need to use Mami's. I open the door and begin to pick my way through her room. I am holding my breath. I mustn't wake Mami, because she'll get a terrible fright and scream. I bump into something. Very lightly. I can't remember what. Mami's scream freezes me to the spot and my mouth opens and I scream, too. Lupo is there in the instant. He makes little whining sounds, pushes his body against mine. I sink into my knees and he licks my face. I cling to his hairy sides with my fists.

*

THEY BROUGHT US COMICS. By the time we were enrolled at the Shanghai American School, we had gone without formal education for three months, but we knew about Mickey Mouse and his heroic antics. And there was Minnie Mouse, come to life at last, singing *I was born to love you*. We had become acquainted with Superman and Captain Marvel, invincible defenders of American justice, and the ordinary city guys in whom their transformative powers were concealed. We got to know Roy Rogers, Hopalong Cassidy and Tom Mix and the law of the Wild West. But my favourite was Don Winslow of the U.S. Navy, who was perennially engaged in defeating his Japanese counterpart, Toguchi, in the war of the Pacific. This was getting close to home. Don Winslow was, in every way, a competent officer. His white uniform and cap were immaculate, even when he was sinking in quicksand. His off-sider, a marine called, simply, Red, was overweight and sloppy, if good-natured. I admired Don Winslow and wanted to be like him and, in my fantasies, I was. But Red embarrassed

66

me and I think it was because I knew I was actually more like him. Victory came to Don Winslow in every episode. His prize was always waiting for him: the exquisite Mercedes, woman of every hero's dreams.

For my eighth birthday, in November 1945, Mami took me to the movies. We saw *Thirty Seconds over Tokyo* and Van Johnson played the part of the airman whose plane crashes. When he gets back to America, his wife comes to meet him. Her eyes sparkle. He stands up and comes crashing down on the floor, because in that moment he has forgotten about his amputated leg. I cried when that happened.

That film was also about the war in the Pacific. B-25 Mitchell twin-engine bombers had to take off from an aircraft carrier, but couldn't return to it to land. They had to bomb Tokyo and then make a run for the China coast and hope for the best. I could easily recognise a B-25 when one flew over the house. Its twin tail fins were a sure mark. Some bigger four-engine bombers also had twin tail fins and they called them Consolidated B-24 Liberators. One flew so low over our garden, it straddled the whole sky between the willow trees. Its propellers chewed the air and kept all that metal aloft on outstretched wings. Consolidated B-24 Liberators made you gape.

We would lie in bed at night, Rabe and me, listening to the drone of their engines down at Lunghwa aerodrome. It would come and go, the individual voices rising and falling, throbbing in our ears as their sound waves overtook each other, settling in again, wavering, becoming steady. "That's a B-24," I said. "You can tell, because it's got four engines." "No, it's not," Rabe said. "It's bigger than that. It must be a B-29 Superfortress." We listened to the engines coming up to full throttle and singing in perfect unison. "It's taking off!" I said and held my breath. When the pitch dropped a little, I knew the ship had become airborne. *It's away!* I gasped for air, but already the next one was tuning its engines and taxiing into position at the head of the runway.

The kids at the American school were a mixed bunch. Some had come from the liberated camps, the ones Captain Milne spoke about, where the Japanese had held American families. Some came from the Hongkew ghetto. There were Polish kids, White Russian kids, Hungarians and Estonians. And there were the children of American servicemen whose families had come from the States to join them in Shanghai.

Richard Jones was one of them. He became my friend. He taught me how to pitch a baseball. Then he taught me to bat. When I made third base, he ran over and held up my arm. The next time I managed to make it all the way home. He traded me an American flag for my Japanese one, which I smuggled into school wrapped up in my sweater. "This'll go down swell when I get back home," he said and wrapped it up in his. I tied the Stars and Stripes to my bike. I learned the meaning of the stars and could recite the names of all the states. I learnt to sing *The Star-Spangled Banner* and *America the Beautiful*. But for all my devotion to comics, I only scored an E for Reading in the first quarter.

Gitty Gilbert sat in the desk beside me. She giggled when I read aloud from our school reader and pronounced the word *sometimes* phonetically, giving it four syllables. When I sat down, feeling the flush on my cheeks, she nudged me with her elbow. She held out a package of CLOVE chewing gum below the lip of the desk and pushed out a piece. I met her

68

eyes and she smiled. I reached for the piece, but her thumb wouldn't release it. It was planted squarely over the initial C of the name on the wrapper. Her nail was bitten quite low. She nudged me again. "Read it," she whispered. As I did so, I felt the flush in my cheeks all over again.

Through the open door of his room, I saw Captain Milne packing his bag. "They're sending me back home," he said. "I've gotta be off in the morning." He came towards me and was about to extend his hand, but I had to turn away. I was already in my room when I heard him say, "I'll come say so long later. OK, Till, ol' buddy?"

I am lying in bed, awake. The clock on the landing strikes ONE. A while later it strikes ONE again. The aeroplanes at Lungwha don't let up. Their engines rise and fall. They throb as their waves pass each other. Now they wind up, for real, this time. They don't waver. They come to full pitch, singing in perfect unison. A Consolidated B-24 Liberator is taking off. The bed lifts, sways from side to side, then rises to the ceiling. The clock strikes another ONE. It is half past one in the morning. I am still fully awake.

I got up early to say so long, but Captain Milne's room was empty. Except for his mattress in the dust cover, rolled up and tied with string on the bed. A note was tucked under it. It read:

To Till
Sweet Dreams
Till The Clouds Roll By
Capt. Milne
(Your Flying Tiger)

69

My mother

Captain Richardson had an oil furnace installed. "Sylvia's going to be here by Christmas," he said. "She's used to being snug back home."

It was a steel box, about twice my height, an army khaki. It had levers and wheel valves and gauges and a little window, through which you could see the fire. It sat squarely in front of the fireplace in the sitting room downstairs, with a big metal flue disappearing into the wall. Where the flue bent, it had lots of tapered segments all welded together to make a curve, so that the smoke didn't have to go round a corner. The furnace hummed when it was going, which was night and day.

I wondered where they would put the Christmas tree, because the furnace now stood where we always had ours. Nowadays, of course, we had ours upstairs in our bedroom. We left our door open and the heat from the furnace came soaring up the stairs and filled our room with a wallowing warmth and a smell like the exhaust from aeroplanes.

"Can you be up by four-thirty in the morning?" Captain Richardson said one day. "I'm taking a plane up to see if I can spot Sylvia's ship. You kids can come for the ride."

The inside of the C-46 was a windowless hull that slanted steeply up to the cockpit. It only had a few folding seats along each side and you could see the ribs of the fuselage like the inside of a whale. "Is this your plane?" I asked Captain Richardson. He laughed. "Might as well be, number of times I've flown the old workhorse over the Hump." He made the propellers stutter into life. One side first, then the other.

"She's his ol' babe alright," said Captain Hamilton. He was co-pilot. "I've flown the Hump a few times myself and, believe me, you get kind of fond of your ship for bringing you home again in one piece."

The noise was terrific as the engines wound up. Everything started to vibrate and creak with the effort until they reached full throttle and the C-46 rocked and strained and sprang free. Captain Hamilton threw a last glance over the lap belts that

tied us into our dicky seats and Captain Richardson's "Ol' Babe" pressed forward, feeling out the bumps in the tarmac, heavily at first, getting lighter, then flipping them away below us as the fuselage levelled and brought the end of the runway into view through the bulbous nose cage. In a moment we were lifting over villages and fields. Then we were high over the Whangpoo River. "At 2,000 feet," Captain Richardson shouted. Three American warships and an aircraft carrier lay at anchor surrounded by a dense mosaic of sampans, Shanghai's water rickshaws. Freighters of all sizes crammed the docks and tankers waited their turn to berth at the Pootung petroleum wharves. A fleet of dredges worked the channel in mid-stream. The sun rose and silvered the wake behind motionless junks in the brown water. It threw a yellow tinge over the haze that clung to the city. Captain Richardson adjusted our course so that we weren't flying straight into it.

The engines lost their deep thunder as we left the river on our right for the comeliness of the fields and the known earth. Then, without warning, the horizon tilted and all those flat fields swung up on the left and filled the windows in the cockpit. The engines slackened and I could feel the plane dropping and suddenly there was the river mouth before us. No sooner had the horizon settled into place with the sun hovering above it than it tilted again, the other way this time, sending it hurtling behind us on a wheeling rack of sky. Captain Richardson had his head screwed round to the right, where Captain Hamilton was trying to read out the names of ships in the Whangpoo heading upstream towards Shanghai. I clambered in beside him and saw our wing tip in the window, poised above the water as if wanting to dip into it. Ships, much larger now, wheeled slowly round it, their names and ports of home unravelling in the stern.

Captain Richardson smiled and Captain Hamilton gave the thumbs-up and the C-46 did another complete round of a twin-stacked vessel in mid-stream, with Sylvia radiant on the deck, waving a silk scarf and squinting into the morning sun.

SHE TURNED OUT TO BE MUCH MORE BEAUTIFUL than I had imagined. Small, delicate. Her hair hung loose and kicked up from her shoulders, shining golden, revealing a long neck. Her nose kicked up, too. Her eyes were quick, shimmering behind dark lashes that could flutter as she tilted her head to look at you. Her lips were thin and very red and quickly lost their smile when Captain Richardson showed her the portrait that Mami had done from the photo. "There's a likeness, honey," she said, "but it's just not me." It wasn't. The formal bearing, the steadfast gaze, the larger-than-life image had missed the mark. "More Hamburg than Carolina," Sylvia said and turned it to the wall.

When they met, Mami was gracious, hospitable even, as though she were the hostess and Sylvia the guest. She coolly invited her to make herself at home and to send Rabe and me upstairs when we got too much to bear. Sylvia had been trying to formulate a reply when she turned abruptly to her husband and slid her hands over him to touch her fingertips together behind his neck. "If we're going out to dinner, sweetiepie," she said, "I'd like to start getting ready. Will you help me choose my evening dress? I'll need someone to iron it."

She said, "Excuse us," as she led her husband past Mami and up the stairs, leaving her standing in the sitting room, where she had entertained the wives of diplomats at countless receptions and where she now had no business to set foot at all. Mami didn't move. We stood and watched her in silence. She was just starting up the stairs when Captain Richardson came back down and stopped halfway.

"Ilse," he said, "Sylvia would like to invite your kids to come with us. It's going to be a Christmas affair at the Sennet, for families. Santa Claus is going to be there."

I saw my mother in a no-man's land, her back to us, facing the American. "I think they should stay home tonight," she said. "It is the third Sunday of Advent. We are having guests. It is our tradition."

Captain Richardson's smile was awkward. He shifted his weight onto the other leg, wincing a little, then placed his hand on the balustrade. "We won't be home late," he said. "It's just going to be a fun evening."

"Please can we go?" Rabe and I spoke simultaneously and I felt like a traitor. Mami turned toward me and her look told me I was. Then she lowered her eyes and said in a tired voice, "Alright, if you want to."

"Tell your wife thank you," she called out just as she heard Captain Richardson close the door to his room. Then she started up the stairs a second time and continued to the top without turning around. We followed, after she'd climbed two or three flights, letting the choked air that she trailed behind her exhale its burden. Upstairs we heard her telling Amah to wash our hair and make us ready to go out.

*

CAPTAIN RICHARDSON SAT AT THE WHEEL OF THE BUICK and waited. Rabe and I disappeared into the back seat. "Captain Richardson,—" Rabe began, leaning forward to get closer, but the captain didn't seem to want to listen. A little impatiently, he said, "Can you please just call me Bill?"

76

Rabe didn't pursue his question. It probably wasn't important anyway. What had happened just now was that, for the night, we had become family. I stopped sulking because we weren't going in the Jeep and admitted to myself that the ivory steering wheel and dashboard of the Buick were very beautiful, as were the cream coloured door linings with those padded grips. Not to mention the creamy leather upholstery, which gleamed in wonderful contrast to the dark blue exterior, and I thought we were the luckiest boys in the world. When the house door opened and Sylvia stood in the light of the porch in a red dress and silver mink stole, I was ready to concede that the Buick had been the right choice.

Bill leaped out and guided her into the car, whereupon it instantly filled with her dreamy perfume and tinkling laughter. Boy came down from the house to hold open the driver's door and Bill, at ease in a dark suit and tie, sat heavily in behind the steering wheel. Boy slammed the door shut and sealed us in so close that it made my ears pop.

The Buick began to move. I reached for the strap on the door pillar and pulled myself up so that I could see over the seat rest and watch the car's bonnet as it reached into the night. It tapered a long way out in front and its shiny emblem, like a gun sight, scanned the bushes in the glow of the headlights, then steadied and took aim straight down the centre of the street.

It had begun to rain. The city wiggled in the reflections of neon lit facades spilling music into the street among the swish of cars all black and chrome on white walled tyres and umbrellas popping up to shield brocaded ladies alighting from their running boards with a flash of naked thigh. Hot inside the Sennet, Sylvia slid the mink from her bare shoulders and Bill pocketed the numbered tag. He introduced her to friends. She introduced us, making us feel special. We remembered not to bow. Waiters brought drinks, very smart Chinese youths with Brylcream and tight trousers. I knew to ask for an ice cream soda. Rabe said he'd have one, too.

The women's talk skittered around the table, very fast, trills of laughter interspersed. I found it hard to follow. A sudden hush and "Ho, ho, ho!" from an oversized Santa Claus. Richard Jones rushed at me from out of nowhere and whispered into my ear, hands cupped, all breath and excitement, "That's my dad!" He ran off, turned, pointed, laughing. I noticed other kids from school with their moms and dads. I kept a look-out for Gitty Gilbert. I didn't straight away notice the little pile of sweets on the table in front of me. Richard, was that you?

Sylvia shooed us from our places to join in the scramble that was now besieging Santa Claus. When I turned halfway, it was the question *Are we allowed?* that she read in my face and she nodded wildly, her face exploding with a soundless *Yes*, her lady friends echoing her, soundlessly. When the scramble was over, Santa Claus held out an orange in each hand and Rabe said *Thank you* as he took his and I remembered just in time to say *Thanks!* Then he gave us two more. We stuck them in our pockets to take home.

Bill Richardson stood by the bar and held out a drink to Santa Claus. Richard Jones led his mother by the hand and delivered her to Santa, who slung an arm around her and kissed her long and hard on the mouth. He held his drink high in the air as he did so, as though proposing an endless toast, and didn't spill a drop. Then he took a microphone and began to sing in a voice that didn't seem to be his, it was too light and high and sweet for such a big man.

I'm in the mood for love
Simply because you're near me
Funny, but when you're near me
I'm in the mood for love.

Then the band played and Richard's mom and dad danced the first dance, he still in his Santa outfit, guiding his wife around the wooden dance floor as if they were weightless. People clapped when the dance ended.

I was glad the American ladies didn't ask about my mom and dad, what with her being left on her own and him stuck in Kiangwan Camp awaiting repatriation. I wondered whether Richard Jones thought Bill and Sylvia were my parents.

Bill Richardson had taken the microphone and was saying something I couldn't hear. Then the loudspeakers made a shuddering sound and I saw him smile and a moment later his deep voice filled the Sennet and everyone stopped talking. He swayed a little as he sang:

Ol' man river, that ol' man river
He must know somethin', but he don't say nothin'
He just keeps rollin'
He keeps on rollin' along.

And then the second verse and then:

You an' me, we sweat an' strain
Body all achin' and wracked with pain...

I loved that bit. Loved to hear Mami singing it, the way Bill did, the way Paul Robeson did, with a heavy beat. "My mother knows that song," Rabe piped up and Sylvia hushed him and people turned their heads. When Bill had finished, he came across to our table and took Sylvia's hand. "May I have this dance, honeymunch?" he said. They looked wonderful, Bill so handsome and she so lovely in that red dress. The dance floor filled, while Rabe kept the ladies at our table entertained. Oh yes, they were soaking up his stories. If anyone had asked them to dance, they would have stayed put. How I wished he would keep his mouth shut.

"Once, when my mother was just getting out of the bath, Bill Richardson opened the door and she just stood there, holding up the towel in front of herself, and Bill Richardson began to laugh, because he was looking in the mirror on the opposite door behind her back." It made me cringe. It had the ladies in fits. "Wait till Sylvia gets to hear that story," I said to him when we got outside. But, judging by the silence in the Buick on the way home, I guessed that she already had.

*

MISHA BRENNER'S STACCATO came hammering down the stairs as we entered the house. I couldn't tell whether it was laughter or just the way he talked when he got excited, in his Russian German. A woman's voice ran through it. That was Maria Blödorn. We found her reading aloud from a book of German Dadaist poets.

80

Schinkel purzel funkele
pinkel furzel stunkele

Mami lay back on the latex mattress, over which she had spread a Chinese rug. She looked wonderfully relaxed, a happy laughing Mami, waving us in through the door.

Misha took down a painting from the wall and unrolled a silver screen in its place. He adjusted the projector and brought an image into focus. PICASSO was all it said. There followed a crazy lantern show of paintings. Most of them were of women. They looked as if Picasso had taken them to pieces and put them back together wrongly on purpose. Misha said that was the point of it. If you painted a woman as you saw her, that would be all you got, but if you took her apart and then put her back together in a new way, you'd be saying something about her that only you could say and so the painting would be about you and her. She might be looking straight at the painter and sideways at someone else at the same time. What would that say about her? I wondered whether Sylvia would have liked Mami's portrait of her better if she had approached it that way.

Maria Blödorn stood up and folded an arm behind her head. "I could have been Picasso's model," she said. I looked at her, tall in her black trouser suit, her hair combed close to the skull and gathered in a bun. She was right. It was the skull that did it. The sense of bone. The way her brow extended straight down the bridge of her nose and overhung her eyes like a precipice. Picasso could play with ideas like that and I was beginning to do so myself.

Maria Blödorn poured the rest of the vermouth and picked

up the Chesterfields. Misha took one and lit hers with a silver lighter and then his own. "I'm sorry, would you like one?" he said to Mami, who seldom smoked but liked to be asked. She took one and tapped its end on her thumbnail, not just a couple of times, but on and on, so that Misha had to wait with the lighter. Then she put the other end in her mouth and felt for the loose strand of tobacco with her tongue, making a pained expression. Misha held the flame into the space between them.

I close my eyes and the flame is still there on the inside of my eyelids. When I open them again, it is dark. I have pulled the bedcovers over my head. I press the palms of my hands into my eyes and watch the muddy puddle spread out from the rim. I press harder and it gets lighter, patterns weaving across. Then it is a luminous blue, like looking into a bright universe, seeing forever into distance. You have to keep the pressure on your eyes perfectly steady to maintain that image, because, if you relax it even slightly, a cloud spills over and everything becomes dark.

I am listening to violins playing, muffled, through the wall and through my bedclothes. Mami's dark sound and Misha's brighter one, weaving in and out of each other. I recognise the music, because Mami has been practising it, the slow movement from Bach's double violin concerto. It's the kind of music that, if you go to sleep while you're listening, it comes along with you and you can go in and out of sleep as often as you like and it will still be there.

When I woke, the house was vast and silent. Just the clock echoing on the stair. I pumped my ears with the palms of my hands and it was like the pressure of the door closing me into the Buick. The creamy light, the softness, the smell of leather. And now Bill Richardson and Sylvia dancing at the Sennet. Smiling, flirting with each other. Every now and then they'd slip around the corner and out of reach. Then I'd hear Mami whispering. She'd be saying *Alright, alright, go if you want to.* Her voice tired.

It is late. I'm returning home. Strange. I must have been away. It feels like a short time, yet the place has changed so I hardly recognise it. An old woman stands in the door of a dilapidated cottage. There are bits of washing on a line. All kinds of old things clutter the yard, as if they were left lying there a long time ago and no one has bothered to come and pick them up. A wheelbarrow on its side with a broken shaft, an upturned bucket, a ladder with rungs missing, a rusted cross-cut saw with no handle at one end. Next to it a saw-horse. Bits of cut wood. Shards of broken drainpipes. A collapsed mound of straw, a rake, a pitchfork. The woman looks over her shoulder as she enters the cottage. It is my mother. She says something, I can't hear what. The open mouth of a drain exhales a dull breath, hopelessly.

I hate this dream. Things falling apart. But I can't wake from it, because there is another dream that has to come through. I know what it's going to be. It's always the same. The clutter of stuff has gone. In its place is emptiness. I am alone. It is night. Nothing moves. High up in the empty sky there is a full moon, a perfect circle of light. Or maybe just a bright point, smaller than any star. I'm holding a line in my hand. It goes all the way up there. It is infinitely fine and silent. Like a thread of silk. A single filament of silk. Yet between my fingers it is warm and smooth and round, like living flesh.

83

All the way down from the sky a whispered sound comes sliding. My mother's voice. This time I can hear it. It says:

Biggi, you're alive!

And I wake.

My father

I woke to the sound of Amah singing. It was her favourite song, about the little boy who returned from his wanderings because he loved his mother. Amah sang in German. It made us laugh, because she had picked up the words phonetically and they had odd little slips and slurs to them. She placed a pot of rice on the table and arranged the bowls. "Breakfast," she said.

We pulled on our slippers and dressing gowns and sprinkled sugar mixed with cinnamon on the steaming rice. Amah poured hot milk from a saucepan. She beamed. "Today have milk. Mishabrenner bring big tin powdermilk. Good one." We were lucky. It was more usual to find the original contents had been replaced with rice flour. You had to look out for the tell-tale solder plugs at the top and bottom of the tin.

Amah removed the wrinkled skin from the hot milk before pouring mine. "You should eat that," Mami's voice admonished from the door. She, too, was in her dressing gown and was tying her hair up with a head scarf. "It's the best part," she said and took the teaspoon from Amah and licked off the skin that clung to it. It nearly made me gag. Amah went to get the tea.

"Did you have a lovely time last night?" Mami said. We remembered the oranges and put them on the table. "From Santa Claus," Rabe said. "There were lots of children there and they got all the sweets."

"Why don't Bill and Sylvia have any children?" I asked.

"It's a sad story," Mami said, "but they can't have children. Bill Richardson was wounded during the war. You know that he flew dangerous missions over the Himalayas—"

"We flew in his C-46. We know!" Rabe and I cut in to lay claim to first-hand knowledge of dangerous missions.

"He received a bullet wound here," Mami said, indicating her groin, "from Japanese fighters."

The C-46 had had a well-worn look, like a truck or a piece of machinery. Like Captain Milne's Jeep. Unlike the Buick. Yet I couldn't remember seeing bullet holes, even patched-up holes or broken glass in the nose dome. Maybe the Jap fighters attacked from below and got him through the seat.

"Has he still got his joy-stick?" Rabe said, showing off his new word from school.

"His what?"

"OK, his willie." Rabe made it sound patronising.

Amah had come in and was pouring green tea for Mami. The smile on her face said she'd caught the gist of the conversation. She was using our new teapot. The black one Rabe and I bought for Mami at the market. She cut off the flow with a deft lift of the spout to keep it from dribbling.

"Yes, he has." Mami managed to sound matter-of-fact. "But the wound was deep."

That did it. Rabe crossed his legs. I simply went numb. I must have gone pale, too. "It's alright now," Mami said. "It just means he'll never have children."

I tried hard to stop picturing Bill Richardson naked with a bullet wound in his groin. To a nine-year-old boy, a willie is a willie and you can have fun with it. But a grown-up man's penis is quite another matter, even without a bullet wound. I saw my father's penis once, when he was still with us, maybe three years earlier. I have never told anyone about it before.

It happened like this. I had been watching Mami painting her toenails red. While she waited for them to dry, I sorted through the silk scarves and handkerchiefs she kept in a tall chest of drawers. I unfolded them to admire them and then folded them up again. In the very top drawer, she kept her jewellery box. It was padded and embroidered. I lifted it down and began looking at all the necklaces and brooches. I had my favourites. I held up the one with the blue flower petals, like glass, so you could see the light through them. Mami draped a silk scarf over my head and pinned it with the brooch. Then she painted the fingernails of my left hand.

"Sit still so you don't smudge it," she said.

"How long does it take to dry?"

"About a minute."

"Is a minute a long time?"

"No, but to a small impatient child it can seem a very long time," she said and left the room.

I held my hand up in the air. I remained sitting on Mami's bed for what seemed close enough to being a very long time. Then I got up to look at myself in the mirror. What I saw was a young girl with my face. I began to fumble with the pin, but my red fingernails mocked my frowning in the mirror. My hands stopped working. They moved forwards when I wanted them to move backwards towards my chest. Everything seemed back-to-front and I needed a pee and those were my father's footsteps coming up the stairs.

The moment I had shot under Mami's bed I knew I had sealed my fate. I thought of clambering out and pretending to be looking for something. A button, for example. But Daddi was already in the room. Besides, how could I let him see me like this? I tried not to hold my breath because, sooner or later, I would give myself away with an almighty gasp. And probably wet myself. So I panted lightly like a dog, making no sound at all.

Daddi's feet rounded the foot of the bed. His heels had skewed the leather uppers at the back of his slippers. He kicked them off and removed his dressing gown. Oh my God, I thought, he's going to get into bed. Going to read the paper in bed. But the next thing he did was pull his pyjama cord and let the pants crumple down around his feet. Then he stepped out of them. I could see Daddi from the waist down and he was naked.

I was staring at his penis. I probably stopped breathing then. It hung heavily, a serious, living part of my father's flesh. This was much more than a thing to pee or play with. It could make babies happen. It actually made *me* happen. And Rabe, too. All around it there grew a mighty forest of black hair, making it look like it belonged to a savage, some kind of wild man, a man never to be trifled with.

That man was my Daddi. And here was I, spying at him from under Mami's bed. Stealing from his savage nakedness a sight that was never intended for my eyes. Any savage would kill for such a crime. Without a moment's thought. *Kill.* My urge to pee left me forever.

"Have you seen Didi?" came Mami's voice from the door.

"Didi, no." They still called me Didi then. Only Amah is allowed to call me Didi now. And that's because she has real trouble saying Till.

Mami went through to the verandah, where the cyclamens grew. "Didi?" she called and then, under her breath, "Strange," and mercifully exited.

Daddi was dressing. I should say, I was watching the lower half of Daddi dressing. Then he came towards me. He sat

89

down on his bed and dangled his feet only inches from my nose and pulled on his socks. Then his shoes. The top of his head brushed against the fringe of the bedcovers when he did up his laces. It smelt of cigarette smoke.

Daddi took ages to get ready. He made three false exits, each time turning back for something. I fabricated a story to account for my disappearance and was still rehearsing it as I crawled out of my hiding place. I don't remember what it was, but it would've been a good one, in case Mami asked. But she never did, so I didn't get to use it.

I got the brooch pin undone without the duplicity of a mirror. In any case, there wasn't one in our upstairs bathroom. But there was a nailbrush and a cuttlefish bone from when Mami had kept canaries. It took some time, with the aid of these instruments, to remove the red from my fingernails. The crescent traces that persisted along the cuticles eventually vanished with a little help from my teeth.

*

BILL RICHARDSON AND SYLVIA now slept in Mami and Daddi's old room. I saw inside it once. I had been sitting on the stair doing a drawing of Lupo, who was lying as always just outside their door, fast asleep. My drawing showed Lupo's balls very clearly. I never wanted anyone to see it. So, when Sylvia came up the stair, I turned it over and slid it under my thighs.

"What're you drawing?" Sylvia said.

Lupo had got up. "I was just trying to draw *him*. It's not very good."

90

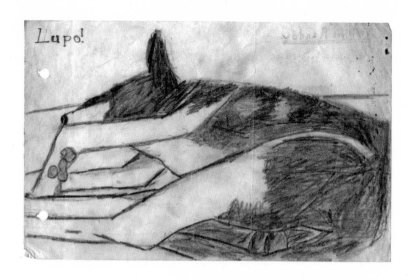

Sylvia went into the room. She stood with her head craned round to face the mirror while she struggled with the zip in the small of her back. "Would you be a honey and help me with this?"

I had never imagined a woman's waist so small. Nor her dress so tight. "The zipper's stuck," I said. "I can't do it. Sorry." I bolted for the door.

"Thanks for trying," I heard her say as she closed it behind me. *Whew!*

Only the zipper was still stuck inside there, somewhere. In that room.

What I had noticed was that they'd moved their beds together. I was glad about that. If they couldn't have children because of Bill Richardson's bullet wound, at least this way they could snuggle up together and keep each other warm as they went to sleep.

My drawing pad was still lying on the step and I bent to pick it up just as Captain Mantoux came barging out of his room.

He was our new American. He was followed by a woman I'd never seen before. Lupo greeted them, his tail wagging, his nose nuzzling into the woman's groin.

"This is my wife Stella," he said. "Stella, this is Till."

"Till? Wherever have you been all my life Till now?" she giggled. "I say, what've we got here?"

I was holding the drawing by my side, but she whisked it out of my hand. "Why, this is simply gorgeous," she said. "Darling, isn't this simply gorgeous?"

I recognised her now, from Mami's portrait. But, if Mami had misjudged the playful kitten in Sylvia, she certainly fell short of finding the full-blown lioness in Stella. The captain looked up into her face and smiled a shy smile, but said nothing. "Wait till I show Sylvie," Stella said and stole away with her prize.

"Can I have it back please," I called after her. "It isn't finished."

"Sure," I heard her say as she disappeared into the Richardsons' room. I hated her for that. Those two haven't got children either, I thought, oozing venom and hoping they never would. But, by the summer, her light cottons had begun to show a roundness that Mami said meant a baby was on its way.

I had forgiven Stella by then. In fact, we'd got to like each other. She even asked me to do a drawing of her. But I never saw her baby because, by the late summer, Stella and the captain had left for the United States. The week after, Bill Richardson and Sylvia left, too. They left Lupo with some friends of theirs and I never saw him again. The following week, it rained so hard, Rabe and I got drenched on the way to school. We had to wheel our bikes through knee-deep water. The school's principal saw us as we passed his house and invited us in. He wrapped us in huge towels until our clothes had dried. His boy served us French toast and cocoa. The week after that we were expelled from school.

Mami never said why. We knew it couldn't have been because of anything we had done. You could tell a kid that was setting himself up to get thrown out. My reading had improved from an E to a B and I always got an A for attitude and deportment. And the day of the downpour, we had been very polite to the school's principal and thanked him for his kindness.

SHANGHAI AMERICAN PRIVATE SCHOOL		
53 Avenue Petain, Shanghai		
School-Year 1945-1946		
PRIMARY SCHOOL		

Report of scholastic standing for __Till R. Von Rendow__ Grade __Third__
1st quarter, 1st semester, 3rd quarter, school-year.

Subject	Rating	Remarks
Reading	E	
Spelling	C	
Language	C	
Oral Recitation	C	
Written Work	C	
Penmanship	B	
Arithmetic	B	
Drawing	B	
Science	C	
Geography		
History		
Music		
Attitude	A	
Effort	B	
Deportment	A	
Neatness	B	
Chinese language	A	

This sheet is used for reporting progress in Grades I through VI, hence it lists all subjects given in those grades. The marks indicate those subjects taught in the grade to which your child belongs.

The grade of A means exceptionally good, B above average, C Average, D passing but below average, E Incomplete either because of late start, slow progress, or sickness. F-definitely failing.

Teacher's Signature ___Pauline___

SHANGHAI AMERICAN PRIVATE SCHOOL		
53 Avenue Petain, Shanghai		
School-Year 1945-1946		
PRIMARY SCHOOL		

Report of scholastic standing for __Till Von Rendow__ Grade __Third__
1st quarter, 1st semester, 3rd quarter, school-year.

Subject	Rating	Remarks
Reading	B	
Spelling	B	
Language	C	
Oral Recitation	C	
Written Work	B	
Penmanship	A	
Arithmetic	A	
Drawing	A	
Science	C	
Geography		
History		
Music		
Attitude	A	
Effort	A	
Deportment	A	
Neatness	A	
Chinese language	B	

This sheet is used for reporting progress in Grades I through VI, hence it lists all subjects given in those grades. The marks indicate those subjects taught in the grade to which your child belongs.

The grade of A means exceptionally good, B above average, C Average, D passing but below average, E Incomplete either because of late start, slow progress, or sickness. F-definitely failing.

Teacher's Signature ___Pauline___

I wondered if it was somehow connected with the man who came to visit not long after. Mami had been acting a bit strange for some days. She disappeared for hours on her bicycle, while we stayed at home with nothing to do. She didn't play her violin in the evenings. She hardly even talked.

On the morning of the visit she kept us close. She led us downstairs, where nobody was living now the Americans had gone. I recognised the man. He had been at the house before, years ago, probably one of Daddi's circle of friends. Mami invited him to sit. He greeted us with a tight-lipped sort of smile and when we didn't respond he pulled a funny face to make us laugh. It made me scowl. Amah brought tea and sat down with us. The man looked at Mami with his eyebrows raised and waited. I guessed he wanted to talk to her alone.

"I asked them to stay," Mami said and crossed her arms.

"You will know that I was at Kiangwan Camp with your husband," he said after a while. "Excuse me, your ex-husband. With a whole little German community, in fact. We set up a committee to run it and make representations to the Chinese authorities." I was thinking it sounded just like the consulate all over again, when the man turned to me and said, "Your Daddi was chosen to be their spokesman." He gave his tight-lipped smile again. "I was elected by the camp committee to represent the German nationals remaining in Shanghai. In this capacity, I am responsible for organising their repatriation."

There it was. That word again. The ship was to sail in three weeks' time, the man said, and he had placed us on the passenger list. He added that refusal to be repatriated would be regarded with disfavour by the Chinese authorities.

"We're staying," Mami said.

"How will you survive financially?" he said. "Consider your two sons."

"I *am* considering them," she said. "We will manage. In fact, I have just enrolled them at the Shanghai British School. They are starting school next week."

Was she *bluffing?* I looked across at Rabe and he nodded his head as if he'd known all the time. He had. I could feel it in my tummy. Like a cramp.

Mami stood. She seemed taller than usual. Her arm came up to show the man to the door. He scrambled to his feet but didn't move. "There's one more thing," he said.

He rested his hands on the back of his chair. "Your ex-husband is coming to see the children. He has been handed over to the Americans. You can expect a phone call from the prison authorities to make an appointment." He took a step towards her, bowed and offered his hand. "I am here to help you," he said. "Don't forget."

Mami didn't take it. Instead, she led him to the door. This time he followed. When he had gone, she went upstairs, leaving us hanging. I heard her bedroom door close.

Amah gathered us up. "I make banana fritters for tiffin[1]," she said. "You come help me." Rabe followed her into the kitchen. I went upstairs. I stood outside Mami's room and listened. She was moving stuff around. I could hear her saying things under her breath, whispered things. Muffled sounds. Silence. Then, "Mami?" I said.

"Wait." Her voice, very quiet. "Oh well, you can come in."

Mami sat hunched on her bed, staring at the wall. Picture frames and canvasses scattered all over the floor. Above the skirting board the wallpaper had been curled back. The hole in the wall was dark. Out of its emptiness Mami's voice seemed to come in a whisper. "They're gone," it said.

"What?" My mouth dry. "The gold bars?"

She doesn't answer, or maybe I can't hear her. I want to

1 lunch

95

touch her, but I can't find my hands. My bottom isn't sitting on her bed. The floor has vanished beneath my feet. The room has emptied, become white. Nothing moves. There is no sound.

TILL???

I sat up. "Amah is making banana fritters for tiffin," I said.

Mami put a hand on my shoulder. "Come on, let's go get them."

Afterwards, Mami talked to Amah. She didn't talk to the other servants. They were still there, all except Coolie, who had gone up country to take care of his sick father. Amah said she had once overheard Cook and Boy talking about Coolie. Coolie had boasted of having hidden some gold watches. The hiding place wasn't in the servants' quarters, Amah said, but somewhere in the house, where no one would think of looking. She didn't know where. Only Coolie knew the place.

"Maybe, Missie, you put Daddi's gold bars in same place belong Coolie's gold watch," Amah said. "He very lucky man, that Coolie."

*

FROM OUR BEDROOM WINDOW we watched two Jeeps arrive. They were the kind I'd first seen downtown with Captain Milne. A solid roof, white, with two large letters in dark blue: MP.

Daddi sat on the sofa he had once used to bolster up the window against shattering glass. He wore a loose jacket over cotton trousers that were too large for him. He greeted us in

English with a heavy drawl, trying to sound American, but it just sounded funny. "Got a kiss for Big Daddi?" I actually thought he looked smaller than before. His hair cut very short. His hands and wrists bony out of loose sleeves. He dangled them over our shoulders. His kiss was stubbly on my cheek.

I ran upstairs, returned with a story book and asked Daddi to read to us. A story about ducks. In German. Daddi unbuttoned his jacket pocket and put on a pair of glasses. He looked funny. He wiggled his eyebrows and rumpled his nose to make us laugh. "Ah, it's in German," he drawled. "I haven't got any German glasses. Don't you have any English books?"

"We've got comics," Rabe said. "Do you want to see our comics?"

"Ah, you have comics. Comics is all we get to read where I live, too. OK let's see what this book is about." He had switched to speaking German. "I won't need my glasses for this. It has lots of pictures."

Then suddenly it was like Tuesday nights in his study before he went away. Rabe and I sat dead still while Daddi read, until it came to the places where the ducks had to quack. It sounded so real, the way Daddi quacked, we giggled and squirmed and got him to read those bits over and over again. Each time he did so, it got even more real and he added hisses and the peeping of the ducklings and the hoarse voice of grandfather duck. I wanted him never to stop.

But he couldn't stay. Mami told us to say goodbye and sent us upstairs. I turned round and gave him a wave. The next time I saw him was when I was twenty-four.

"I didn't want you to see him handcuffed," Mami said. "There were two MPs waiting to take him out to the Jeep."

Then she told me that Daddi had married Tante Alix and they'd had a baby. Mami couldn't remember the name of the baby. But he was my younger brother and they called him Didi, like me.

Becoming British

Their years in the Japanese internment camps were not just remembered, they were etched into their angled bones. Like elbows and fists that boxed. Knuckled fists. Fast and light, these boys carried no puppy fat. Rabe and I were the enemy and we were outnumbered, outmanoeuvred and outrun. When the Russian boy came to our help, he too became their enemy and we became friends. Oleg didn't box, but he could catch a flying fist and twist it into an arm lock. When mobbed, he ran, not fast, but with a loping stride that could take two or three sprinters along and send them tumbling down in a heap. An ally to be reckoned with. No teacher ever intervened. We talked to Mami about it and she enrolled us with Massimo Morelli for wrestling.

Massimo Morelli displayed his twice life-sized image in a cut-out sign mounted above his gate. We passed it each day on the way to school. The cut-out had on a pair of blue shorts, but presented the rest of Morelli's body to the street. Very muscular, with skin that shone as though oiled. His head was turned towards his flexed biceps, which he studied with steadfast admiration. When I told Amah we were going to him, she laughed, but she covered the laugh with her hand.

We did chin-ups and press-ups and learned wrestling holds that we practised on each other. We learned how to use our own weight against a lighter opponent. In the playground of the Shanghai British School we began to command respect. We ploughed through the terror of flying fists and brought our adversaries down. We pinned them to the ground and made sure they felt it when we knelt on them. Oleg was our champion. He loved the new tactics and paid no heed to cries for clemency. *Get off, you're hurting me* was met with his *So now is my turn.* It may have appealed to him as a kind of justice, but it cost him a blood nose from an unguarded quarter. Oleg recoiled, spun round and came down on his knees, the curve of his back protecting him like a wounded animal's, his head buried in his hands. He didn't move. The blood between his fingers was a very bright red. We gathered round, as much to shield the slain from view as to attend to his rehabilitation. Someone placed a key on the nape of his neck. *They taught us in Brownies* was the explanation. Another offered his handkerchief, waving it at Oleg as if he might catch sight of it through the top of his head. "You can keep it," he said. "I don't need it." Oleg still didn't move. *If only the bleeding would stop before the end of break* was the hope that united us. And it probably would have, had not Oleg made a sudden lunge in the direction of the offender and fallen on top of him just as the bell rang.

Oleg explained to Miss McGregor that he often got nose bleeds and that they soon passed. The boy with blood all over his shirt said he'd tried to get Oleg to hold up his head to stop the bleeding. The silence that followed was a white stone wall. Only a stifled giggle breached it before the girl with the red

100

hair had time to slap her hand over her mouth. Heads turned. A slow stain rose up her neck and spread over her cheeks.

Miss McGregor eyed her. "You wanted to say something?"

There was no reply. Would she tell? Very gently, Miss McGregor repeated the question and the girl said, "Please ma'am, can I have back my key?"

The incident didn't put an end to the fighting. It changed it. Where it had been a free-for-all, it now became subject to rules. It was alright to bring your opponent down, but not to hurt him. If he cried out *You're hurting me!* you got off. If someone shouted *Pax!* it meant he wasn't in the fight any more and you left him alone. Rabe made the counter-demand that two (or three or four) against one was unfair and only single combat was allowed. It was a radical demand, considering the odds we'd been facing, but it stuck. And it turned the fighting into a kind of ritual or game and, as with all games, we got bored with it and eventually gave it up. Except for Oleg, who hadn't had enough of the action and kept picking fights. I even had to intervene when he persisted in beating up a boy I'd started playing marbles with.

By the end of term, in December 1946, the fighting had given way to more civilised contests. Michael Brisk brought his soccer ball to school. It was leather and was laced up with leather thongs. We kicked it around and did goal practice and he taught me how to dribble the ball (he even wore the right kind of boots) and I found it impossible to get it off him, he was so clever with it. Then one day I did and afterwards he shook my hand and I noticed for the first time how he'd rounded out, his arms no longer like sticks or bones, and he congratulated me and I knew I had taken a fair stride forward to becoming British.

And there's another thing that was going on, watched out of the corner of my eye. The girls had started playing hockey. Us boys kept away as if it was somehow beneath us, but I couldn't help stealing little glances at them. They had their skirts tucked into their bloomers and they chased the ball on long bare legs and whacked it with their hockey sticks to make it fly and leave behind a *crack!* on the air and the umpire shouting *Sticks!* Must be a British thing, I thought to myself, a game British girls played. I recognised the ones from my class, but I'd never spoken to a single one of them. They were part of a whole other world, whose windows had remained shuttered, but whose shutters were beginning to rattle.

In the last loose days before school broke up for the year teachers invented tasks to keep us occupied. Oleg suggested we make a Union Jack. "British flag," he explained. "I like to make British flag." So we cut out the crosses of St George, St Andrew and St Patrick and overlaid them on a blue ground, exactly as shown in the Encyclopaedia Britannica. Then we turned it over and did the same on the other side. The flag looked impressive and I thought about the Japanese and American flags that had fluttered in turn from the rear of my bike, but dismissed the sequel that that thought suggested. Not only because it couldn't possibly flutter, being composed of seven layers of heavy paper, but because I was older now and it seemed a childish thing to do. Miss McGregor was full of praise and got Oleg and me to explain to the class the significance of the crosses and how they went together, showing different widths of margins on their arms. They seemed to have had no idea.

Except for one. "Please Ma'am, that flag isn't right. The

wide margin always has to be on top nearest the mast. On that flag it'll be on top one side but down on the other."

She had stood to make her point, her face bright, her eyes sparkling (brown eyes like mine), meeting mine for the first time ever, for only an instant, before their lids came down to cover them. Then she folded her skirt under to sit.

Not until after school—watching Oleg do up a hexagon nut with a spanner while his other hand held a screwdriver into the slot to stop the screw rotating—not until then (and sounding as casual as I could) did I ask him, "Oleg, do you know that girl's name?"

"Please you don't always call me Oleg," was what he gave me for a reply. "Can you say Ollie? Only my father, he call me Oleg."

I waited for a moment. "Do you know that girl's name, Ollie?" I said.

"That girl with key she put here?" He slapped the back of his neck. "Name is Elizabeth Adams."

"No, not her. The other girl. Today," I said.

"Who? Oh, you mean about British flag? What you call? Union Jack?" Ollie looked up from his Meccano. I nodded. "You like her?" His eyebrows two tall dark arches over his eyes. "You can have. I give to you. Too smart for me, that girl. Top of whole class always," and he brought his brows back down to concentrate on his nut and screw. Maybe he didn't know her name. Maybe he was shy of girls, like me.

"Please you hold me that nut while I tighten bolt. Thank you. You know what is it called, this bridge? It is single span arch girder bridge. My father he teach me to build this bridge. My father is engineer."

Ollie's single span arch girder bridge spanned from the dresser (with an old schoolbook under it so as not to scratch the varnish) to the back of an armchair. I estimated the span at about three feet. "Hundred metres," Ollie said. "See how strong." He proceeded to load the bridge up with books from his father's bookcase. "All in Russian," he laughed. "You can't read anyway." He passed the books through the triangulated spaces between the red and green perforated struts and piled them up on the traffic deck of the bridge. "Each one is ten ton truck," he explained. "Twenty-five trucks is two hundred and fifty ton load." The bridge never even squeaked. When his father came in, he laughed. They talked in Russian. Ollie's father had exactly the same eyebrows as Ollie. He shook my hand and spoke to me in Russian and Ollie told him to stop and they both laughed.

I thought a good deal about that bridge and the ten ton trucks and Ollie's father (did he have a mother?) and I wished I could have been more like Ollie. Ollie knew what he was doing and what he would be doing when he grew up, while I sat there, gazing out of the classroom window and getting an F in arithmetic and forgetting to bring home my report and not even managing to find out that girl's name.

So, when the next school year began, I decided not to gaze out of the window and concentrated instead on what was going on in class. By the end of the first day, as a direct result of that decision, I had discovered that the girl's name was Ann Murray and, by the end of the first term, that I could equal her in English composition and beat her in arithmetic with straight A's. But, despite it all, I still hadn't managed to speak to her. I looked at her a lot, but I never once caught her looking at me. Ollie teased me about it and laughed when I blushed. His turn to blush came when his English composition earned him the bottom mark in the class and Mrs Anderson, our new form teacher, took up half the lesson going over the use of the definite article. I didn't think he'd ever learn to use it and I imagined that, as an engineer, he would probably get on perfectly well without it.

*

SPRING CAME EARLY in those young days and the weeping willows that bounded the playing field kicked it in with a flurry of green. The groundsman made a running track around the field and the clanking and whirring of the mower blades carried with it the fresh smell of cut grass. Baskets up-ended it into hillocks and we dived into them and tumbled, flung grass in fistfuls and stuffed it down open shirt collars until the hillocks had all but vanished into the strewn field.

A sandpit appeared in the corner of the grounds, but this time the ban was announced before we had a chance to claim it for our use. It shattered my vision of tunnels and secret chambers and castellated turrets, but it opened my way into the unexpected realm of unaided flight. A wooden take-off board had been embedded into the ground at the end of a mown strip, but well clear of the sandpit, making a no-man's-land between them that only the weak-hearted would ever set foot in.

Accelerating arms and legs along the runway, inner engine racing, the take-off board thumps below me and I am airborne, pulling up my knees as I cross the no-man's-land, holding my course, slowing time right down with all that pillowed air steady beneath me, then bringing legs forward, coming in now, aiming for a hummock in the sand where my feet will imbed, knees giving, feeling the landing soft but firm, rising again, turning and seeing Ann Murray with the measuring tape. *It's a record!* she cries.

After school I practised high jump, setting the bar at waist height and knocking it down again with my trailing leg each time I jumped. I remembered the senior boys at the American school. They didn't do the scissors jump like we were taught. I knew, because I'd watched them. They rose into the air and dived over the bar and somehow rolled round it. It was called the western roll. I tried it. With each try, I set the bar up a notch. Finally, I dived over it at shoulder height and rolled in the air, taking my time, coming down into the sand that I'd carefully mounded and breaking the fall with my right arm and the back of my right shoulder. There was never anyone else around. Learning to fly was my secret.

I lay in bed at nights, counting each measured pace on the approach and feeling myself lift into the air, rolling around the bar, never quite touching it, then slowing right down until there was zero motion, as if that split second before beginning to fall could hold for an infinity. And then I was flying over the playing field and everyone was there and I flew among them and over them, so close, I could have touched them, but no one saw me, no one noticed anything at all. And I was as naked as the day that I was born.

*

106

MRS ANDERSON READ US A STORY. When she'd finished, we had to write it down in our own words. This is how it went. A farmer had been burning off his field, when the fire got away and set light to a copse of pines. The animals that lived in the copse fled and one of them, a marten that had four young ones holed up in the bole of a tree, set about to evacuate them to safety. She had found a suitable place on the far side of the copse and was just returning to retrieve the last of her little ones, when she was overcome by a fierce wave of heat. For a moment she struggled and then her feet let go and she fell to the ground.

Ann Murray had entitled her story Sweet Marten. I hadn't thought of a title. I was too moved by the story and had to hold back my tears as I wrote the closing sentence:

> *And that was the end of the poor*
> *brave bird and of her little ones,*
> *who were still too young to fly.*

Mrs Anderson was very kind about my mistake and couldn't stop smiling, while the girls couldn't stop giggling. But they all acclaimed her decision (still smiling) that my effort warranted a top equal with Ann's.

The spring term report placed me sixth out of a class of thirty-four and described my work as very satisfactory. I took it straight home to show Mami. "Where has Mrs Anderson studied?" she said. It stumped me. "Anyway," I told her, "my place in the class is good, isn't it?" Mami closed the report along the fold and scanned the title page. Mrs Anderson's handwriting gave me as *T. Randow, Primary III.*

107

SHANGHAI BRITISH SCHOOL
REPORT 1947 .

Name J. Randow

Form Primary III

Age as at 1st Jan. 9 years 2 months

Average Age 9 yrs 3 mths

	No. in Form	Position	Percentage	Parent's Initials
Jan. — Feb.	37	6th	70%	I.v.R
Mar — Apr.	34	1st	73%	I.v.R
May — June	34	4th	76%	I.v.R
Summer Exam.	33	6th	76%	I.v.R
Sept. — Oct.	36	7th	72%	I.v.R
Nov. — Dec.	35	8th	80%	
Winter Exam.	35	5th	81%	

Standard for Year

A.=V. Good C.=Credit P.=Pass F.=Failure

GENERAL COMMENT

Spring Term Very satisfactory work

Summer Term Good steady work.

Winter Term Most satisfactory

C. M. Anderson Form Master/Mistress.

	Jan. Feb.	Mar. Apr.	May June	Exam.	Sept. Oct.	Nov. Dec.	Exam.
Eng. Comp.	A	A	A	C	C	A	A
Lit./Reading	C	C	C		P	P	
Writing / Grammar							P
Dict./Writing	C	A	A	A	P	A	A
French Comp.	A	C	C	A	C	A	A
French Gram.							
Arithmetic	A	A	A	A	A	A	C
Algebra							
Geometry							
Nature Study / Science		A		C			A
History & Script	C	C	A	C		C	C
Geography / Recitation	C	P	A	C	A	A	A
Chinese/Latin	C	C	C			C	
Scripture							
Phys. Training	P	P	A	P	C	C	

A.=V. Good C.=Credit P.=Pass F.=Failure

20.6.47. I.R

A. Crow M.A. Principal

"It depends who the others are that you are comparing yourself with," Mami said and handed the report back to me.

"You have to initial it," I said and pointed to the blank box. Mami unscrewed her old Pelikan fountain pen, posted the cap on its end and wrote her initials in the box:

I.v.R.

She reached for the blotter and rocked it back and forth over the initials. Then she blew on them.

"There you are," she said.

Tien Mu Shan

My next major venture into English composition concerned the prescribed subject: My Summer Holidays. We had taken the train to Hangchow and a bus to the village of Linan. It lay within sight of the three mountains, Si Tien Mu Shan, Tung Tien Mu Shan and Mokanshan. Sedan chairs took us to the foot of Tung Tien Mu Shan, the eastern peak with its eyes turned toward heaven. There we stopped at a tea house set in a garden surrounded by trees. A new team of bearers was waiting to take us up the mountain.

The ascent was steep. The wooden seat I sat in hung level from the bamboo poles that flexed between my bearers' shoulders. There was no canopy as on the sedan chairs of the plains. These chairs were made for the mountain, just as the mountain had made the sun dried calves of the man who climbed the path in front of me. I asked the bearers to set me down. Mami said I had insulted them. I only wanted to lighten their load. They begged me to get on again before we rounded the last bend and came in sight of the monastery that was to be our home. The abbot and all the monks had gathered in the forecourt. They folded their hands together and bowed several times and led us inside. We sat down at a long table and all drank tea together.

I woke to the sound of the prayer bell. The shutters opened with little effort and revealed an inner courtyard under a square of sky. Through the lattice gate on the far side I could see the silhouette of a monk and the bell he was striking. Behind him the morning sky brightened and then the gate opened and the monastery came alive with movement and the slap of bare feet on stone. The chanting of the monks wakened the day and through the open gateway I saw a new sun taking its first peep at the world and breaking out into the fullness of the morning.

"Get your clothes on," Mami said. "It'll be cold out there."

We stood on the edge of the world and squinted into the sun across a dazzling quilt of cloud. Two peaks broke through it and cast their shadows over it. "I've told you about Omei Shan, haven't I?" Mami said. She had. But I liked listening to her stories about the time before we were born. "Tell me again," I said.

"Omei Shan is a mountain in Szechwan, not far from the Himalayas. It is twice as high as Tien Mu Shan. It took us three days to get to the top. We stayed at monasteries like this one. We never saw the sun. A freezing mist clung to the mountain day after day and then, on the afternoon of the third day, we reached the summit and all at once we were standing in full sunshine."

It must have been something like this, I thought. "The sun was behind me and it threw my shadow over the layer of cloud below," Mami went on. "I spread my arms and my shadow did the same down there on the cloud and it seemed to be calling to me to fly into its arms—" This was the bit I liked best. It was so much like the poem Mami often read to us. It was by Heinrich Heine and in it a man climbs the ship's

110

railing, believing he has recognised his long-lost beloved in the window of a house at the bottom of the sea. He stretches out his arms and is about to dive in, when the captain grabs him from behind and pulls him back. *Doktor, sind Sie des Teufels?* the captain cries.

Mami's story goes on. "—I took a step forward, when I suddenly felt a hand on my shoulder and someone pulled me back from the edge, shouting, *What the devil's got into you?*" Which is exactly what the captain says in the poem by Heine.

In my English composition I described how we climbed the steep path to the summit of the mountain. There were pools up there, brimming full, and you could imagine that they really were the eyes of the mountain looking up at heaven. They never blinked and the dragonflies that skimmed over them left not the faintest riffle to mar their watch.

I also wrote about the salamanders in the mountain rill on the way down. We played with them and let them slither over our tummies. They seemed to like that. Mami said it was because they enjoyed the warmth. I left that bit out. I left out all the bits about what Mami said and did. They didn't seem to fit.

But I added the story about Garn.

Garn had first appeared in Linan. We had got off the bus and the charcoal burner on its tail exhaled its last choked breath into the evening air. The dust of our arrival enveloped a group of men drinking tea outside a shop. One of them leaped towards us. He was naked except for a rag about his loins. He stopped when the chain snapped tight around his neck. The man arched his back and spat into the air across a gap of five or six paces and got Mami on the front of her shirt. The madman howled and rolled backward and his captors dragged him back writhing over the scarred ground.

A young Chinese man with the soft face of a boy came running towards us. "I sorry, I sorry," he said. He wore a shirt and tie and tight trousers with a transparent plastic belt and patent leather shoes, like a city spiv. "You come please," he said, making scooping gestures with his hand. "You come please. I am Garn." He picked up our bags and we followed him.

A minute later we had our night's lodgings arranged for us and Mami was brought a basin of hot water and soap to wash her shirt. All the rooms gave on to a courtyard and Mami put up a line in the doorway and pegged up the shirt with travellers' pegs.

Garn led us to a restaurant. Its front was an open wooden grillage that faced into an alleyway. It could be closed off at night with wooden shutters. We sat overlooking the alleyway and watched young couples as they passed. A waiter with a pair of metal tongs offered us steaming towels. Then the soup arrived. A cool breeze came in off the alleyway.

"Who is Garn?" I asked Mami.

"Just a pimp," she said. "He picks up a cumshaw at both ends of the deal."

"Did you give him a cumshaw?" I said.

"No. He's bound to turn up again."

I hoped he wouldn't. The image of his face with those soft features stayed with me. His mouth particularly and his rare grey eyes. I thought I caught sight of that face again the following day in the tea house at the foot of the mountain. But when I looked a second time, it had gone.

The story I wrote about Garn in my composition took place on the day of our departure from Tien Mu Shan. I was heading down the mountain after the others (I wrote) when he appeared on a side path. With small scooping gestures he made me follow him along the path. It led to a shrine the size of a market stall. It had a roof like a temple with a bell hanging from each upturned corner, only one had gone missing. I could see that there had been a seated figure in it, something befitting a Buddhist shrine. The lotus flower was still there, but the figure was gone. A coloured poster had been pasted up at the back of the shrine, depicting a boy in an ornamented robe and with ornaments in the pigtail that sprouted from his shaven head. The boy had a soft chubby face and he smiled as if he wanted to tell you a secret. I wanted to run away, but Garn had taken hold of my hand. I felt his grip tighten when I pulled, but managed to twist out of it and get free. I ran down the path and didn't look back until I had got to the bend, but I already knew he wasn't following me. Garn had vanished.

When I caught up with the others, they were drinking tea at the tea house where we'd stopped when we first arrived. They hadn't missed me at all and I decided not to tell them anything about my adventure.

Mrs Anderson got me to read my composition to the class. She praised it for its detailed descriptions. The kids listened without interrupting, but couldn't seem to understand why I hadn't told anyone what had happened. "You should've told," one said. "That man was trying to kidnap you." "I'm sure I would have told," said another. "I would never have been able to keep it to myself." Then Ann's voice: "Why didn't you tell?"

"I don't know."

The fact was, I did. I told Mami and Rabe and Frau Wenzel (she had come with us) the whole story, just as I have written it. I blurted it all out, all the stuff about Garn, that he'd grabbed hold of me and tried to take me away and how I'd struggled and not a word of it was true. Except the poster in the shrine. I had stopped to look at it, because it didn't seem to belong, and at the empty space where the Buddha figure should have sat, but Garn had nothing to do with it. He wasn't even there. I had decided to walk by myself and was already lagging behind the others and it didn't bother me at all until I came out into the open at the foot of the mountain and they were nowhere to be seen. I was still on elevated ground above the flat fields and could see for miles. Peasants worked in the fields, isolated dots that seemed not to move. There was a group of people in the distance. I knew they could never have got that far. I ran after them, anyway.

I followed a path between fields. An old man with a hoe looked up as I passed. I didn't stop. I kept my eyes on the group of people ahead and ran hard. When I got close there was just a peasant and his wife and a couple of children in a cart. They looked at me, foreign boy lost. I turned away and followed another path as if I knew exactly where I was going. I willed every futile step as if there were weights on my feet. I got further and further away.

It was Garn who came for me. With little scooping gestures he beckoned me to follow him and he led me to the tea house in the garden surrounded by trees where the others were waiting. "Where have you been?" Mami said. Just like that.

The place is full of people talking and laughing and drinking tea. I am small and dumb and blind with rage. Partly at them

114

for talking and laughing and drinking tea, but mostly at myself for flying into a panic like a three-year-old that lost its mother. *Everyone's staring at you. Look at you! God, you're almost ten.*

I said, "It was Garn!"

"*Till?*" Mami's tone was earnest. "Tell me what happened."

And there, in front of all the bearers and Frau Wenzel and the man with the soft face and the rare grey eyes, I made up the lie that was supposed to cover my shame. From the moment I had said his name I knew it was too late to stop, but when Mami flew at Garn, packing in every punishing phrase she could muster in her scant Chinese, and he screwed up those soft features as though in pain and said not a word in his own defence and all the bearers looked on bewildered, I pleaded with her not to go on, it hadn't actually been quite like that, Garn hadn't meant any harm, please don't, *he wasn't even there...*

But it was all too late. When Mami finished she turned to the assembled bearers, those of the mountain and those of the plain, standing in a circle as though witnessing an execution. "What are you staring at?" she said. "Pick up those bags and let's get going." Frau Wenzel paid for the tea and the tea host pointed to the mountain bearers, who were still waiting to be paid.

*

IT WAS HOT IN THE PLAINS. The afternoon sun slanted below the fancy canopy of my sedan chair and burned me. Mami and Frau Wenzel were discussing tea. The fields through which we moved (or would be moving once we got going again) were tea plantations, Frau Wenzel pointed out, and Mami made us all chew on the tips of leaves she'd picked. "The only thing that quenches thirst," she said. But it wasn't my thirst that needed quenching. It was the sun in my face and the eyes of the mountain in the back of my head. It must have turned them away from heaven and fixed them on me, because I had offended one of its children. Maybe Garn could see through the eyes of the mountain. Maybe the tears that welled out of his grey eyes had come down from its brimming pools. Maybe they were what I could feel on my own face, too. Only they felt burning hot.

Garn didn't turn up in Linan this time. In a way, I knew he wouldn't, although it was unlikely that Mami would have given him his cumshaw. I wasn't going to ask her. To my amazement, our rooms were waiting for us and a table had been made ready for us at the restaurant.

"How do they always know when to expect us?" I asked Mami, but Frau Wenzel answered. "You've heard of the bamboo telegraph?" she said. "The peasants working in the fields—you've seen them—are never much more that a hundred paces apart. They can call to each other over that distance. Usually there's nothing much to say, but when travellers like us come along, they talk to the bearers and pass all the news along the line. It gets to wherever you're going way ahead of you."

"But it was the same when we got to the monastery and there are no fields up on the mountain," I said and turned to Mami. "Yet the abbot and all the monks were waiting for us."

"Sometimes that's just the way it is." Mami had no answer.

"I think it's like this." I came out with these words of

wisdom. "I think there's you and then there's the story about you. And they're not always the same or in the same place or at the same time."

"Mountains have secrets—" Rabe said, ignoring me. He gave Mami a knowing look. "—and sometimes lies—"

Well, I had both and I was sticking to them. Thank God, the food arrived and I hoped that, in all the clutter and the clatter and the steaming dishes, the subject would be dropped.

"—like the story about Don Winslow." Rabe, of course, couldn't leave it at that.

"So?"

"We're eating now, so please stop it." Mami put an end to it.

But I knew I'd be hearing more about that one later. I didn't really mind, because that story wasn't really a lie, it was just something I had made up on the spot about the American fleet commander out of the comics. I had told Rabe that Don Winslow and the lovely Mercedes had stayed on the mountain recently on their honeymoon. It was top secret, I told him. Not even the navy knew about it.

"C'mon, you're making it up," Rabe had said. "They're not even real, just comic book characters."

"Yes they are. The abbot showed me the house they lived in, near his own house," pointing vaguely.

"You didn't go to the abbot's house, did you?"

"Of course. The abbot invited me and gave me sweets and we talked for a long time."

I had been enjoying Rabe's curiosity and knew it wouldn't be long before Mami got wind of the story. That night in Linan she sat by my bed and asked me what had taken place between the abbot and me. I had trouble keeping my eyes

117

open and could still feel the undulation of the sedan chair in my bones. "He was nice to me," I said and turned on my side. "He is a very nice man."

"What *happened*?"

"Nothing," I said. "You and Frau Wenzel were having an afternoon sleep and Rabe was reading or something, so I went for a walk. There is a pavilion up the path on the edge of the cliff. You know, where we watched the sun rise. I sat down there and I could see for miles and miles. I didn't notice the abbot arrive. He sat down beside me and told me the names of all the villages. He pointed out Linan in the distance. I couldn't believe we had come all that way. He told me the names of the rivers. He said he often came to this pavilion and sometimes he kept his eyes shut so that the view wouldn't take all his attention. Then he stood up and asked me to follow him. He said he wanted to show me something. So we went further up the slope. He pointed out a little red house with a verandah and said it was the summer house of a very dear friend of his called Mei Lan Fang, maybe I'd heard of him. Have you?"

"He is a famous singer of the Peking Opera," Mami said. "He sings in a very high voice and he does the roles of women. I think he dances, too."

"Well, he's the abbot's friend," I said.

"Is that all he wanted to show you?"

"No. We went to his house and he gave me some sugar candy and lychees. He showed me his library. He has lots of books in English and Chinese and he has been to university. He knows lots of famous people."

"Anything else?" Mami said.

There wasn't anything else. Why couldn't she let me go to

sleep? "We played chequers," I said. "But I didn't know the rules he played. Oh, and then he showed me how to write Tien Mu Shan in Chinese. He used a brush and ink and he taught me how to write the characters. They mean heaven, eye and mountain. I wasn't any good at it, but he guided my hand with his hand and then I could write almost as good as him. He made me write the names of the places we saw from the pavilion. He said if I wanted to stay at the monastery, he would teach me all the Chinese characters and I would be able to read his books."

Mami can't have said anything to that and I just nodded off. I seemed to have been asleep a long time when I heard her say, "And there never was a visit from the commander of the American fleet?"

I could feel a funny little smile stealing across my face and didn't try to stop it. I opened my eyes and Mami was looking back at me with a smiley look of her own and it was that look that I loved more than anything in the world.

No, I said.

Home again

The pedicab came to a stop outside 131 Columbia Circle and we clambered down. The driver watched Mami as she counted out the cash and handed it to him in a wilted bunch. Then he unloaded our travel bags from the carrier and dumped them down where he stood. The canvas sack with our bedding rolled over in the street. He swung the pedicab round and stood on the pedals while he guided it between potholes. He aimed a perfect arc of spit into one of them. I guessed Mami can't have tipped him.

Amah appeared at the back door and made no greeting. She hurried towards us on her tiny feet. "Missie," she said, "foreign people come stay in the house. One lady, she go catch baby. Very soon."

Olga met us on the landing as we emerged from the servants' quarters, lugging our stuff. "My name is Olga Bortoluzzi. How do you do? Mr Leto said to expect you." Her smile was girlish but a little tired. Her hair hung down over her bare shoulders and the bulge in her tummy lifted the hem of her frock halfway up her thighs. "Please excuse me," she said. "It is so hot." Her English was perfect. "I would introduce you to my husband, but he is asleep. His name is Armando. He is Italian."

A door opened. "Oh, and this is Gaetano. Gaetano Gavazzi," Olga said, "Armando's friend. He is staying in that room." The man smiled and bowed. "Gaetano Gavazzi," he said, as though we might have missed it. He looked apologetic as he said it. Mami nodded. I suppose she was wondering how many more people had moved in while we were away. She opened the door to her own bedroom and peered in as though expecting it to be full of strangers. Everything must have been as she'd left it. The bed, the easel, the table with the paints, the trunk, the canvases against the wall. Slowly she closed the door.

"I expect Mr Leto has advised you," Olga said. "My parents are arriving this Sunday by train from Harbin. They will be moving into that room. My parents, of course, are Russian."

I am staring at Mami's profile while she stares at Olga. Her face shows no feeling. It might have been cut in stone, that strong nose, eyes set back under half-shuttered lids. Time holds its breath, becomes internal, like a life being remembered. She stands.

Olga tugged at her frock where it clung to her and wiped the perspiration from her face with moist hands. She didn't meet Mami's eyes. How could she? She had just told her to move out of her room.

A crooked smile curled Mami's lips and she said, "I move out tomorrow." She started up the stairs to the top floor, lugging the canvas sack behind her.

On the half landing, she stopped to wind the clock and tipped the pendulum into life with her finger. Then she lifted the handset of the telephone and tapped on the cradle. She asked the operator the time and said thank you. She moved

122

the minute hand forward on the clock face and waited for the clock to chime all the hours and half hours as she passed them. Before she had finished, the telephone rang. "Oh, Frau Wenzel," she said (they never got on first name terms), "I hope you had a happier homecoming than we have had." While Mami recounted the events of our homecoming to her friend, we went on upstairs. Someone scurried out of the bathroom and into the attic, closing the door. Our bedroom looked strange after two weeks away and seemed smaller. Rabe thought so too. "It's because we've grown," he said. We looked at our things with renewed interest. Rabe at his paper and balsawood scale model of a stunt plane out of *POPULAR MECHANICS* and I at my scored and folded card replicas of a Fairchild glider (which really did), a Northrop Flying Wing (which only tumbled until I made a harness and pulled it along at running pace, making it rise and soar like a kite) and, lastly, a Luscomb Silvaire (darling of the air), all circling lazily on their blue threads in acknowledgment of my revisiting breath. It was good to be home.

Mami came in. "Frau Wenzel has invited us to a garden party on Sunday. They are putting up the volleyball net. You will go to choir in the morning and will have time for a rest after lunch." Mami was back in charge. "Tomorrow is Saturday and we will work together to move all my things up from downstairs. I will sleep in the pink room from now on and I can set up my painting things in the attic. We can tidy it up a bit."

"There's someone in there," Rabe said. "We saw someone go in." Amah came up the stairs with green tea for Mami. She placed it on the table in our bedroom. "Missie, very sorry. I no can do anything. Old lady, she move in next door." Amah hung her head and, when she looked up, there were tears in her eyes. The clock chimed. Something ridiculous, like thirteen. "Oh, for God's sake, I didn't even finish setting the time," Mami said and started off down the stairs again. "Missie, you not forget drink your tea," Amah said. But Mami had clapped her hand to her ear and was listening once again to the operator's time report. Then she resumed moving the hands of the clock through all the chiming hours and half hours. "You boys get this sack up the last flight of stairs," she called from the half landing. "I don't see why I should have to do it when I've got two strong boys just fiddling with their toys." We heard the attic door burst open, followed by rapid footsteps and muttered phrases, Italian, maybe. A small woman in a nightgown stopped at the top of the stair and looked down at Mami. "Is very much noise, loud talk, clock making *dong dong dong*. Please, is impossible. I have to sleep. Yes?" Mami closed the glass lens over the clock face and introduced herself. "I am Ilse von Randow." She sounded very superior. The little woman did not return the formality but spun round to head off back into the attic. As she did so, she passed us and her face was grey and lined like a spider's web. A tangle of hair shrouded it, wiry, in two tones of grey. Her tongue spat out dry, unsounded words. We noticed the whiskers on her chin. But it was the eyes, the yellow eyes with one black pupil slotted sideways like a goat's, that gave her away as a witch.

*

124

WE COMPLETED THE SHIFT in the morning and spent the afternoon whispering because we didn't want the witch to come out again. Mami went back downstairs after I thought we'd finished. I followed her. Crouched by the skirting board in the empty room she had her hand in the hole in the wall, feeling around one last time. Then she pasted the wallpaper down and held it in place until the glue had dried enough to let it go.

On Sunday morning Rabe and I cycled off to school, where we left our bikes chained to the bike stands and climbed on the bus. Actually, it wasn't a bus but an army transport with a wooden bench along each side and a canvas awning over the top.

The driver was about to lift the tailgate in place, when a man in a beige suit (open jacket, waistcoat buttoned up except for the bottom button, gold watch chain showing), climbed into the transport, nodded at us cheerfully and sat down. His legs were short, so that his feet hung clear of the floor and dangled as the bus moved, like a small boy's. "Rolly Chamberlain," he said and listened to our names as we spoke them back in turn. "I'm sure you've all seen me in church. I'm a great admirer of your choir and have obtained permission to travel to church on your bus." We couldn't help smiling at him, the way he spoke to us. "In our family, you see, no one has ever been able to afford a motor car, so we have always travelled by bus, or walked. I've never ridden on a bicycle, because I've never been able to reach the pedals. What?"

He was right. We had spotted him in the congregation, seated alongside the British High Commissioner and his wife. The High Commissioner's record was fifteen yawns during one sermon. Rolly Chamberlain took it a step further by falling asleep for the duration. He didn't wake until we sang the hymn *Sleepers Awake.* It was really hard trying to sing when we were shaking with laughter. We told Mami about it, but she just said, "That's not a hymn, it's a Cantata by Bach. Maybe they don't know that." Mami didn't have a high opinion of the musical culture that surrounded our church choir. She only ever came to hear us once. It was a carol service and she had come with Misha Brenner. I tried to spot them during the recessional but they had gone. Later that evening, she said, "Do you really like those songs? I have not imagined my sons singing music like that." So I sang her the opening bars of *God Rest Ye Merry Gentlemen,* because I knew exactly what it was she disliked about the English carols. *"Schrecklich, schrecklich,"* she said and I followed that with *The Holly and the Ivy* and *A Virgin Unspotted.* "Stop, stop, stop! It is like your church bells, hard notes like stones," and she imitated the rapid descending scales that rang from the belfry as you entered. "Have you forgotten our German church bells and our Christmas songs, like music for the soul?"

Of course I hadn't forgotten. We had sung *Silent Night* in the carol service and it had brought a lump to my throat. Even now my eyes were misting over and I left Mami's question unanswered. It wasn't her fault. She hadn't had the initiation into becoming British that Rabe and I had had. But she'd made it possible for us and we'd made the grade. It just meant we now had two separate worlds.

Rolly, as he asked us to call him, belonged to that other world. He knew a lot about the Holy Trinity Cathedral. He had been treasurer during its restoration after the plundering by the Japanese during the war. He told us he had once been presented with an invoice by a Chinese craftsman, who had carved a perfect replica from photographs of a wooden eagle for the lectern from which the lessons were read. The invoice, Rolly said, was for *One piecee holy chicken!* It made him chuckle merrily, interspersing little explosions of *What?* and, of course, it made us laugh as though it had been the funniest story of our lives.

*

"BACH NEVER PLAYED A NOTE LOUDLY. Instead, where a note needed to be emphasised, he expanded it." The words of Api Brenner, my piano teacher. He had written them in German in the front of Bach's *12 Little Preludes for Beginners.* He had obliterated the words *for Beginners* with vigorous strokes of blue pencil.

On Sunday afternoon in Wenzels' garden, he is shirtless and his indigo blue shorts hang from his waist. His brother Misha is half a head taller and wears white shorts. He pounds on the volleyball with his fists. Api returns it on slender wrists. His wiry black hair stands out from his skull the way it does when he is conducting. Kurt Wenzel and his wife are the owners of this piece of land, which they call their garden. It is tenanted and cultivated by a Chinese market gardener, who also maintains the formal grounds. He brings us tea and lights the mosquito coils under the table as dusk falls. Api lives here, too, in a single roomed cottage. There are two upright pianos in the cottage, each with a narrow bunk above it. There is also a small table with an ashtray and two chairs. When the

quartet get together to play, two of the players have to sit on piano stools. Then the room is full. Mami and Misha play violin, the Landauer boy plays cello and I can't remember who played viola. Probably Api, when he wasn't playing piano. In and out of my sleep up there in the bunk, the music rose and fell and when we lit the oil lamps on our bicycles to pilot our

way home, the night was already half gone.

"What does it mean, *He expanded it?* How did Bach expand the note?" Api placed his finger on the music in front of us. "The three descending bass notes are a repeated figure throughout the C minor prelude," he said. "You are a singer, so sing them with me." We started with *La, la, la.* Then he invented words like *Stay with me* and *Be my friend* and *Hear my prayer.* He finally settled for *Ach, verzeih!* and we sang that for all the remaining bars. "Come, I show you something."

Attached to a rafter above his table was a cocoon made from little sticks and stalks bound together with a fibrous web. The shiny black head of a caterpillar showed at one end. It reminded me of the dead baby in the straw bundle. "Yesterday when I was having my dinner, I watched that caterpillar coming out of the cocoon. Just a little way, so it could go back in again. It arched its body like this," Api said and stretched his arms over his head. Then he bent forward and put his hands flat on the table and slid his head over them. He did it slowly several times like someone praying for mercy and each time he said, *Ach, verzeih!*

"The first note, *Ach,* that is you (or the caterpillar) calling out to God. This note is not the loudest, but the most expanded. Not longer either, but feels longer. With the second note, the caterpillar turns inward, becomes humble, smaller. On the last note, it breathes out the last of its breath. It has said everything it needs to say. No pedal! Very important." As Api spoke, the caterpillar came to life and flexed its tufted segments, showing its underbelly and hundreds of tiny feet. "Look," I said and pointed. "Aha." Api rolled his dark eyes and flashed his smoke-stained teeth. Because he had a slight

129

130

squint, it made him look like a clown. "The caterpillar knows. And he teaches us: it is never just the notes, there is always a prayer also. Now, when you go home and play that prelude, remember him."

I have never forgotten him. It did strike me as I packed up my music that Api's story would be utterly lost on Rolly and all those people that belonged to church and choir. But he had already put his hand on my shoulder and pulled me up by the door. "Misha says you shouldn't sing in the English choir because it will spoil your music. But I want to tell you this: there is no thing such as bad music. Only there is bad playing and bad singing. Always when you play or sing, listen to the music what it wants to say. And always make a beautiful tone. Then your music can only get better and better. That I promise you."

*

"MISHA SAYS there is a really good French music teacher at the Catholic school, Ste Jeanne d'Arc. His name is Father Anselm or something like that." Mami's opening gambit had Rabe and me on the alert. Misha was having quite a lot to say. We waited for her to go on. "They also have a choir, a very good one, I'm told, and the music they sing is ancient music. You remember Palestrina—"

"We don't want to sing in a different choir," Rabe cut in. "Why does Misha hate our choir?"

It really made a difference, Rabe being two years older than me and his question stopped Mami in her tracks. I watched her straighten and bite her lip. It was something she'd started doing, something that told me that everything was not alright. Instantly, I got a sick feeling in my stomach.

"It's not just about the music," Mami said. Her voice was steady. "You will have to change schools. The money is not there to keep you at Shanghai British School. You remember the gold bars that were stolen? They were for your education. I can pay for you to go to Ste Jeanne d'Arc, which only costs very little, because it is a Catholic church school. I can pay the Jeanne d'Arc fees for both of you for one year, maybe two, and then we have to see what happens."

I know this can't be true. This moment that is going on right now isn't real. I can sink down into that sick feeling in my stomach, but it isn't really *my* stomach. I don't have a stomach. There is nothing down there and nothing below me at all. But I'm sinking into it anyway.

"I have spoken to your headmaster, Mr Crow. I have told him." Mami's words bring me back. I stare at her. So it's already happened. We're leaving school. *Our* school. We're going to Ste Jeanne d'Arc. We're going to be cycling along with those foreign kids, those French speaking kids, and I don't know a single one of them. *And* they're all *boys.* "I don't even know where their school is!" I cried.

"It's not the end of the world," Mami said. But I knew it was.

"It *is* the end of the world," I said.

There was the sound of a baby crying and a woman's voice humming a reassuring kind of hum. Then a knock on the door. "Mrs von Randow, I want to show you my baby. Can I come in? Her name is Silvana." Olga turned, still patting the baby on its bottom, and Mami smiled at the flushed face that lolled on Olga's shoulder. She made soft cooing sounds at it and found its hand and let it close around her finger. Mami had wanted a girl. She often told me that and I watched her take Silvana, quiet now and impossibly small, into her motherly arms.

"Olga says you are welcome to practise on her piano, unless the baby is sleeping," Mami told me later. "But after school is alright."

What school? I said.

*

RABE AND I LAY AWAKE. I knew his thoughts were churning, like mine were. He said, "Are you awake?"

"Yeah, and you?"

"Yeah."

After a while he said, "What do you think about going to Jeanne d'Arc?"

"Mami says we have to," I heard myself say into the darkness. But it didn't sound like my voice. I had no voice.

"Think of me," Rabe said. "I'm supposed to be preparing for my Cambridge School Certificate next year. I won't be able to do that at Jeanne d'Arc."

The clock's tick-tock marked time on the empty stair. A slit of light underlined the door to the pink room. I thought about Capt. Milne, who had slept in that room. Mami was there now. She would be sleeping on his mattress. It was mine, really. He had given it to me.

"Do you like Misha?" I said.

"Not very much," said Rabe. "Do you?"

"Sometimes I like him. But I wouldn't want him for a father," I said.

134

"What makes you bring him up?"

"You know—Misha says this, Misha says that. I think Mami likes him."

"He tells really weird jokes," Rabe said.

"Like how!"

We tried to reconstruct a story Misha had told about two brothers who took their dead uncle on a train. They propped him up in a seat with a newspaper in his lap. They couldn't find him when they came back from the diner and some rough guys who had got on the train said, "Oh yeah, the old man, he got off at the last stop." Mami couldn't stop laughing when Misha told the story. But it wasn't even funny.

"I like Api though," I said.

"Aw c'mon, Till," Rabe said.

"So how 'bout Onkel Siegel?"

"He's gone. Anyway, I thought he drove you mad."

"He did," I said. "Remember how he used to do that puzzle? You know, the one with all the geometric shapes?"

"What did he do?"

"You must remember," I said. "He skewed the pieces so they wouldn't fit together but leave gaps between them. Then he stood some pieces up on end and wedged them into the gaps. I told him that was wrong, but he just laughed and said *Nein, nein, so ist gut.*"

"I remember that," Rabe said and laughed.

"In the end I always had to laugh, too."

It's funny how you keep your eyes open when you're talking in the dark. I must have shut mine then, maybe for a split second. Maybe for half an hour. Suddenly I heard myself say, *Hennessey!* and opened them wide.

135

"What?"

"That's the name of the cognac Herr Maier brings Mami," I said. I tried to sound normal.

"You're dreaming," Rabe said.

"No I'm not. Mami told me he wants to marry her."

"That'll be the day."

"Anyway," I said, "he's dumb."

"What about Rolly?" Rabe said.

The landing lit up and Mami came in. "Stop talking and go to sleep," she said. "It's late."

It was. Mami said good night and I saw her light go out. I rolled over on my side to sleep. "Don't worry about school," Rabe said. "Mami is going to see if she can maybe manage to keep me at Shanghai British School till the end of next year." It was an unexpected turn. I lifted my head off the pillow. "Of course, *you* would have to go to Jeanne d'Arc," he added.

Rolly

Rolly cut the pack and dealt out seven cards each. Then he placed one face up in the middle of the table and the rest in a blind stack beside it. "This is the draw pile," he said. Rabe had shuffled. Only he'd called it 'mixing the cards'. Rolly had corrected him. Just as important as the rules of play were the words that defined it. "In gin rummy one melds runs and suits. Mark the words. To play a hand, one must draw and discard. Not throw out. One can lay off against another player's meld and, should one be able to dispose of all one's cards in a surprise meld, it is called a splash." Rolly demonstrated all of this. "But first you must learn to shuffle." I loved that word, shuffle. Rolly could shuffle really fast and, as the cards feathered under his thumb, they made a sound just like that word, *shuffle*.

Some Saturday nights, Rolly read to us from his favourite collection of poems entitled *RUTHLESS RHYMES FOR HEARTLESS HOMES*.

> *Little Johnny, only four,*
> *Nailed his sister to the door.*
> *Mother said, with humour quaint,*
> *"Johnny, must you spoil the paint?"*

Rolly's style was dry, his words clipped. He read without much expression, holding it back somewhere, where it built like a wave and you sat stock still and listened until the end, when it all spilled over.

There was a young lady named Hyde
Who ate so many green apples, she died.
Inside the lamented
The apples fermented,
Making cider inside 'er inside.

We didn't know what cider was, so Rolly had to explain about fermenting apples. It ruined the punch line, but, by the second or third reading, the meaning had fallen into place and got funnier and funnier every time. And, the more we laughed, the higher would Rolly raise his eyebrows above his round spectacles and chuckle like an owl, "What?...what?... what?"

We'd set off from home in the late afternoon for our Saturday night's dinner at Rolly's. After his Boy had taken charge of our bikes, Rolly would lead us round the garden, where he'd point out the new flower beds he'd had the gardener put down. Perhaps an iced lemonade on the terrace if it was a warm day. A bit of talk about the week at school. At a nod from Boy, it was a visit to the lavatory (not the toilet) and a scrubbing of hands and combing of hair. And so to dinner.

The chilled dew from the Frigidaire clung to the sea shells of butter in a misted silver dish and the comfort of hot bread rolls wafted over them. Rolly broke his bread roll and dipped it into the consommé to show it was right and proper to do so.

But it wasn't proper to tilt the dish towards you to scoop up the last mouthfuls.

"Why not?" I asked.

"That's simple," Rolly said. "If the lady sitting to your left were to have a sudden coughing fit, you might spill the consommé into your lap. This is why one tilts the dish away from oneself."

Rolly carved the chicken and we helped ourselves to the mashed potato and the minted peas. "The only sensible way to eat those is to dab them into the mashed potato on the back of your fork. That's it, or you'll be chasing them around all night. Oh, and if you're lucky enough to get the drumstick, as I see you both are, you may hold it between your fingers by the ends of the bone and chew off the flesh." Rolly nodded in approval. "The King of England does this," he added, "but one does not lick one's fingers afterwards." He held up a starched serviette.

When we had beef, we'd place a daub of English mustard on the rim of the plate. "I'm sure I won't have to remind you to be careful of that," Rolly would say, "unlike the American, who wouldn't heed my words. We had to call the fire brigade, what?"

"I met Mr Colman once," he went on, "the chap who makes this mustard. We were lunching at the Atheneum in London and I asked him how on earth he'd made a living from a commodity of which you only ever needed such tiny amounts. My dear fellow, he replied, I didn't become rich on the mustard that people ate, but on the mustard they'd left on the side of their plates."

When Boy had cleared the main course and returned with the dessert, Rolly said, "Oh, by the way, I shouldn't wish you to form the impression that we've always eaten like this in my family." Boy set down the sliced pears in crystal dishes with scoops of vanilla ice cream floating in a milky slick. "Help yourselves to hot chocolate sauce," Rolly said. "The fact is, my family were as poor as church mice and pudding was something we had once a year if we were lucky."

He dabbed his mouth with his serviette and found a clean fold of cloth to wipe his spectacles. He checked them by looking through them out of the window, fogged them with his breath and wiped them again with the handkerchief out of his breast pocket. Then he put them back on and blinked at us. "You see, I also grew up without a father, like yourselves, so I know what it's like. And I know what hard times are. There were five of us, you see. My elder brother left school when he was thirteen to take a job as delivery boy for the baker in the mornings and a cleaning job at the mill every night. He paid for his brothers' education, including mine. Not that we didn't do our bit. We did everything we could for a penny, short of stealing it. We might earn three pence on a milk run or for doing windows, mowing lawns, sometimes newspapers. The girls did washing and mending for older people in the neighbourhood. Mother was a midwife—you know what a midwife is?—and so she might be out on a call at any time and we were often left to get our own meals. But there was a war on and food was so scarce, we probably only ever had to peel and boil the potatoes. What?"

Rolly noticed that I was running my spoon round and round the dish to glean the last traces of ice cream and chocolate sauce. "You'll go through the crystal if you keep doing that," he said. "You're allowed to leave some in the dish, or your host

140

may feel he hasn't fed you enough and that you're going to get up from the table hungry." Rolly chuckled. "You see, it's a complicated world we live in, isn't it?"

He rose. "Let's go through to the drawing room," he said. "I say, we must have been real chatterboxes or, at any rate, I must've been. A chatterbox, that is. It's a bit late for cards, I'm afraid, so maybe we could just go on chatting for a while longer until bedtime." We sat on either side of him on the sofa. "You know, just because we had hard times when we were young," Rolly began, "—rather like you're having, I might suppose—that doesn't mean they were bad times. In fact I'm quite certain we all thought of them as rather good times. So that, when we got wind that the Council were sending round a child welfare officer because we children had been seen out earning a crust at crack of dawn, well, we were outraged. So, the day the woman officer from the Council was to call, we stayed home from school and hid. It might have been in the garden or under the stair or around a corner of the hall. Mother didn't know about this and received the child welfare officer and a constable, God bless him, at the front door. We let them say their bit and then we let fly. As if out of nowhere, our unsuspecting visitors were being pelted with flour bombs, courtesy of the mill (which the girls had sewn into little bags) and stale bread rolls from the bakery. When the visitors retreated through the garden, armfuls of cut grass showered down on them from behind the hedge. And, as a final touch, my younger brother had let down the rear tyres of their bicycles, so that they had to push them all the way back to the Town Hall."

Usually, when you laugh, it's because something was

really funny, or was said in a funny kind of way. But we were laughing because those kids, they had nothing, yet they stuck up for themselves and they *stuck together* and they *showed 'em!* And when something like that happens, it's *exciting*. And, of course, they *won!* That's quite another kind of laugh. "We were never bothered by the Council again," Rolly said. He put his arms over our shoulders and squeezed them.

"Tell us another story. Please, before we go to bed."

"On Sunday mornings," Rolly obliged (I suspected he didn't want to stop either), "we had breakfast in bed. We tossed up who was to get it and the rest of us piled into Mother's bed, where there was ample room for us all. Breakfast was always porridge, but on Sunday mornings in Mother's bed we got a special treat. I never found out how, but she'd managed to save up a little cream for Sundays and we'd pour it on our porridge and we thought we ate like kings."

Boy brought hot chocolate and said our beds were ready. Rolly had had him set up a folding bed to either side of his own. "Now drink up and go upstairs," Rolly said. "I'll be up in a little while to say good night. You've got to sing like larks in the morning, so you'll need a good sleep. And don't forget to do your teeth," he called after us. "You can have a bath before breakfast."

After our bath (Rolly washing our hair), well groomed now and ready for church (fuelled by porridge and cream), we took to our bikes, thank you Boy, and headed off to meet the choir bus. "Don't let them leave without me, will you," Rolly said. "I'm taking a pedicab and will be close behind you." His kiss now was astonishingly smooth on the skin and scented. "You'll be coming back without me, though," he added, "as

142

the High Commissioner is giving a garden lunch. Must rush now. I haven't even put on my tie. Oh, dear!"

Dean Trivett's sermon rose in waves over the choir stalls. Tommy Blake nudged me and held out a sweet. I shook my head and then put a finger to my lips as he crinkled up the cellophane wrapper and popped the green acid drop into his mouth. Green was lime flavour. I couldn't remember what colour mine was. It was still in my pocket.

I am lying on Rolly's right. Rabe is on his left. The bedclothes cover the three of us. It is strange, feeling this man's warmth, but it's OK. "Have I ever told you you're the most intelligent boys east of Suez?" I hear him saying. His kiss is prickly. He tightens his arm around me and pulls me close to his side. His hand is on my tummy, undoing my pyjama cord. It reaches down. "Do you like it when I do this?" he asks. It feels funny (funny peculiar or funny ha-ha?). Funny peculiar.

Hm? He is waiting for my answer, but I don't know what to say. Then I hear my voice, no more than a squeak.

Yes.

Tommy Blake started. Had I said that out loud? The way he looked at me, something must have happened. Could he tell? Rolly's voice was saying, "You shouldn't really touch yourself, you know, so this is something we will never tell anyone. You know that, don't you? *Hm?*"

I sat dead still. Didn't give Tommy Blake any excuse to pry. But he picked up the shiver that ran through me. I could tell, because he looked at me again. It was strange that Rabe never said anything. He was always the first to speak up when

143

something was wrong. Was Rolly doing the same thing to him? Would he tell Mami? *Was* it wrong?

I reached for my sweet and unwrapped it. It was purple. Blackcurrant. Tommy Blake put his finger to his lips. *Shh!* he said.

"And now to God the Father, God the Son and God the Holy Ghost..." Dean Trivett ended his sermon and announced the hymn. We all stood. I had to sing with the sweet stuck in my cheek.

*

RABE LET ME CATCH UP TO HIM as we cycled home. "We'd better keep mum about what happened," he said when I'd come alongside.

"You mean you're going to tell her?"

"Don't you know what it means to keep mum?"

"I don't get it."

"Mum's the word, OK?"

*

AFTER WE'D EATEN, Mami called us into her room. "I need to talk to you," she said. The potato dumplings turned over in my stomach. "I need to lie down," I said. "It's about your friend, Rolly," she said. The dumplings rolled themselves into a hard ball. "I had a letter from him." I shot a glance at Rabe's white face. "I want to read it to you," Mami added and pulled up a chair. We sat down on the edge of her bed.

My dear Mrs von Randow,

I hope that you will forgive me for interfering with your private affairs. As you must realise, I fell in love with Rabe and Till as soon as I set eyes on them; but it is their nice characters that make me want to know them better. A lot of people in this world need help, but it is not all that deserve help...I know how worrying it is not having enough money, and more especially for school fees, when you know that your sons are worth educating...There was quite a possibility that Till would have to leave the school to enable Rabe to remain on another term. The very idea made me feel sad; and after consulting Mr Crow and Mr Luff I have now paid to the school one hundred and fifty pounds, which should be enough to cover their fees for another year. I hope you will be able to pay something to the school when you can so that my money will last as long as possible. I may go home to England any time now, but I shall not spoil your boys. A little mere male affection will do them no harm, and I have become very fond of them. I hope they will always bring you nothing but happiness.

Yours sincerely,

Rolly Chamberlain

There are some things that, when they happen, you can put a finger on them and say, *this is so.* And there are some you can't. And while you're struggling with them, something else happens and turns the whole thing inside out and you don't know where you stand. But I never had to go to Ste Jeanne d'Arc and both Rabe and I were able to stay on at the Shanghai British School until the day before we left Shanghai. And some twenty-eight years later, Rolly came to my wedding. It was my second wedding, but that's by the bye. My father was there, too. They'd never met before. They chatted together and, of

145

course, old Shanghai days came up, but my father never found out what part the elderly Englishman had played in our young lives. Two years later, they were both dead.

Sons and mothers

Amah stitched white toe caps over her shoes and waited for Bao-jin to arrive. Boy had read her the notice, handwritten in Chinese and bearing the official stamp.

> *To Li Sin-su, next of kin*
> *Li Jerh-lin killed in action*
> *For further details contact*
> *Nationalist Army HQ*
> *Shenyang.*

She dictated a letter to her daughter, adding, *I will wait for you, so we can weep for your brother together.*

*

AMAH LEANED FORWARD and fanned the charcoal stove. Flames started to play over the dark embers and the rice pot lid lifted on its frothing rim. She sat back again and picked up the shoe. She drew the needle out of the fabric where she had secured it in and out and in and out again. She pulled the white thread through to give herself more length and resumed

147

stitching. Such a tiny shoe, I thought. I'm only eleven and it's way smaller than mine.

"Bao-jin has bigger feet, hasn't she?" I said and Amah returned a laugh and fell silent again. She must have come from a well-to-do family, not peasant stock, to have had her feet bound as a girl. "You came from Kiukiang, didn't you?" I said, but Amah only nodded. She was probably thinking about Kiukiang anyway, where she was born and where her parents were buried. Where Jerh-lin was born. Bao-jin too. Five hundred miles up the Yangtze River. Where Jerh-lin must return—must be returned.

Jerh-lin.

"Please, Didi, you open the window. Too much smoke," Amah said. I got up and opened it, but some of the smoke still hung against the ceiling and wouldn't go out. The little Italian woman came scuffing out of her attic and Amah had to pull back her feet to let her through. She carried an enamel basin with bits of washing in it. "You are cooking in the bathroom, yes?" she said and emptied the clothes into the bath. She scrubbed them in some cold water and then strung up a washing line. She tied it to the shower rose and across to the window. She closed the window with a bang and attached the line to the window latch. She had to stand on the lavatory seat to do this. Then she hung up the bits of washing and secured them into the twist of the washing line.

Rabe came into the bathroom and took one look at the arrangement and turned on the shower. It gurgled and choked a few times and then coughed up a bile of rusty water over the lace-edged garment the Italian woman was just hanging on the line. She swung at him and caught him in the face with it.

Strega! he shouted. The woman froze. Amah froze too. I turned to stone. Rabe ran his hand over the reddening flare on his face and studied it as though expecting it to be smeared with blood. He grabbed the sodden garment from the woman and twisted it so that it rained on the floor. Then he doubled it back and twisted it again. It looked menacing, but he simply held it out to her and, when she didn't take it, let it fall into the puddle on the floor.

Then he walked across to the lavatory, lifted its lid and peed.

"What did you call her?" I asked Rabe when the coast had cleared. "Witch," he said. "I called her a witch in Italian." I gaped. Rabe's voice hardened. "The other day when I was brushing my teeth, she came in with some dirty dishes and just piled them into the hand basin in front of me. She shouldered me out of the way with her sweaty bare shoulder and I said nothing." Rabe took a breath and looked at me as if asking for a sign of approval. "I had to spit the toothpaste in the toilet," he added. "I couldn't even rinse my mouth." Then he laughed. "I mean the lavatory," he said and I laughed too.

*

AMAH PROPPED UP A MIRROR on the window sill and combed her hair. It hung straight and black halfway down her back. She removed the lid from the glass jar beside her bed and dipped a fine spatula of split bamboo into the wood shavings soaking at the bottom of the jar. The spatula flexed as she stirred the shavings through the clear fluid and the fluid clung to the spatula as she lifted it out and smoothed it over her hair.

"I think so Bao-jin come today," she said.

Amah reached for her comb. Her hair divided as she slid its coarse-cut bamboo teeth through it, leaving it ruched and glossy. I noticed for the first time the strands of grey.

"Why you think so?" I said.

"Bao-jin she come today, because yesterday no come," Amah said. She pulled up her hair and twisted it into a bun and secured it with a bamboo pin. "You see," she said.

And, of course, I did. I heard the quiet keening of the two women from behind the closed door of Amah's room and strings of white petals hung from the lintel arch.

*

"MY NAME IS YEH-CHING," said the gentleman. "I believe you employ a person in your household by the name of Mrs Li. I have come to pay her my respects in honour of her late son." He raised the three-tiered basket he was carrying. It gave off a smell of steamed dumplings. He smiled at me from behind heavy spectacles. Mami knocked on Amah's door. "There is a gentleman to see you."

Yeh-ching towered over her though his head was bowed. He said his name and bowed again several times and proffered his gift. He spoke softly. Several times I heard him say Jerh-lin's name. Then Amah spoke and she mentioned her daughter's name and he bowed to Bao-jin and she stood and lowered her head. Bao-jin poured tea from the thermos flask with the bamboo base and the chrysanthemums painted on the metal body. She served hot rice cakes from the three-tiered basket. The door remained open the whole time.

150

"You don't speak Chinese, do you?" Yeh-ching said to me after he'd made his good-byes. "Perhaps I could teach you some time." Mami's door opened and he straightened and brushed the heavy wave of jet black hair from his brow. "I am a friend of Li Jerh-lin," he said. "That is, I was his friend. We trained together." Mami waited for him to go on. He said, "I have suggested to Mrs Li not to try to contact the Nationalist army HQ concerning his death. Shenyang—excuse me, you will know it as Mukden—was taken by the People's Liberation Army the night he was killed. They are now in charge. What I haven't told Mrs Li is that her son wasn't killed in action as the report said. He was executed by the Nationalists. Jerh-lin was a Communist sympathiser, you see." Mami took in a sharp breath. "You needn't worry," he went on. "There will be no reprisals against Mrs Li or her daughter. For one thing, all the records at Shenyang are now in Communist hands."

"How do you know all this?" Mami said.

151

"I have told you I was Jerh-lin's friend," Yeh-ching said.

"If you trained together, why aren't you in the army?"

"They failed me on account of my eyesight. They seemed to think I would be more useful out of the army."

"Do you work for the Kuomintang?"

Yeh-ching laughed. "I am just a schoolteacher," he said. Then he added, "I would be pleased to come to your home to teach your sons Chinese. If you will permit. You have two sons, haven't you?"

"My older son is preparing for his Cambridge School Certificate examinations," Mami said, "but Chinese is not one of his subjects. Maybe Till..."

*

YEH-CHING HAD SET UP A TABLE and two chairs in a room in the servants' quarters. Electricity meters bulked on the wall, humming. Porcelain fuses clung in broken rows and, a little apart, threadbare cables crowded into an iron casing with a bar switch that could knock out the entire house. From the ceiling hung a single light bulb.

There was only one window in the room and Yeh-ching had pasted paper over the window panes. He stood his bedroll into the corner and covered a collection of things that he had stacked against the wall. "You have a radio," I said as he tucked the cloth around it. "Please sit down," he said. "We are going to do some study now."

Yeh-ching rolled out a rectangle of felt in front of me and placed a sheet of paper on it. He poured a little water from an old medicine bottle into the well of his inkstone and dipped the ink stick into it. I had seen the abbot on Tien Mu Shan mountain do this. He rubbed the stick on the inkstone until it made a thick ink. He never got a mark on his fingers, because the ink stick had a paper wrapper. Anyway, he was a very neat sort of person and probably never did a clumsy thing in his life. When the ink was ready, he ran a brush through it and the hairs on the brush became black and smooth and shiny and ended in a long thin point.

"Watch me and then copy me," Yeh-ching said and wrote the character for China. "There are four strokes," he said. "Watch the order of the strokes." I thought he was going to let me use his brush, but he rolled a pencil toward me. He showed me how to wet the point between my lips to produce a dark line. At the start of my second lesson he said, "I have a present for you," and from then on I used a brush and filled sheets of paper with Chinese characters.

I showed Amah that I had written her name and, to my delight, she was able to read it. There weren't many things she could read. Cash notes, telephone numbers, the calendar. Only the bare necessities. But Amah couldn't even write her own name. Now I had written it for her.

I showed it to Mami's friend Heckeline and she told me about a German who had invented the Chinese typewriter. I told her how Yeh-ching had taught me to combine characters to make different words and she said that was how the typewriter could manage five thousand Chinese characters without having to have five thousand keys.

"I've seen one of those," Rabe called out, resting his cello on its side. He hadn't been playing it anyway. The cello was Mami's idea, one of her less successful ones. "I've even typed something on it"—he laid the bow down on the cello—"and it has a very complicated mechanism, you see—"

"You haven't finished practising," Mami said. I was sure she didn't want him to start again, but she said it anyway. Then she turned to Fräulein Gutscheidt.

"There is a young Chinese gentleman who is teaching the boys, well, Till mainly, how to write Chinese. He seems to be living in a room in the servants' quarters. Amah says he's writing a book."

"Is he a friend or did he just appear out of the blue?" Fräulein Gutscheidt asked and Mami explained about his first appearance and his connection with Jerh-lin.

"Well, he's certainly not working for the Kuomintang," Fräulein Gutscheidt said. "More likely the Communists. Lots of young Chinese intellectuals with university backgrounds started collaborating with the Communists. Most of them have probably been shot, like your amah's boy. My guess is that he's lying low until the take-over." She put up her hand and coughed. "I mean the Liberation."

"Just be careful," Heckeline said. "You can't be too careful." Then she noticed I was listening and changed the subject. "We have a surprise for you this evening, Ilse," she said. "The third guest." The door opened and Fräulein Dittberner walked in.

Mami screamed and the other three women joined in and then they all embraced each other and laughed. Through the open door came the hammering of footsteps on the landing and all the way down the stairs. "The little Italian witch, I mean widow. The boys call her the witch," Mami said. "She lives in the attic. A gift from the landlord. Thank God she's gone out. I need a good laugh. But what are you doing in Shanghai?"

154

Rabe had got up and stumbled over his cello. It droned angrily and the bow clattered on the floor. He rushed to the window and opened it. Together we hung our heads out and sang *Arrivederci strega!* to the little figure walking down the street. Suddenly it stopped. Hesitated. Then it turned and strode back towards the house. Rabe shut the window and went back to his cello and began to play. I just froze. The women seemed not to have noticed anything. I heard Fräulein Dittberner saying, "I am staying with Heckeline and Fräulein Gutscheidt for three weeks and then I'm boarding a ship for Hamburg. Not the same one as them. It was already full, so they've put me on a coaster. Stops at every port. Lucky me!" She laughed. "You really should be doing the same, Ilse," she said. "None of us will be needed here when Mao arrives."

She put her arms around Mami. I think they were both crying. But I was listening to the footsteps coming up the stairs. Up the last flight, slowing. Then a knock on the door.

"Signora di Rando, scusa mi. Is necessary *parlare,* how you say? Talk." She paused for breath. Mami stood in the open doorway, blocking it. "You have-a two boys. I have-a two boys. Good boys, *miei ragazzi.* Not your boys—" I don't think Mami said a word. "—they call-a-me *strega.* Is very cruel. I am-a-not liking. Is for me so sad..." The voice faded out. When Mami closed the door, she stood for a moment with her back to it. She met Rabe's eyes. Then mine. Then she rejoined her friends and nothing was ever said about the incident.

*

THE NEXT TIME I WENT for my Chinese lesson, Yeh-ching wasn't there. Just the table and the two chairs. Amah said maybe he'd gone back to Fahwha Court. So I got on my bike to see if he was there. The grey archway brought me into a courtyard overlooked on three sides by an upper balcony. Washing hung from bamboo poles projecting over the railings. Chinese kids drove their hoops over the bedded tiles or tossed diabolos whistling into the air. They stopped when they saw me. An infant started to scream and ran to its mother. An older boy with a shorn head and mere slits for eyes came up and tugged at my bike. I called out that I was looking for Yeh-ching. It was his Chinese I spoke. Women turned their backs or plucked their children from the courtyard. An old man said *Not here, not here!* The boy with slits for eyes didn't seem to have heard me at all and began trying to push my hands off the handlebars. I clung on and he shoved a hand into my face. *Go away!* I shouted. He rubbed his hands together and breathed on them and this time he clapped them both freezing cold against my cheeks. I turned the bike round and swung my leg over it, but his hands had landed on mine and were pulling off my gloves. I swore at him in gutter language and was glad Yeh-ching wasn't there to hear. The boy took no notice at all. I pulled a hand free and tried to grab his wrist with my (by now) ungloved hand, but already he'd got hold of my other glove and vanished into the rear of the building. While I stood there dumbstruck, it occurred to me that he hadn't said a word, hadn't uttered the smallest sound. And as I rode away under the arch I saw the first snowflakes beginning to fall.

*

MAMI AND I CONVERGED ON THE BACK DOOR of our house from opposite directions. There was a fir-tree standing on the carrier of her bike. Snowflakes had got caught in its needles and we laughed together as we untied it and started carrying it upstairs.

"Happy Christmas," said old Ludmilla Vinokuroff as we passed her.

"Happy Christmas," her husband echoed, pushing through the door after her with his pants off. He held a glass high above his head and spilled vodka on his wife. From inside the room came Olga's cry and Armando's avalanche of laughter.

"Where have you been all this time?" Rabe said. "Olga's been up here looking for you."

"I've brought home a tree," Mami said. "Why don't you and Till decorate it?"

We kept our Christmas decorations in a box in the attic. No one answered the door, so we went in. It was very cold in there. The old trunks and suitcases amongst which we had played hide-and-seek in years gone by were still piled up in the dormer on our right. Straight ahead at the far end, a bed stood against the sloping ceiling of the main gable and a commode beside it. In the middle of the room was a table and chair and against the wall a dresser. "Hey, come and look at this," Rabe said. On it stood two photographs in tarnished frames. They were of young men in army uniform. Around each frame was draped a silver chain with a crucifix and in front of each lay a heart made of icing sugar with red decorations round the edge. The hearts lay on green crepe paper doilies that had been trimmed into the shape of a Christmas tree. "Red, white and green," Rabe said. "The colours of the Italian flag." But

I was looking at a small sepia photo tucked into the edge of the frame. It showed two boys about our age with their mum and dad. "What's the bet that's La Strega with her family," I said, "before she turned into a witch?" Rabe was about to pick it out of the frame, but I pushed his hand away. "You'll never get it to stay put again if you take it out," I said. I turned and crashed into the table behind me and only just managed to save the water jug from spilling over the dishes. They were covered in red and white smears and seemed to be waiting to be washed.

I counted my pocket money and set out for the market. I returned with frozen hands and a Christmas tree standing upright on my carrier. Smaller than ours, but, when I'd stood it on La Strega's chair, it looked tall and proud. And when I'd decorated it, it positively glowed.

*

THE LAUGHTER FROM BELOW had turned into shouting. I heard the old man scream, "Where is Armando? I kill him, I kill him." Someone fell over and a door slammed. Then Olga's footsteps up the stair. "Armando is drunk," she said to Mami. She was clutching the baby Silvana. "My father has gone crazy and wants to kill him. Please, can I leave Silvana with you. I'm scared. Thank you. I have to go back." Mami took the baby in her arms and rocked it. It didn't cry. It was probably too frightened, so it switched itself off. That's what I would do. "Thank you," Olga said again.

"Shut the door and light some candles," Mami said. "It's freezing in here. And get Herr Maier's cognac—it's in the cupboard—" "*I know,*" I said. "—and a glass."

I filled the glass and Mami made me pour half of it back in the bottle. It wasn't easy and a small puddle formed on the table. I licked it up. Silvana stared into Mami's face with wide eyes. I wound the old gramophone and put on a record. No Christmas songs. The Harmonious Blacksmith. Händel. Then I took Rabe's place at the window and he got the box of matches and lit the candles on our Christmas tree. "Why are there only three candles," Mami said, "and so few decorations? Must be Till's minimalist look again. Is that it?" Rabe shrugged his shoulders. I shook my head.

It was getting dark. Snow circled in the light of the streetlamp and mottled the street. The record stopped. Mami went on humming the melody and rocking the baby. Then she laid her in *my* bed and tucked my featherbed around her. She poured herself another cognac. Rabe looked at me and shook his head. I shrugged my shoulders. Then a pedicab rounded the corner.

I gave the signal and Rabe got up and left the room. He seemed to be gone an age and I could have sworn I heard La Strega's footsteps on the stair. And then I could. I really could this time, just as he came in and shut the door behind him. He put the matchbox down and gave me the thumbs-up. We listened as she crossed the landing and arrived at her door. Then silence. I could see behind my closed lids a vast attic bare of furnishings, not quite making out the dingy gables. And in its centre a fir tree, quite small, standing on a chair and bristling with candlelight and stars and sparkling colour.

"*E un miracolo!*" the witch exclaimed, "*Un vero miracolo!*" Then at our door, "*Signora di Rando! Signora di Rando! Veni*

159

subito, come and see!" Mami followed her out. "I been to *messa,* I pray. And look-a-da! *Che belissimo!"*

Rabe and I couldn't look at each other. We weren't even tempted to laugh. Somehow the thing had got much bigger than we'd imagined. When Mami came back into the room, she just said, "You rogues, my sons are a right pair of rogues." Silvana stirred and Mami picked her up. Amah appeared at the door and asked if she could bring the dinner. "Yes, but first you make warm this bottle." She looked startled, but immediately understood.

The Italian woman collided with her at the door. *Scusa mi!* In her hands she carried two icing sugar hearts wrapped up in green paper doilies. She didn't say a word, although her lips moved as if she were speaking. She placed one in Rabe's hand and cupped his other hand over it. Then she did the same with mine. She hesitated before grabbing me and hugging me with her shaking bones.

And then she noticed Silvana in Mami's arms, dimly in the flickering candlelight. *"Ecco un miracolo di piú!"* she cried and crossed herself. *"Una bambina! Una bella bambina!"* She raised her arms to the ceiling and laughed and laughed and laughed.

*

YEH-CHING DID MAKE ONE MORE APPEARANCE at the house before he disappeared for good. It was more than a year later, after the Liberation. He was accompanied by a woman officer in padded clothes and a cap with the red star on it. They were talking to Amah, bowing their heads. I wanted Yeh-ching to notice me, but he never once looked in my direction. They posted notices on the back door with cataracts of Chinese writing on them. One had just three large characters in gold on red paper. I recognised Amah's name. Then they bowed again and left. The rumour that Yeh-ching had afterwards gone to organise a co-operative in Inner Mongolia must have come from Bao-jin, because she had been posted up north on a farming commune. I remember that she had been confused, because a friend had told her that he was again teaching at a secondary school in Shanghai. At about the same time, we heard that he had been charged with counter-revolutionary activities and shot. But no one knew for certain and, in the course of time, Yeh-ching's name stopped coming up any more.

But on the evening of that last visit Mami told us that he had seen to it that the body of his friend Jerh-lin was to be transported to Kiukiang for burial in the family tomb. The dead soldier's status as a hero of the people had been confirmed. Amah was being honoured as his mother. She asked Mami for permission to go to Kiukiang for the funeral. Bao-jin would come, too. They would be away for a month.

When angels fight

part one

In the spring of 1949 the school roll dropped by half. Everyone talked about leaving Shanghai and going to Hong Kong or Australia or Canada or England. It was because of the Communists, who were coming to take over. No one seemed to know a lot about them, just that there was a big army of them sweeping down across the country and that they were headed for Shanghai. "China will soon have a Communist government," Mami said. "That's certain. And the Kuomintang will be finished for good. They've been finished for years anyway and it's time they went. For the sake of the Chinese people." But the kids at school said the Communists would close down all overseas businesses and confiscate people's property. And as soon as they got close enough to Shanghai there would be a war. Already their army was positioned on the north bank of the Yangtze River a hundred miles upstream and they might be crossing it at any time.

On the news, 20th April: "A British frigate, *HMS Amethyst*, has come under heavy fire from Communist shore batteries on the northern banks of the Yangtze River. She has sustained serious damage and is aground. There are reports of heavy casualties..." So they were right. There was a war. It had already begun.

Mr Crow, the school's principal, appeared at the door and the class scrambled to their feet. He nodded to Mrs Moffat and then to us to be seated. The report had just come through from the BBC, he said. A number of British marines had been killed. "There are no further details as yet. Meanwhile, please carry on." Mr Crow again acknowledged Mrs Moffat, managed just in time to stop us all rising to our feet again and walked out, his academic gown trailing behind him.

I looked around the class at the empty seats. In these gaps Michael Brisk and Derek Frost had sat, alongside Gary Walker, Brian Buttridge and Eddie Shaw. And, until quite recently, my friend Ollie. It must feel like this on the *Amethyst*, I thought. Of course, girls had gone, too. Elizabeth Adams the Brownie, Patsy Borgheest, Gaby Gideon. Thank God, Ann Murray was still there, confident, bright. She caught me looking at her, but gave no sign of recognition.

Next morning Miss Penfold, our deputy principal, also in academic robes, talked to our class about the battle on the Yangtze. How the British destroyer, *HMS Consort*, had steamed down from Nanking to try to re-float the *Amethyst*, but had also suffered heavy shelling from the Communists and had to give up the attempt and make a run for it down-river after losing ten men killed. On the third day, she told us about the cruiser, *HMS London*, and the frigate, *Black Swan*, steaming up the Yangtze from Shanghai and also turning back after being hit by Communist guns. There were still more dead and wounded. Miss Penfold folded her hands and got us to stand.

She prayed for the British marines, strength for the living and peace for the dead. Then she sat and talked about the lifeboat from the *Amethyst* that had taken wounded men ashore. It was the only lifeboat that had remained undamaged. Other marines swam for the south bank, which was still in the hands of Nationalist forces loyal to the Kuomintang government. Miss Penfold paused for a moment. Then she said, "The Communists fired on them in the water and a number of them have been hit and are missing." We all remained very quiet.

Mami remained very quiet, too, that evening when we told her about it. It was unlike her to be moved by stories we brought home from school and I was just about to ask her if she'd been listening, when she said, "You remember Hellmuth von Ruckteschell?"

"Yes?"

"You know he was a sea captain. He fought against the British. His ship was one of those raiders. They looked like freighters, but were armed with big guns. In the Atlantic. He sank a lot of British shipping."

"Yes, we know about that," I said. "Daddi showed us pictures of raiders. They were sneaky."

"He couldn't have," Rabe said. "Raiders were top secret."

"Well, after the war, they accused him of firing on British survivors, not picking them up, things like that. He died while serving a life sentence. I didn't tell you. He died in prison in September last year."

"Was it true that he fired on survivors?"

"How should I know?" Mami said. "He wasn't that kind of man. The Germans loved him and gave him medals. The British feared him and locked him up to die. Who knows what

165

happens in a war? When the angels fight, someone is going to get hurt."

"He once told me," she went on, "about a Christmas at sea. He had forty survivors on board and they all celebrated together. Christmas tree, Christmas cookies and for everyone a present. The survivors helped make the decorations. And sang Christmas carols."

"I can remember him telling you," Rabe said. "I was there."

"That's how I remember him," Mami said. "Another time he held a service for their comrades who had been lost when their ship went down. Ruckteschell and his officers and crew stood to attention while they played music on the gramophone and a wreath was dropped into the sea. I know what they played. He gave me the records. You know, the ones in the blue box. Beethoven. His seventh symphony."

"Remember the presents he gave us?" Rabe said. "The puppet called Dopey? For our puppet show?"

"And Michel the sailor," I added.

"His name wasn't Michel," Rabe said.

"Yes it was," I said. "It was written on his cap."

"That was *HK Michel*. The name of his ship," Rabe said.

"Oh yes, now I remember."

Mami took our hands. "He liked you both. Very much. He always mentioned you in his letters."

"We're having a special service on Sunday," I said, "for the men who were killed. We have a choir practice tomorrow." I didn't push Mami to come to the service.

*

166

SUNDAY, 24TH APRIL, 1949. Holy Trinity Cathedral was packed. Officers and marines in white filled the aisle. They bore wreaths and held aloft White Ensigns and Union Jacks from the fighting ships. The organ played. We had to come in through the vestry and file into the choir stalls from the top. Then a trumpet called and the column moved up the aisle at a slow march, holding their caps in their hands. Beethoven! I recognised the piece. Hellmuth von Ruckteschell would have been proud.

When the column reached the altar steps, the standard bearers spread the flags over the carpet and the officers placed wreaths against the altar and on the steps and against the communion rail, until the entire apse shimmered with colour and light. Then the music stopped and the ship's chaplain from *HMS London* performed the funeral rites and everyone remained dead still for a long time. All those hundreds of people in the church and not a single sound.

Then we sang the special hymn we had rehearsed. It was a

setting of the poem by Alfred, Lord Tennyson that begins:

Sunset and evening star,
And one clear call for me!
And may there be no moaning of the bar,
When I put out to sea—

—and ends:

I hope to see my pilot face to face
When I have crossed the bar.

And the *Amethyst* was still stuck up there in the Yangtze River with holes in her side.

*

"SHE SHOULDN'T HAVE BEEN THERE AT ALL," Mami said. "It was the last day for Chiang to accept the Communist ceasefire offer and he let it lapse. Everyone was nervous. Imagine what the Communists thought when they saw a British warship steaming up the river under their noses."

We tried to imagine it. The trouble was, Mami always saw the other side of everything. No sooner were you feeling that you were part of something you really believed in, than she'd find something wrong with it. And if you realised she was right, but at the same time stuck to your belief, you ended up on both sides and that's a very funny place to be (I mean funny peculiar), because you're always keeping half of you a secret. I think Hellmuth von Ruckteschell might have been like that.

Rolly Chamberlain, too. Daddi, probably, come to that.

It was a relief going back to school on Monday, because you didn't have to think too hard and could just go along with everyone else. We had French with Mr Radik and he told us he would be leaving and we booed him, mostly because we wanted him to marry Joan Penfold. She was the deputy principal's younger sister and taught us geometry. When he said he was coming back, we applauded him. We applauded him again a year later, when he actually did. Then we sang at their wedding. They held a wedding feast for us afterwards. Mr Radik was unique. In those days, when people got out of China, they didn't come back. Like Miss McGregor and Mrs Anderson—who had been my form teachers—Miss Walker, Miss Wyatt, Miss Yonin and the venerable Mr Rood. We would never see them again. All the more surprising to have a new teacher walk into class one morning. "I am Miss Schofield," she announced. "I am here to teach you Latin." She had written her own textbook and illustrated it in illumination of the absurd text. A childlike outline of a girl with tears exploding from her eyes and semiquavers emanating from her mouth accompanied the entry: *ululare, to howl: puellae semper ululant.* We each received a cyclostyled copy bound with red string, which we immediately set about to colour in. Later, Miss Schofield became Mrs Wong and turned up to teach us Latin in a padded uniform with a red star on her cap.

On Wednesday 25th May, 1949, Miss Penfold interrupted the class and told us that school was closed until further notice and we were to find our way home as quickly as we could. Reports had come in that Communist troops were about to enter the city. Our parents had been notified.

Mami turned up on her bicycle and waved to us from the school gate. You couldn't have missed her if you'd been at the far end of the grounds. Kids were getting into cars and some of the older ones formed convoys and made a dash for it on their bikes. There wasn't a single pedicab to be seen, so the teachers helped with the evacuation. Miss Darroch squeezed five little kids into her Standard 8 with the Union Jack on the bonnet catch and Mrs Moffat loaded six of them into her Austin 10. Mami rode out into the street right in front of her car and waved to us to follow. She rode hunched forward with her nose to the handlebars, the hood of her suede leather jacket hiding her head.

We had to pedal hard to keep up with her. Even then, a taxi tooted behind me and I had to pull over to let it pass. Some school kids laughed and waved out of the Plymouth's hulk. As I looked the other way, I thought I had caught a glimpse of Ann Murray on the far side of the taxi. She wasn't laughing or waving. She was looking the other way, too.

We turned out of Avenue Haig and followed the line of closed house fronts along Rockhill Avenue. A woman was gathering up the last of the washing off the balcony rail. It made her look like a patchwork quilt. The man who made *da-bing* brought in the table and chairs and shuttered up his stall. A bicycle wobbled over broken kerb-stones and disappeared between two houses. The woman sitting on the crossbar had to pull in her feet to get through. Life and colour were draining from the street.

By the time we reached Columbia Circle, it was empty. A shot rang out as we rounded the corner, and then another. But Mami had slowed right down. "They're just firing into the

170

air," she said as we came alongside. "They're nervous, that's all. You notice we didn't see one military vehicle or a single road-block. You boys stay at home for a few days. By Monday it'll all be over and you can go back to school."

By Friday, Mami had decided it was time to take a look. "You two might as well come along," she said. "There's safety in numbers." We rode up Amherst Avenue and found it deserted. In the alleyways of Fahwha village, we could see kids playing, but they didn't come out into the street. Round the corner of Columbia Road, a mobile vegetable stall had been set up, just below the brow of the bridge. Buyers jostled each other, waving wads of cash. When a man pulled up on a bicycle towing a cage of chickens, their voices rose, only to be drowned out by the screams of the birds swinging homewards by the neck. "He'll be doing well today," Mami said. "People have to eat."

On Rockhill Avenue, the discarded khakis of what had been the Nationalist army lined the banks of the roadside drainage ditch. We rode as far as the *da-bing* stall, but it was still shuttered up, so we turned back. Mami waved me forward. "Don't look now," she said. "Remember that man with the glasshouses you dropped a stone through? A couple of days ago he was still flying the Nationalist flag. Take a look at the replacement. You'll be seeing it around. That little red flag will be doing a brisk trade, mark my words."

On Sunday, we went out to take another look. An armed column of soldiers was moving down Rockhill Avenue towards us, under an enormous red banner. A red Jeep flanked the column and the five-pointed gold star blazed on its bonnet. I wondered if I'd once sat in that Jeep when it had sported other

171

colours. Once again it had come in victory and a thousand little red flags gave it a hero's welcome. Food stalls opened and women and young girls proffered bowls of rice and noodles to the soldiers. Even the *da-bing* man was busy folding the flatbreads over the deep-fried cornmeal braids and handing them out to be passed on to the troops. But they only tossed their heads back and half closed their eyes as if in bliss and strode on. If they were tired or hungry, they kept that hidden behind the mask. A soldier passing close to me had his lips parted in a smile like a small boy toting his first air gun. I noticed that his feet were dragging on the street. I thought about the defeated Japanese troops I'd watched with Captain Milne some years before. I was looking at the bright side of the same old coin. And that brightness was what the revellers now saw, who welcomed them with bowls brimming and flags waving and lots of teeth showing. Was this not, after all, the army that was bringing liberation to the people?

On Monday, just as Mami had said, we were back at school and everything continued as normal and before we knew it the summer holidays were upon us.

When angels fight

part two

It was the eyes, pale between dark lashes, paler still in the bruised hollow of her left eye, that stopped me at the foot of the stair. Fugitive eyes, catching just long enough to make a mark. To hold after she had looked away. With her head turned, the bone showed in the line of her chin, seeming to accuse. Then her hair swung across and hid it from view. A thin arm dangled from her summer frock, showing a prominent elbow. The other one was in a sling, with the forearm held out at an angle in front. Her classmates left a gap around her as though they were afraid they might snap it off. At the top of the stair they turned toward the assembly hall. The afterimage of the girl's eyes still held after her back was turned. And then, just before she vanished, there they were again, catching mine. How did she know I was still watching her?

Mr Crow took the assembly. He welcomed us back for the autumn term. We sang *Awake, Awake to Love and Work* and a song he had composed himself that went:

Pull, pull, all of you pull together,
For it makes of work and play so much more fun...

We found that one a bit patronising, but he conducted it with such enthusiasm, we had to go along with it. Into the silence that followed he said, "I have good news. *HMS Amethyst* has got away." We shuffled and muttered to each other while memories regrouped like bits of dreams. "No one knew anything about it until the other day," he went on. "She had slipped away and run downstream under cover of night and when she'd made the open sea, she broke radio silence for the first time in weeks and announced *HAVE RE-JOINED THE FLEET OFF WOOSUNG. GOD SAVE THE KING!*" Mr Crow's arms brought us to our feet and we sang the national anthem. I hoped no one would hear us and take it as an act of aggression. *HMS Amethyst* may have got away, but *we* were now stuck behind Communist lines.

The junior classes filed out of the hall first. Since they were at the front, they had to pass the more senior classes on the way out. I kept a look-out for the new girl with the black eye and her arm in a sling, but she was nowhere to be seen.

At playtime I saw her coming out of the girls' lavatory. This time our eyes didn't meet. She just walked right past me and out into the playground. At least I knew I hadn't been dreaming. Besides, she was two classes below me, together with kids like Janie Robson, Diana Newcomb, Heather Richards, Tommy Blake and Paul Kwok. Primary III kids. I was secondary I. I went out into the playground by the opposite door.

Minooh Shroff from Delhi was showing some kids how to bowl (he liked to wear his cricket whites for that) and Brian

Pickles the Yorkshire lad was their batsman. They were new boys and, come to think of it, the only boys in my class. Them and me. The girls kept to themselves. They formed patrols, seven wide, arms linked over each other's shoulders. Ann Murray, Lily Hunter, Monika Müller, Jennifer Dobson, Vera Eynstone, Antonina Kolnichenko and Natalie Menchikov in butterfly yellow summer frocks swept along the margins of the grounds. You had to step aside to get past them. Others played hopscotch in squares marked out along the joints between paving slabs with classroom chalk. Some skipped. They tucked their skirts into their bloomers and their legs betrayed not the slightest effort as the rope whistled through under their feet.

I picked my way past them and stopped when I got to the end of the school building. This was where we used to play marbles, in the paved recess between two wings of the hall. Gary Walker had been the marbles champion. No one played here now. I had a couple of marbles in my pocket and tried some shots, but it felt silly on my own, so I put them away and just stood staring at the wall opposite. When the girls came sweeping around the corner, I pretended I was only passing through. They drank orange squash and munched sandwiches. Monika Müller's were black bread. Lily Hunter always had a packet of potato chips. Ann Murray sipped Culty Dairy chocolate milk through a straw. That must have been nice. There was a picture of that very bottle outside the Culty Dairy shop. If I, too, had had something to eat or drink, it wouldn't have been so bad standing there on my own. I could be reading the label on the bottle when people went by. They might even start envying me. But when you're just standing around doing nothing, no one's going to envy you. They probably think there's something wrong with you.

AUTUMN CAME and the wind swirled the leaves around and piled them up into the angle of the walls. I kicked them in the air, sending them flying again.

"D'you want a ginger biscuit?"

The girl took one from her lunch box and held it out to me. The black eye had gone, but for a brownish mark above the cheekbone. The sling was gone. Her pleated tunic fanned out from below the tied sash showing bandy legs. The winter weight fabric was newly pressed. Navy blue. The profile of a horse's head glinted on the white shirt.

"Thank you," I said. I took the biscuit and snapped it between my teeth.

"Mummy always puts ginger biscuits in my lunch," she said.

"We never have bisquits," I said.

Then I saw her smile for the first time. "Did you call them *bisquits?*" she said.

I didn't get it. "You just said, *bis-quits,*" she articulated the syllables. Then she began to laugh. She spun round and grabbed Janie Robson by the hand. She pulled her up to the wall opposite and whispered into her ear between her hands, all breath and giggles, then threw back her head, hair flying. I heard the thud on the wall.

"You're *bleeding!*" Janie cried.

I could see the red stain spreading along the collar of her shirt. Her hand reached back and slid through her hair, glistening. Janie gave her a handkerchief and told her to hold it to the wound. Then she took her arm and led her away.

I found a red mark on the roughcast of the wall. The bell still hadn't gone, so I resumed my place in the corner and took another bite of the ginger biscuit. Then I felt sick.

"She's probably a haemophiliac," Rabe said that night. "The slightest wound, they can bleed to death."

"How d'you know?"

"You'll be doing Physiology too when you get older," he said and I wished I hadn't told him anything.

"You don't even know who I'm talking about," I said.

"Oh yeah?" he said. "Her name is Elizabeth Berge, she's ten years old, she was in boarding school in England before she came here, her mother knows the Poggensees. That's where I met her, OK?"

I hated that. Rabe getting twenty steps ahead of me again. I pulled the bedclothes over my head and decided to have nothing more to do with the girl.

At playtime next day, I thought I'd just have another quick look to see if there really was a bloodstain on the wall, but couldn't find one. So I left the place. I walked around the school building in a counterclockwise direction. That way I'd have less chance of bumping into the girls' wing patrol, because they always went counterclockwise too. I bet myself I'd do two complete circuits and make it back just as the bell rang. If anyone was expecting to find me in the usual place, there'd be no one there. Oh well. On my second lap there was. I spotted Jane before I got anywhere near the corner. Acting as lookout. The bell didn't go. "Sorry about yesterday," said the girl occupying my spot.

Tommy Blake and Paul Kwok went by carrying hockey sticks. "PT next," said Tommy Blake. "So what?" she said. He turned round and laughed at her. I called after him, "I thought that was a girls' game." It was Paul Kwok who turned round and laughed this time. "Wanna play then?" he said. Instantly I was back at his fancy dress party. We were much younger then, but some things never get forgotten. Like the way Mami had dressed me up as a Chinese bride, all in pink with tassels on my hat and a powdered face, while the other boys had eye patches and cutlasses or cowboy outfits with home-made six-shooters stuck in their belts. It was the worst party of my life.

The bell rang. "I better go," I said. "Wait," cried Elizabeth Berge. "Will you write something in my autograph book?" I took it from her. "Oh, and I'll throw these out if you don't want them, because they go soggy." She thrust her lunchbox at me. The bell had stopped ringing and I was still picking bits out of my teeth when I walked into the classroom.

Tommy Blake came up to me the next day and put his hand to my ear and whispered, "Get her to lift up her skirt for you," and, laughing, ran away. Elizabeth Berge saw him go. "I don't like him," she said. I handed her the autograph book. She opened it at the page where I'd drawn waves breaking on a headland. On the opposite page I had written *In A Kingdom By The Sea* and my name. She looked puzzled. "Can I write something in yours?" she said. "I don't have one." When my birthday came, she gave me an autograph book of my own. "Go on, open it." She'd drawn a horse and signed it. Under her name, in brackets, she put *The First*.

I wondered why Tommy Blake had said that. Was he trying to tell me she'd lifted up her skirt for him? Was she wearing bloomers at the time? Or underpants? Or nothing at all? It was the way he laughed that made me wonder.

"How did you break your arm?" I said.

"I was coming out of a jump. When the horse's head came up, I was still going down. I blacked out and fell. But it's all better now. Don't look so worried."

I wasn't worried. Not exactly. Not about that, anyway. Yet there was something about her. If it was true, what Rabe said about her being a haemophiliac, then maybe I ought to mention it. But I was listening to her stories about her horse and the dogs and the goat and even the pig, so I didn't.

"When I grow up, I want to live with animals too," I said.

*

I NO LONGER MINDED THE GIRLS from my class patrolling past in their ridiculous squadron formation, all in navy blue serge now, with their drinks and their snacks. Of course, I did have my ginger biscuits. I even pronounced them correctly.

When the puddles froze, Elizabeth Berge and Janie Robson jumped on them and slid the slippery shards of ice down each other's necks. They did it to me, too. When the girls came past, Elizabeth Berge did it to Ann Murray. She shrieked. "Find someone your own age to play with and stop acting like a *scamp*," she said. She had to undo her sash to shake it out, but it must have slid down inside her bloomers. I looked away. I knew that nothing would ever be the same again.

The scamp shook her hair back and her chin accused the sky. Her pale eyes reflected it for an instant and then the bell put an end to the scene.

We had football last period. I jumped up and down in the goal, trying to keep warm. I always played fullback or goalie, because I wasn't good at sprinting. It winded me. We were short of players and I looked around for Ann Murray. I couldn't see her anywhere. That meant we were making up two teams out of eleven girls and two boys. Three, counting me. The forwards had to do a lot of running, just because of the sheer distances between them. I had nothing much to do in the goal. The ball was forever being kicked over the sidelines. I was thinking about what happened at playtime when I saw Ann coming from the school building. I got that pit-of-the-stomach feeling.

Ann Murray was heading straight toward me. It was taking her ages. When she finally got close, she said, "Miss Penfold would like to see you at her office."

Miss Penfold smiled. The kind of smile adults use to make you feel at ease when what it really means is that you're about to feel more uneasy than you can remember. "Come in and shut the door. You may sit down. I only wish to have a chat. Now, Ann probably told you she'd spoken to me about Elizabeth Berge. You see, younger girls sometimes don't understand that girls and boys of your age can get to know each other and enjoy getting on with each other in, shall we say, a more mature way. And so they can make a nuisance of themselves simply by trying to get attention. You understand that, don't you?"

"They were only playing. With the ice." I said.

"Yes indeed," Miss Penfold laughed. "There have been other things as well." She looked at me as if I was supposed know what she was talking about. I didn't say anything. "So I shall just have a chat with Elizabeth Berge before the end of the day (oh my goodness, it's getting close) and I'm certain it will all rest there." She stood up. "Did you wish to add anything at all?"

Yes, that I was feeling sick. That there was something smutty going on and I bet Tommy Blake was involved. It made *me* feel smutty now, seeing Elizabeth Berge at playtime every day, letting her put ice down my back, enjoying her ginger biscuits. As if I should have known better, a boy of nice character that I was. That's what Rolly Chamberlain had called me. And if I now let Miss Penfold have a chat with Elizabeth Berge (how could I stop her?), what would that say about my nice character? *Hm?* I knew what Elizabeth would say. That I had betrayed her. I would, too.

And what about Ann Murray? I wished it was true, what Miss Penfold said about us getting on with each other. What did she say? In a more *mature* way? What did she mean by that? We never even talked to each other. It was all a big mistake.

Miss Penfold held the door open. "Did you?" she said.

"No ma'am," I said.

*

I UNLOCKED THE PADLOCK and pulled the chain out of the spokes of my bike with a clatter. I watched the empty walkway. Then I passed the chain through the wheel again and locked it to the bike rack. I paced across the concrete yard and back again. Through the arch I could see Elizabeth's chauffeur in the forecourt. He was pacing, too. He must have seen me, but we kept our distance. I, because I didn't want to have to explain to him what was going on, and he, because he wouldn't have felt entitled to penetrate any further into the school grounds. Everyone else had gone. I unlocked the chain once more and wound it round the saddle strut and fastened the padlock. I perched myself on the saddle with my right foot on the pedal and rocked the bike back and forth as if I were about to leave. Then she appeared.

Along the walkway, past the boys' lavatory, past the closed tuck shop, down the concrete steps. I caught her sideways glance as she turned under the arch. It was just enough to tell me she'd been crying. Into the forecourt, ignoring the chauffeur, her deliberate steps signalling that this hurt had been put there by me. I waited till she had gone out at the gate, her chauffeur walking behind her. Then the sound of the Austin 7 passing through its gears down the street.

It didn't bring her to school the next morning. Nor the morning after. And then on the third morning a bump from behind. "Hey, guess what!" and Ann's face beaming at me. "We're rehearsing Alice tonight. D'you know your lines?"

"Yes."

"I was going to be your Queen, the Queen of Hearts, but they insisted I do Alice."

"D'you know yours?"

Her face was a sunburst. "Try me!"

"Have you guessed the riddle yet?"

"That's not your line. That's the Mad Hatter's."

"I know his part too. *Have you guessed the riddle yet?*"

"No, I give up," she said. *"What's the answer?"*

"I haven't the slightest idea!"

We laughed. Through the arch, up the concrete steps, along the walkway, past the tuck shop, past the boys' lavatory.

"I think you might do something better with the time than wasting it in asking riddles that have no answers," she panted. Over her shoulder.

Into the foyer and up the stair. *"I dare say, you never even spoke to Time,"* I said.

"Perhaps not, but I know how to beat time when I learn music."

"Ah, that accounts for it," I said. We doubled over, caught our breath. *"Who are you talking to?"*

"Now you're the King," said Ann. *"It's a friend of mine—a Cheshire Cat. Allow me to introduce it."*

We rattled off more lines until I said, *"Don't look at me like that,"* and she said, *"A cat may look at a king."*

On the night, she gave the line a special touch, so that I quite forgot the disembodied Cheshire Cat grin and saw only Ann, who had skipped onto the dais and was masking the Queen beside me. She let her hand light cat-like on my shoulder and rested it there.

Before the curtain, the Queen got her revenge. *"Hold your tongue!"* she shouted at Alice.

"I won't!"

"Off with her head!"

There was a commotion and the executioner knocked over one of the corrugated cardboard columns flanking the Queen's throne. One of the guards bent over to pick it up, when the seam of his tights burst, revealing his underpants. The gardeners knocked over their pot of red paint and the White Rabbit skidded in the spill, becoming wildly spotted. My giant playing card of the King of Hearts finally stopped cutting into my chin and flicked off my beard instead. We fell upon the Queen's tarts when the curtains swept across and were caught eating them as they parted again. We spotted our parents and waved to them. They whistled and threw streamers onto the stage.

Ann's father came backstage and she ran across to him in her underwear and threw her arms around him and he kissed her on both cheeks.

A couple of days later, when the crazy lines and the lights and the laughter had begun to settle, I had a dream about Ann. Everyone was getting changed in the foyer at the foot of the stair that went up to the hall. Ann had stripped right down to her bare skin and no one was taking any notice of her except me. I was staring at a tiny black shield that covered Ann's most naked part, as if it was telling me that this was as far as my burgeoning imagination was allowed to take me.

Bonjour,
Mme Elters

Madame Elters was late that day. On any other day she would have come breezing in hard on the bell like a galleon under sail, her cheeks puffed, the full mid-sail of her bosom extended. *"Bonjour mes elèves!"* "Bonjour, Madame Elters," on our feet. *"Asseyez-vous, s'il vous plait."* A clatter of seats, desk lids, pens. A scuffling of feet, textbooks, exercise books. Madame Elters the while scanning the class blue-eyed, then her bare arms upwards as though hoisting the Tricolour, hands all a-flutter. "You make me so 'appy, this class is my best out of the 'ole school. A special gift for me!"

But this day it didn't happen. The show was off. To be truthful, the operatic overture was not our taste. However, it was hers and we played along with it for her sake. It was probably very French, we thought, and we could excuse that the same way we excused our mothers, those of us who had German, Russian or Jewish mothers. But Madame Elters had stood us up. Had left us holding our special gift and not bothered to appear. She would discover that this was something we wouldn't excuse so easily.

Someone began the revolution by flying a paper dart and Brian Pickles fired paper pellets at it with a rubber band. Jeanette Dobson tiptoed up to the blackboard and wrote in bold letters:

BONNE JOUR
MADAM ELTERS

Monika Müller stood up and said, "Jeanette, that is not right. It should be one word and not—"

"Yes we know," Antonina Kolnichenko weighed down on the German. "Is a joke. You don't understand?"

Below the greeting Jeanette Dobson added:

COME ON TALLY-VOOOH!

Then she picked up the duster and started to rub it out, but Minooh Shroff grabbed it from her and posted himself at the door with the duster in his hand. Tiny Jill Wilkinson did an imitation of Madame Elters entering the room, with all the associated gestures and salutations. The class applauded her as she strutted across the podium and thumped herself down as heavily as her little frame allowed on Madame Elters' chair. She sank below the desk but instantly rebounded to a false alarm from Minooh, all teeth, and us pointing to the door, in league. Jill Wilkinson turned white and set off an explosion of laughter from the class. *Shhhhh!* we hissed and the idea shot into my head: *Let's stick a drawing pin on her seat!*

Into the silence my words escaped and nothing would ever bring them back. Eyes fixed on me. Someone said, "There's one on the notice board," and I could see it there, stuck into the cork all alone, doing nothing. But I didn't move. *Go onnnn!*

From somewhere behind me, Ann Murray shot to the front of the class, shining like an angel. Straight up to the notice board, then across to Madame Elters' desk, hesitating. *She's coming!* Minooh hissed from the door and Ann placed the pin.

A scuffle, then silence. Jeanette's voice sounded weakly, *The duster!* But it was too late. By the time Madame Elters came into view, we were all back in our seats.

Her entrance was unremarkable, as if part of her had remained absent. We stood up noiselessly as she spoke her greeting and replied in our best French, but without sparkle, *Bonjour, Madame Elters.* Then she sat.

We stared at her. We held our breath. Nothing happened. She looked from one to the other of us, frowned a little, didn't tell us to sit. She reached for her bag and pulled out a book and placed it on the desk in front of her, never taking her eyes off us. Then she opened it and rocked the chair forward. That did it. With a short cry of *Ah!* she erupted out of it and reached behind her, ran her hand over the seat cushion and found the pin. "*Que diable!* I cannot believe," she said, holding it up, her eyes crossing. "I never will be able to believe this."

My right knee twitched. I was sure she would notice. She placed the pin on the front corner of her desk where we could all see it and sat down again. After a backward glance. She coldly scanned the class, nodding her head like someone to whom a grim truth has just been revealed. "Who 'as done it?" she said.

She got no reply. "*Eh bien*, I will wait for the 'ole lesson for you to say who 'as done this," she said, "and you will continue to stand." She leaned back in her chair. "Then I will call Miss

187

Penfold and I 'ope I will never see this class again." And with that she switched off.

Leaving us stranded. Fallen from grace, condemned, dishonoured and disowned. Where had I heard that before? Byron? Yes, Childe Harold's Pilgrimage. The piece about the ocean. The one that ends: *Without a grave, unknelled, uncoffined and unknown.* I ran the whole verse in my head. Still standing. That's what comes of being late for school. I was always getting to school late and Miss Penfold got me to learn one line of poetry for every minute I clocked up late each week. I was amazed how they mounted up. She chose long poems and put a pencil mark where the week's quota finished. Over a period of a few weeks I had the whole of Milton's l'Allegro off pat. That was quite an achievement. It begins:

Hence, loathed melancholy...

and then goes tumbling out into the fields:

Zephyr with Aurora playing...

(I never really got that at the time). Then:

Come and trip it as you go
On the light fantastic toe...

down to this bit:

While the ploughman, near at hand,
Whistles o'er the furrowed land,
And the milkmaid singeth blithe...

That was Ann. The milkmaid. She's right behind you, waiting for the moment when she must break and say, *I did.* Up before Miss Penfold again, the two of us, me crying, *Please m'am, it was my idea, I'm to blame!* There we'd be, in our more mature way, as she'd called it, and I'd still have no idea what she meant by that. As for Madame Elters, just sitting there like

188

a big iceberg with the pin in front of her quietly pointing to the sky, *how could she!* She's got the whole class standing, not a cough or a hiccup, no one asking to go the lavatory even, while all the time a time bomb is ticking away under our feet and time is running out. God knows how long we've been standing.

It was me.

Everyone reacted. I don't know what they did—made a sound, moved a muscle, caught on fire? I had no idea. But something happened and the ripple ran through the class like a zephyr through a tall field at daybreak. And Madame Elters? Her eyes opened so wide, I worried they might pop out.

You???

The silence was complete. You could have heard a pin drop. *A pin.* She riveted me with her eyes. *Is it possible?* shaking her head in disbelief. Then she rose. She had grown. "The rest of the class sit down." It was her and me. She moved forward, towering above me on the podium. "My favourite pupil, you do me such an unkind thing?"

Et tu, Brute?

"You 'ave been my friend always, my lovely friend. And now you stab me 'ere in the 'eart. From this moment, you are not my friend. You are a beast."

The word hit home. "At the end of the class you will go with me to Miss Penfold. Until then, get out." She pointed to the door. *Get out!*

I moved like a condemned soldier, following the direction of her arm. I could feel the eyes of the whole class on me, but didn't turn around. As my hand went out to take the doorknob, I heard Ann Murray's voice.

"Please, Madame Elters, he didn't do it. I did."

I half turned. Ann had stood to say it. She was looking into Madame Elters' shocked eyes. Then I saw her hang her head. Her hand came up to meet it. She sucked in a big breath, wet and urgent. "I'm sorry," she said.

"Is it true?" Madame Elters' voice was soft.

"Was not Ann's idea to do that," Antonina Kolnichenko said, remaining firmly seated. "Was whole class. We tell her to do it. I mean, we told her to do it."

But Madame Elters wasn't listening. She was looking from Ann to me and back at Ann. Then she turned away and stood with her back to the class. She blew her nose and tucked the handkerchief into her bosom. She noticed the writing on the board and seemed to be reading it over and over. Then she faced Ann.

"And did you write this, too? What does it mean?"

"No, I did." Jeanette Dobson had risen to her feet. "It doesn't mean anything. It was supposed to be funny." A giggle skittered through the room and lightly brushed Madame Elters' lips. She reached for the duster.

"Oh, I have it. Here it is," Minooh Shroff was out of his seat, passing it to her, making a very slight bow. "Sorry."

"I know it is not correct, the way it is written," Monika Müller said, "and I tried to—" But Madame Elters had already erased the text.

"And do we 'ave any more confessions?" she said.

Brian Pickles stood. "I fired them paper pellets, Miss, what's on't floor out there, but I'll be gathering them all up after class, I promise tha'." Madame Elters put on a friendly expression, but she had never been able to understand a single word he said.

We looked round at each other and tried not to show how much we wanted to laugh. But when Ann's eyes connected with mine, it wasn't to laugh, it was something else, I didn't even know what. Something *keener*. Jeanette Dobson knew alright. She was smiling and she wasn't trying not to show it. We were all so drunk on amnesty, we completely forgot about tiny Jill Wilkinson, who had slid under her desk in shame with only her flushed ears showing and seemed never to want to be seen again.

"You are my little devils, all of you," Madame Elters said with an unsteady smile, "but you 'ave golden wings. Like the angels." She reached for the book on her desk and began to leaf through it. *"Eh bien, prenez votres plumes et écrivez sous dictée."* We hated dictation, but this came like a new lease of life. I crossed to my desk, but Madame Elters stopped me. She thrust a piece of chalk in my face. "You do the translation," she said. "On the blackboard." Then she began. *"Le petit prince s'en alla a regarder encore les roses..."* I knew this story. I could translate this. I wrote on the board:

> The little prince went off to take another look at the roses. "You are beautiful but empty," he said. "One couldn't die for you. A stranger might think that my rose (and I mean my rose) looked just like the rest of you. Yet in fact she's more special than all of you put together. Because she's the one I have watered, because she's the one I have protected from the elements, because it is for her that I have killed the caterpillars (except the ones we saved to turn into butterflies), because she's the one I listened to when she criticised or scolded and even when she said nothing at all. And that's because she's my rose."

191

*

WE WALKED HOME TOGETHER that day. It just happened. I was riding my bike, trailing the day behind me, and there was Ann. I swung the bike across Avenue Haig and got off and started walking beside her. She gave me a smile. I wheeled my bike on the outside. Our feet kept time on the flagstones. I looked at her. She looked back. Just glances, really. We still hadn't said anything by the time we came to Route Ferguson. We turned left. "You'll be able to meet Taff and Gwendolen," she said. Then she laughed. "They're our Welsh terriers. Do you have dogs?"

"We used to have wire-haired terriers," I said, not giving away that it was seven years ago, when my father was there and we had the run of the whole house and the garden. "We don't now."

"They're my father's dogs, really," she went on. "He's—well—nuts about dogs."

I could see the place now, a little way ahead. A cream coloured two-storeyed villa with gardens. "The house and garden are Mummy's," she said. "She's crazy about interior decoration. She had my room painted a buttercup yellow with blue-and-white curtains. A light blue, like the sky. It's so bright. I love it." I pictured Ann in her bedroom. "My mother adores flowers and she has flower arrangements everywhere."

She pressed the white ceramic bell button on the gate's square pillar. The dogs danced against the wrought iron bars, yapping. Ann wasn't taking any notice of them. She held out an envelope with my name on. "I forgot to give you this," she said. "It's an invitation—from my mother actually—to a

192

party we're having Sunday after next. It's our farewell party. You see, we're going to England. I hope you can come."

A day of collisions

"Hello, you're Till, aren't you? A thorn among the roses, eh? Please come in. What I mean is, they're all girls in there. Sure you won't mind. Oh, by the way, I'm Ann's father. Follow me and we'll go try and find Ann. Looks like Mrs Murray is busy with the ladies. Sure she'll spot you, though, dying to meet you she is. Oh, and that's Taff and Gwendolen, the fair one's Gwendolen. So, now you've met them. Show me the dog and I'll show you the master, eh? Well, we did it the other way round. Come and shake hands, miffed he is with me, old Taff. Thinks he owns the place."

I followed him into the house where Ann lived. Sunlight fell through the wisteria in the window. The terriers slithered down off the sofa, where silken dragons writhed and shimmered in the dappled light. I knelt on the rug and shook the little paws and thought of Ann holding the same paws in her hand and of the lucky owners of those paws seeing Ann and being near her every day of their lives.

And when I looked up, there she was. "I knew you'd like them," she said. "Looks like they like you too," she added just as I jumped up and blurted out, "Thanks for inviting me," which I hadn't wanted to say at all, there was nothing at this moment that I wanted to say, it just popped out, because it was the kind of dumb thing that tends to pop out of my mouth when I'm stumped for words. I hoped maybe she hadn't heard, considering we had spoken over the top of one another. Then I said, "Yes, I do." She gave me a puzzled look. "Like your dogs," I said. "And the sofa with the dragons—and the flowers—the flowers are beautiful, just like you said. And the rug. That's a really nice Chinese rug."

Thank God her father had vanished. That he hadn't witnessed my embarrassing inventory of approvals. "And your father's nice too," I added before I managed to put my decision into effect to keep my mouth shut.

And all the time, Ann had stood in front of me and smiled and said nothing, just waited for me to stop rambling and take notice of her which, of course, I was doing, only it was too much for me, I needed to throw up a screen of words about rugs and sofas, anything to shield me from the sudden reality of Ann.

But she waved her arm and in one sweeping gesture took in the rug and the sofa and the folding screen (with more silken dragons) and the entire dining room behind it and brought a new and final reality to bear down on them. "All this," she said, still smiling, but with a raw edge to her voice, "all of this is being packed up next week and put on board a ship. And them, of course." She dropped into her knees and picked up Gwendolen. "They're building a large crate for them so they can be together on the trip. They're not permitted on the train, you see."

But that would be next week and next week hadn't begun. There was certainly no sign of it. Before me stood Ann, cradling

Gwendolen, the fair one, two streams of perfectly plaited gold sliding across the dog's untamed wiry jungle, where my fingers now played on Gwendolen's tummy, touching occasionally with the back of my hand the other hair that was Ann's. I wondered if she could feel my touch. If those long braids were as much part of herself as the combed strands springing from that narrow white pathway where they parted, where my eyes and not my fingers were given leave to play.

"What are you looking at?" she said.

"Nothing," I said and shrugged.

"D'you want to hold her?" she said and handed me the dog. "I'll be back in a moment."

Did she think I had found a hair out of place? Spotted a flake of dandruff? On Ann's head? It could never be. On my own, yes, I had even been turned away from the swimming pool at the YMCA and told to go wash my hair. But Ann?

She had left me with Gwendolen, who struggled in my arms until I put her down, whereupon she shook herself and clambered back on the sofa opposite Taff, who had repossessed his end of it some while back, and there she arranged her coat and licked away the human scent and went to sleep.

The women's voices had grown louder. I could pick Ann's mother's, so like Ann's, but with the patina that deepens the voices of grown-ups. She was welcoming Mrs Richards, who had just arrived, and there was Ann, greeting Heather at the door. *Of course*, I thought, she'd heard the doorbell, she'd been expecting Heather, she'd gone to open the door, that's all. And she would be back, as she said.

The women clearly all knew each other. Mrs Newcomb (I'd already spotted Diana in the garden), Mrs Allington, Mrs

Edwards, Mrs Bumstead (her husband chatting with Ann's father outside) and Shirley Grey's mother, the only Chinese apart from the servants, in brocaded red silk, her jet black hair coiled and pinned above her head for added height. She was the only one I hadn't seen before, but it was easy to pick that she was Shirley's mum. All the other mothers were familiar from school functions, church or Country Club parties. I could even tell you the makes of their cars, most of them. And, as though on cue, my own mother popped into my head like the ghost of Hamlet's father, not to be forgotten.

She'd turned up at school once, my mother, just as my class was filing up the stair to the hall for assembly. She had spotted me, singled me out from where she stood on the upper landing. She was waving to me, her face alive, happy to see me, teeth showing, her arms cutting the air like someone signalling from afar. How could I later explain to her why I had looked away, leaving her to perform her solitary act to the mute consternation of my classmates? I mean, picture her in her square-shouldered leopard half-coat, spots and all, the brick red head shawl wound round and round her neck and knotted bulkily under her chin, bicycle clips on her trouser legs and those sturdy leather shoes. Come to think of it, just her face even and her facial expressions, which were outspoken in themselves without her having to speak out at all, these alone made her so different from everyone else's mother, they might have come from different planets. Not that I was ashamed of her, I wasn't. It's just that, by being who she was, she pulled the covers off who I was, the ones I'd worked hard to put in place, that earned me my identity as one-of-us among my schoolmates.

Ann's mother was making her way towards me. Her face was like the sunshine. "Ann has spoken so much about you," she said, "and I simply adored you as the King of Hearts."

I fumbled with nice words for a reply, but couldn't get them out. She said, "You live in Amherst Avenue, don't you?"

"Yes ma'am," I said, "but we have to call it Fahwha Lu now."

Mrs Murray laughed. "Yes, I suppose you're right. I had better make sure we're still living on Route Ferguson, hadn't I? Not some unheard of Chinese street name. Imagine if they tried to rename the Bund! Oh well, it won't matter to us soon." She must have registered something in my expression and added, "Oh, I'm sorry, I didn't mean that carelessly."

"We actually live in Columbia Circle and I don't think they've found a new name for that yet," I said, ignoring her bleak reminder. "It runs off Amherst Avenue."

"Oh yes, I know it well. We used to visit the Ricketts, who lived there. Did you know them?"

"Yes, I knew Robin Ricketts. They had an Armstrong-Siddley. His mother was an actress and we saw her in *Gioconda Smiles* at the Lyceum Theatre. It was smashing!"

"Did you really?"

"We also saw the ADC doing *The Man who came to Dinner*. He's in a wheelchair, you see, and no one seems to have any idea who he is. He turns out to be quite a card and he has the whole dinner party on its head."

"I can just picture it," she laughed. "You must have loved it. It sounds so wonderfully—burlesque." She watched me as I took in that word.

"Like *Alice in Wonderland*," I said.

"Quite so."

Maybe Ann really had talked about me. Her mother seemed to know a lot about me. "I can see you're quite a Thespian," she said.

I didn't know what a Thespian was, but went on. "I want to do Hamlet for the end-of-year show. I saw the film with Laurence Olivier as Hamlet and that's what I want to do. I even know who's going to do all the different parts. Ann—"

I have tripped myself up. I am falling. Like Alice down the rabbit hole. Cold, dark and bottomless. Only it's not about Alice, it's about Ophelia and it isn't the rabbit hole, it's her grave. And Ophelia isn't there. Only the dank smell of freshly dug earth.

> *I loved Ophelia: forty thousand brothers*
> *Could not, with all their quantity of love,*
> *Make up my sum.*

Ann's mother was looking at me steadily. I feigned a smile. "I was just remembering," I said. "You see, I've already started learning my lines."

Ann grabbed me by the hand. "You're freezing," she said. "Come on, we're all waiting for you outside." She pulled me away from her mother. I ventured a hasty apology, but let Ann lead me through the French doors to the terrace and out into the afternoon, where the others were gathered around a table covered in sandwiches and cakes. I had never touched her hand before.

*

I SAT IN A RING OF GIRLS on the lawn and Ann sat beside me. We told stories of the supernatural, of unexplained mysteries and ghosts that people had really seen and felt the cold that hangs around them. I told the story of a dog at home on the ranch. His master was fighting in the war on a distant front. They were just talking about him, hoping for a letter soon. The dog started pacing restlessly around the room, then parted the curtains where they overlapped and peered out into the night. There was a full moon and it had been snowing. The dog scratched on the glass and his tail began to wag and someone let him out. They watched him standing dead still some way off, his head raised as though picking up a faint scent. Then they heard him howl, a long, slow howl into the night. When they called out to him, he disappeared into the shadow of trees, where he howled again and again and listened for an answer, but none came. Next day they received a telegram that the man had been killed in action. They worked out the time difference and it was exactly the moment when his dog had begun agitating to be let out.

"That must have been a German Shepherd dog," Monika Müller said.

"It was," I said, although it had actually been a collie in the story by Albert Payson Terhune.

"Is it a true story?" gasped Lily Hunter.

"Of course it's true," said Ann and told us a story her father had told her about a collie somewhere in the Highlands of Scotland, who'd come after his owner when he'd gone south to find work as a rigger in the shipyards at Newcastle-on-Tyne. The dog had appeared one night, whimpering at his door, so thin, it was a pitiful sight. He'd gone missing from his home in the Highlands three months before.

When we ran out of stories we recited our favourite poems. Someone began:

> Drake, he's in his hammock and a thousand miles
> away...

and we all joined in:

> Capten, art tha sleepin' there below?

When no one could remember the last verse, Jeanette Dobson came in with:

> You are old, Father William, the young man said...

and we managed to get through the whole thing, shouting the last line:

> Be off, or I'll kick you downstairs!

Shirley Grey gave us the first verse of Gray's Elegy in a plodding beat. She was in a younger class than most of us and we applauded her when she'd done. "There's thirty-two verses of it," she said, "and I only know the first."

I continued the pastoral theme with a stanza of Alexander Pope:

> Happy the man whose toil and care
> A few paternal acres bound,
> Who loves to breathe his native air
> On his own ground.

It left a bit of a hole and Ann rushed in to fill it with:

> I must go down to the seas again, to the lonely sea and
> the sky.

She delivered the whole poem down to the last couplet, the sparkle in her eyes melting just a little, her voice halting:

*And all I ask is a merry yarn from a laughing
fellow-rover
And quiet sleep and a sweet dream when the long
trick's over.*

We were now twelve, going on thirteen. We had come
through five years of school together and shared a history. Out
of uniform and on the brink of our futures that were about
to scatter us over far-flung continents, we experienced each
other in a new light. Lily Hunter and I had shared a desk as
far back as Primary III and exchanged doodles on scraps of
paper. Now she slid back a stray teaser of her newly waved
hair and checked the fasteners on her earrings. She wouldn't
be thinking about those doodles now. The jade looked nice on
her skin.

Vera Eynstone, her hair cut like the Sphinx, was explaining
something to Shirley Grey. The younger girl gazed solemnly
into those steadfast features. I did, too, because I had never
before noticed the life in them, nor the warmth in the eyes
they shielded. Neither of the girls noticed me watching them.
Jeanette Dobson did. The class clown, bringer of laughter, she
watched the world from behind that mask and saw everything.
She watched me now as I looked down at Ann's knees, square
and neatly folded together close to mine. Their closeness
aroused in me a plump push out of childhood into a new place.
I hoped Jeanette hadn't noticed that.

Someone took photographs, but I have never seen them.
In any case, they could never have captured that afternoon in
Ann's garden as I remember it, when we were all together for
the last time.

Ann said her goodbyes at the gate. "I'll see you at school over the next few days," she said. There was a graciousness in her voice well beyond her years. "I'll miss you all terribly when we're gone."

I smiled and thanked her. I wanted to shake her hand, but couldn't reach her any more.

*

THE BACK STAIR CUT A STEEP SHAFT through the inner darkness of the house. At the seventeenth step there was a landing with a passage into the servants' quarters off to the left. I could hear the electricity meters humming in the room where Yeh-ching taught me calligraphy. There the passage turned left again and ran straight on until it ended in another room. That's where Amah now lived.

I didn't take it. I continued up the stair. I counted the six steps to the top. I felt for the light switch, but the lamp was dead. My hand fumbled for the doorknob. I had done this a thousand times, but I was rushing it and I could feel my heart beating and then the door opened and I went through into the house.

Even if you couldn't see, you'd know. You could feel it through your feet. You could hear it, smell it. *Your* house. I closed the door and shut out the black hole. Maybe I shut it in, what difference does it make? The last bit of sunlight glinted off the sweeping balustrade. "Bobchik, come," said Ludmilla Vinokuroff to the rumpled dog she led. Her old lady's limp garments reached down to her slippers and she had to pull them up to manage the stairs, revealing her white bones. From the room where Mami had slept and painted her portraits came the sound of old Vinokuroff coughing.

I reached the top landing. The *click-clack* of the flying shuttle now sounded through the door of what had been Amah's room. The room across the landing from our bedroom. The room in which she had been since the beginning. "We are living in a factory, yes?" said the Italian widow as she hurried past. Her sardonic chuckling followed her all the way down the stairs.

Mami sat at her loom. I saw her through a cascade of knotted cords that raised and lowered the heddle frames. With each change, Mami sent the shuttle flying through the shed of the warp, trailing a thread behind it. She thumped it home, alternated the shed and repeated the cycle. A bolt of fabric formed on the forward roller. Mami stopped and released the ratchet, wound the cloth a few notches on and locked it again. She saw me and laughed. "How long have you been standing there?" she said.

"Not long."

"How was the party?"

"Nice," I said.

"Did you have nice things to eat?"

"Yes. Cakes. Sandwiches. Coca-Cola."

"Did you play games?"

"No, we just sat and talked."

"Have a look," Mami said. She ran her hand over the pink-brown-and-white chequered fabric. "For curtains. The Poggensees commissioned it."

"Weren't they the people who built the loom?"

Mami pointed at the STUDIO SEAGULL label on the side rail.

"That's them," she said. "They also have an interior design business. Mrs Berge runs it. Oh, by the way, she rang to invite you to Elizabeth's birthday party next Sunday."

"What? Who?"

"Elizabeth."

Mami went on weaving. When it hit me, it had the force of trains colliding. I left the room. Through the bedroom window the sky had the colour of an empty bucket.

The railway line

It was a much younger party. A huddle of amahs perched on stools outside, drinking tea. No mums and dads. Mami the only exception. Inside, chatting with Mrs Berge and Robert Oates. The Poggensees were there, too. They'd be talking shop. We played games in the garden. Elizabeth gave horse rides, wearing jodhpurs, leading the mare by the reins. We pulled carrots from the carrot beds and fed them to the pig. The pig chomped up the carrots and made the girls laugh. Before dusk we played hide and seek. The dogs had to be locked away because they kept sniffing us out in our hiding places. We played the variation of the game where you could free yourself by breaking cover and running back to the base. Elizabeth was it. I was comfortable in the hedge and stayed. The turn passed to someone else. I hadn't even been missed. There was a rustling in the foliage. Then a voice in my ear: "They'll be going home soon. Can you stay?"

Janie Robson was the last to leave. Elizabeth took me upstairs into her bedroom. She left the door ajar and we could hear the grown-ups talking in the sitting room downstairs. She pulled a cardboard box from under her bed and picked out photographs to show me. Black and white Brownie Box contact prints with wide white borders. Horses, a goat. A brother named John in British Merchant Navy uniform. A snapshot of herself sitting in the bows of a dinghy holding the oars. Her legs apart, showing underpants. "Who took that?" I said. She said his name, a friend of John's. "He shouldn't have," I said.

Then she showed me her autograph book. "Remember doing this?" She held open a page on which I'd done a drawing and written: *In A Kingdom By The Sea*. "What does it mean?" she said.

"It rhymes with *Annabel Lee*."

"Who's she?"

"She's his girlfriend. They live by the sea. You should read the poem. It's by Edgar Allan Poe," I said. "It's one of my favourites."

"I want to live in the country," she said. "I'll show you."

Elizabeth rummaged among the photographs and sorted a number of them into her hand. "Sit here." She thumped her free hand on the bed. On the space beside her. "This is where I want to live," she said. "Yorkshire, the moors. That's Robert."

"Your father?"

"Tell you some other time. This is me on his horse."

You couldn't really see because the picture was very small, but there was a big horse and a small rider sitting bolt upright and holding a riding crop. The countryside was broken by rocky outcrops and there were no trees, only rough looking grass. It went on forever. I took the photo in my hand. I could see now that it was Elizabeth. Her chin cut an angle into the sky.

"It looks wild. Uninhabited," I said.

"We stayed at a croft. Below the moors. There were sheep and pigs and lots of animals. Dogs. And stables with six horses. Here's a picture of it, see?"

Snuggled into a friendlier landscape, the croft looked warm and inviting. "I could live there, too," I said.

"Well, I'm going to live there," she said. Her tone had hardened. "I prefer animals to people anyway. I'll keep horses."

It felt as if she was locking me out. "I like that white horse," I said.

"That was my horse," she snapped and stuck the photograph at the back of the pile. She ran through the remaining ones without comment. Her face was red. She kicked the box back under the bed.

"One day," I said, "I'll give you six white horses."

*

I KEPT A SUITCASE UNDER MY BED in the house in Columbia Circle. In it I had packed the most important things. If anything happened, me and my suitcase were ready to go. I wrote a list of the things and headed it INVENTORY. I checked it often to make sure everything was still there. Like my scrapbook of cars. Chryslers and Cadillacs—priceless clippers of the city streets. Bright red Pontiacs on whitewall Indians going places, their stern-faced chieftain cresting the silver-streaked bonnet, streaming feathers behind him. Dreams of a new frontier for a tenderfoot like me.

My books. The *Rhyming Dictionary*, present from Heinz Heinemann of the Western Arts Gallery. *Nu' kannste aber dichten!* he'd written in it *(Get writing those poems!)*. Also from the Heinemanns, *The Adventures of Sajo and her Beaver People* by Grey Owl (Wa-Sha-Quon-Asin). All the wildlife adventures of Ernest Thompson Seton (Lobo, King of Currumpaw and his beautiful mate, the white wolf they called Blanca. Tito the Coyote. Krag, the Kootenay Ram). The collie stories of Albert Payson Terhune (Lad of Sunnybank, Treve, a singular dog, and Bruce, the slow learner who turns up trumps). Jack London: *White Fang, Call of the Wild*. Well-worn westerns featuring Hopalong Cassidy and Tom Mix.

Two torches, one with batteries. A wooden box with Minnie Mouse on the lid. Inside, a storm-trooper's whistle from Daddi, the black and gold Sheaffer fountain pen from Sylvia Richardson, two propelling pencils (a Waterman and a little gold one, very pretty, also from Sylvia Richardson). My piano music (Short Preludes and Fugues by Bach and the Notebook of Anna Magdalena Bach). A picture of an

American film star (very beautiful) out of LIFE magazine. A large volume called *Modern Flight*, a flying manual from Bill Richardson. A map of Shanghai, my autograph album with Elizabeth's drawing of a horse still the only entry, my drawing of Lupo and a photo of Amah.

I couldn't remember ever having lived anywhere else. This room, in which we ate and slept and did our homework and played with friends, had always been our room, Rabe's and mine. The gallery of Spanish faces had always gazed at us from the painted wall above the blackboard and the meadows where bulls engaged in timeless combat under the distant hills had stretched from the beginning in a continuous cyclorama around the remainder of the room. Ferdinand, the young bull, had sat under the cork tree, sniffing flowers behind Rabe's bed even when we had had the run of the whole house and all the

servants and Daddi were there. Now, Mr Leto the landlord (the man without a face) wanted us to leave. Probably, we just couldn't pay the rent.

We rode out into Hungjao to have a look at a vacant apartment in the *Deutsches Heim* where Dr Mengert had lived. Where lots of Germans had lived. Where some still lived, waiting for their exit visas. It was a four-storied block of concrete and glass, very modern. Bauhaus style, Mami said. The concrete painted white and a deep red. It was surrounded by trees that lost their leaves in winter and the bare branches made scribbles across the taut geometry of the windowpanes. Some of the steelwork around the windows had begun to rust and the stains ran down over the walls as on an old tanker in dry dock. The apartment had glazing that reached full height from the bare concrete floor to the concrete ceiling and open-weave curtains, no longer quite white, screened it. The prospect of living in so uncluttered and uncompromising an architecture excited me.

However, things turned out otherwise. Miss Darroch, who taught junior classes at our school, offered us her house, as she was leaving for England. "It's all you can do with a house these days," she had said to Mami when Miss Penfold introduced them. "You can't sell it and if you leave it empty it just falls into the hands of the so-called People's Republic and they wouldn't know what on earth to do with it." Mami signed an agreement which concluded: *The above licence to occupy is subject to payment of the above peppercorn rental and further to the provision that you pass on this right to a new tenant in the event of your no longer requiring it and subject to the same terms as the above.* Or something like that.

212

The house stood in a lane with six or seven others. It was a two-storied villa with a Spanish tiled roof and white stuccoed walls. A climbing rose entwined the wrought iron grille that guarded the circular living room window facing the lane. The verandah and balcony overlooking the garden had been closed in with rows of wooden windows in faded red on rusting hinges. The Newcombs lived directly across the lane from us, the Diestels at the end of the lane and the Eynstones at the bottom of a tee. The houses were all two-or-three-storied and in a variety of styles. One, that was occupied by a Chinese Route Army officer and his family, had wide timbered eaves, like a Bavarian chalet. Mami said it reminded her of Hitler's retreat in Berchtesgaden. The comely Edwardian country houses to either side kept a respectable distance.

You entered the lane from Hungjao Road and it ran parallel to the railway line. Our house stood close to a tall bamboo fence painted with pitch and behind it ran an overgrown ditch that supplied mosquitoes in the summer. From the ditch rose a steep embankment to the railway tracks. A signal on top of a post with an attached ladder clattered into position to foretell the passing of trains. On our side of the tracks ran a narrow mud path. It didn't go anywhere. Just followed the tracks.

Every morning at 11:20 the southbound express went past the house. Foreigners on their way out of Shanghai would catch their last glimpse of the places they'd known and after that the crowded villages of Siccawei and Lungwha with its dark pagoda, the straggling fringes of Shanghai and then the

endless fields of crops. Mami would tell us when we got home from school, I waved to Maria Blödorn today or Fräulein Dittberner. Weekends, I would watch from the balcony and wave whether I knew anyone or not. Then, as the guard's van diminished down the tracks, the barrier rails at the Hungjao Road crossing would be lifted and all the waiting carts piled high with watermelons, cabbages and persimmons from Hungjao and beyond would begin to move across. Some of the carts were more like an oversized wheelbarrow made of wood with the heavy spoked wheel turning through the middle of the tray. The baskets of produce were stacked around it and tied together. The peasant worker guided it from behind, his earth-brown hands balancing the heavy shafts, while his wife pulled from the front with a rope over her bent shoulders. Water buffaloes pulled heavier carts while their drovers lashed their flanks with sticks. Pedicabs surged past them, their drivers shouting abuse at the peasants, while truck drivers honked at them in turn and bicycles wove through whatever gaps they could find or forge with the steady ringing of bicycle bells.

I had stood among them once, pressed up to the barrier rail with my bicycle doubled up beside me as the train came thundering toward the crossing. Next moment I was enveloped in a hiss of steam and the locomotive came to a shocked standstill in front of me. The shockwave impacted the couplings and passed, carriage after carriage, all the way to the guard's van and back again. People started shouting and gesticulating and the news came through from the other side of the train that someone had gone under the wheels. The body had been cut clean in half.

It was a time of suicides. People had begun to panic under the pressure of purges to rid the New China of new crimes. In fact, there was nothing new about them, just the old traditions newly renamed crimes. Like holding on to family land, wheeling and dealing (what the Chinese do best), hiding the gold, taking bribes or even the time-honoured cumshaw that made the Chinese world go round. Now everyone had to go to 'struggle sessions' where they would be pressured to make public confessions of their crimes. Or to indict others. There was nothing new in that, either. Sentences were handed out at mass trials and the offenders shot.

Amah went to *kai-wheh*, as the struggle sessions were called, and so did Mami's weaver from Siccawei. They may have had nothing to confess, but were expected to go nonetheless. I worried about Amah, that she would be targeted because of her position with a foreign family. I asked her about it and she just laughed. She had her ways. She might have been thinking of Yeh-ching's handwritten notice she'd saved off the back door of the old house. I smiled. I remembered how she'd dealt with the evangelists who had been campaigning for converts. "Why you go so many times to make you Christian?" Mami had asked her. "Every time I get Christian," she had replied, "American lady she give me 5000 yuan." It wasn't much, but it would buy a catty[1] of rice.

There was a cluster of open-fronted wooden houses along both sides of Hungjao Road close to the railway crossing. They had an upper storey where the family lived, while the ground floor was a shop. At the entrance to our lane was an eating house with the smell of hot peanut oil. It was always filled with men bent over bowls of noodles and tofu and the noise of conversation. Across the road, a few paces further up, was the rice shop where Amah bought our red rice. It was a short-grained rice with reddish traces left by the husks and Mami preferred this to the polished rice as it was more nutritious. "I can't understand why the Chinese insist on eating polished rice," Mami would say. "Beriberi, vitamin B deficiency. You can just see it coming."

Alongside the rice shop ran a muddy lane that led to three tall-gabled brick houses with clipped eaves, each set in a garden surrounded by a bamboo fence. But for this and the muddy lane, you might have been in England. In the third of

1 Chinese measure of weight, just over a pound.

these houses I had not long before made a solemn promise of six white horses and by this unconnected circumstance Elizabeth and I became close neighbours.

"I've made a list of our differences," she said out of the blue. We were in the hay pavilion with the warm smell of last summer. She pulled strands of hay from her hair. "And there are twenty of them."

"Hm?"

"Twenty differences. See if I can remember them. One: I like horses, you like donkeys. Two: I like the country, you like the sea. Three: I like Pepsi, you like—what d'you call it?"

"Sarsaparilla. Come on, I've only had it once."

"Still."

"Let's go inside," I said. "I'm cold."

"I like the cold." Her breath made a wisp of fog, rose-tinted in the curtained light from the sitting room window overlooking us. They'd be talking about us in there, I thought.

"I like this time of day, when the sun's gone and it's not yet quite dark," Elizabeth said. "I hate the bright day."

She was pushing the count up. It must be twenty-two by now. "I don't," I said.

"You can go inside if you like," she said.

I didn't. She sat up. "You know that Christmas hamper my Mum gave your family?" She watched her hand as it raked through the hay.

"Of course. It had a ham in it."

"Did you eat it?"

"Of course."

"That was Berriman." She shot me a sidelong glance. Accusing.

"Your pig?"

"Mum lied to me. She said he'd gone to live with the Poggensees."

"That's where Fragile went. You know the chick I had? He grew up into a rooster."

"What's the bet he ended up in the pot, too?" Elizabeth pulled some hay over herself and hugged it like a blanket. "I was sick for days after our Christmas dinner."

I wanted to move a little closer to her, but she had already scrambled up and opened the pavilion door. "It's pitch black out here," she said. "Are you coming? I'm really scared of the dark."

We didn't head for the house, but crossed by the stables. A horse stamped inside. Elizabeth walked quickly and I let her get ahead. When I caught up, she'd stopped by the chicken coop and was bent over, coughing. She kept her back to me. The chickens stirred in alarm.

"Let's go inside," I said. If we'd been older, I would have put my arm around her.

"You can go," she said and started away. "I'm going up to bed."

I joined the adults on my own and managed quite well to hide my feelings. That wasn't easy, because there was a whole jumble of them running around in my head. Or wherever. The adults were looking at maps and glossy black-and-white brochures showing sheep-studded hillsides. "This is New Zealand," Mami said and, "This is Australia," said Mrs Berge. "Sheep as far as the eye can see," said Robert Oates.

"Is Elizabeth not with you?" Mrs Berge asked.

I tried to sound matter-of-fact. "She's gone to bed, I think."

Mrs Berge was about to get up and check, but Robert

Oates stopped her. "Leave her be, Eileen," he said. "I'm sure Pip 'ere needs a break." And instantly the door opened and Elizabeth walked into the room.

"Speak of the devil," said Robert Oates, rising from the couch. "Why don't the two of you sit down 'ere and make yourselves comfortable? Must be better than the hayshed. Been tumbling in the hay, 'ave we?" He teased a strand out of Elizabeth's hair. "Liza been leading you astray? First you come in 'ere with the hay sprouting out of your bootlaces and now the lass 'erself's got it all through 'er 'air."

Elizabeth spun on her heel and vanished behind the slamming door. "Oh, Robert, that's enough," said Mrs Berge.

Pip and Liza, I said to myself. I liked Robert.

*

I WROTE A POEM FOR ELIZABETH and set it to music. It was called *My Little White Dove*. I wrote out the piano part on music paper and put the words under it. The last verse went like this:

> *My little white dove*
> *At night the moon doth shine*
> *And tells me that I'm yours*
> *And you forever mine.*

She got me to play it on her piano. I was too shy to sing it. So we sat on her bed and played card games. Beggar my neighbour. The door to the bathroom was open. "Can I use it?" "Sure." She removed her pants from the floor. "Sorry," she said. "You see, I have this game when I get undressed for a bath where I pull down my underpants and kick them in the air and catch them in my hand. This morning I missed."

"That's exactly what I do," I said and added it to my list of all the things we had in common. I closed the bathroom door and stood over the lavatory. Nothing. I flushed it anyway.

"Do you like baths?" she said as I came out.

"Yes and how! But our bath only has cold water."

"So how d'you wash?"

"I squat in the bath and pour cold water over myself with a pitcher."

"You're crazy," she said.

"We used to go to Bubbling Well Road for a bath. A friend of my mother's lived on the eighth floor of Hubertus Court. It was very modern, with big windows. You could see right across the city and over the Whangpoo."

"You didn't just jump in the bubbling well?"

"What? Oh, I see, no. But the woman who lived there said that in a typhoon the water in the bath would sway from end to end, because the building moved with the wind."

"And did it?"

"I don't think so. I used to make it sway on purpose, just by moving my body. Once I made it go over the edge. Anyway, the architect who designed the building had lived in the apartment before her. He was very famous. He said it was perfectly safe."

"Why did you stop going?"

"The woman left."

"I'm not surprised. What was her name?"

"Mrs Amann. She taught my mother to weave."

"You can use *my* bath if you want."

Whatever I was going to say stuck in my throat.

"Why was your chick called Fragile?" she said.

"We lived on the top floor in our old house. Fragile had his bed in a cardboard box with a net tied over the top. He would stick his head through the mesh and cheep like crazy whenever he saw me coming and then his feathers got caught on the way back and he'd be stuck. Each day I took him down to the garden so he could pick about and scratch and all that. He just always followed me round."

"So?"

"So what?"

"His name."

"Sorry. I forgot. The cardboard box had a picture of a broken glass on it. And in large letters: FRAGILE."

"You're crazy," she said. "What's your dog's name?"

"Wölfi. He's going away soon. To Hong Kong."

221

"You can wave to him when he goes past," she said. And then, "Sorry, I didn't mean that. We're going away soon, too. Our exit visa has arrived. I meant to tell you. It only happened yesterday."

Dum-dum, went my heart and I could say nothing.

"I don't want you to wave to me when we go past," she said.

They were gone within a week.

*

"YOU KNOW SHE WAS ADOPTED?" Mami said to me one day.

"Elizabeth?"

"Her real mother had put her in an orphanage. She was three years old."

"And her father?"

"He was a fugitive from the Nazis. He vanished to America."

"*Fugitive,*" I said.

Mami went on. "Later Mr and Mrs Berge divorced and Mr Berge returned to Norway. Robert Oates became her third father."

"Why didn't he go to Hong Kong with them?" I said.

"He's waiting for his exit visa. He will join them when he can," Mami said. "I didn't know any of this," she added. "He told me."

Elizabeth.

*

THE NEWCOMBS ACROSS THE LANE from us had a new baby
boy. "Mummy wants to invite you round to see him," Diana
said. She beamed. "His name is John."

Andrea and Frances Diestel and the Eynstone sisters
were just leaving as I arrived. Diana's mother beamed at me
exactly as Diana had done. I shook hands with her. A German
governess held the baby and let me touch his fingers. Diana led
me into the garden and I missed her dog. "Where's Scarum?"
I asked. "Kicking up daisies," she said. I didn't understand at
first and she pointed to a patch of raised turf up against the
hedge. "We wanted to take him with us when we went," she
said, "but he grew old while we waited for our exit visas. We're
still waiting. It's been almost three years now. Daddy's just
about given up."

We walked back to the house. "John's cute," I said as I
left. Diana was beaming again. I wanted to hug her. It was
the times. Everything we'd known was coming to an end. And
the end couldn't come soon enough. We were all standing in a
long slow queue for departure with no assurances as to when
it might be. We were afraid to look to either side as we waited
and we were too young to be looking back.

"Come quickly and look at this." Mami drew me to her and
we looked through the windows of the closed-in balcony down
toward the railway crossing. "He's a fisherman," she said. She
pointed to the man crossing the lines. Balanced on his shoulders
was a long bamboo pole on which sat nine black cormorants
and I caught the sparkle of the rings around their necks. "He
sends them out to catch the fish. They can't swallow them
because of those rings, so they bring them back to him." As
the pole sprang to the fisherman's stride, the birds bobbed up

223

and down, their wings rising a little to each bounce. And so he passed, his straw sandals, his loose black shirt, his calf-length black trousers, his peaked bamboo hat and his cormorants taking him wherever he was going, wherever he had always gone. "I want you to take a good look at him," Mami said. "Once we're gone from here, you will never see that again."

Rabe and I lie awake in the dark and wait for the night train; for the moment when it comes round the far bend and its headlamp lines up with our window. Then the window bars start to make a slow pass across the ceiling. Silently. The light cold, the shadows strengthening, the rails beginning to hum. The signal falls with a clatter. Now the room is full of light. We can hear the chuffing of the engine coming closer, working itself into a climax as it plunges past the house and then the rumble of the goods train, wagon after wagon after wagon repeating the clacking of wheels over the joints in the tracks and the comfortable shaking of the bed.

Those same windows afforded me a view, one morning about eleven o'clock, of Mrs Newcomb in a full-length leopard coat, walking along the mud path that followed the railway line. There would be friends to wave to. Mrs Newcomb's tall elegant figure nonetheless looked misplaced at the edge of the tracks and I left the window, not wanting her to see me. When the train went by, I heard the couplings slamming against each other and the shock and hiss of the brakes. When I looked out, I saw the leopard greatcoat tidily folded in the rough grass on the rail embankment and, under a carriage, part of what was left of Diana's mother.

Wölfi

Wölfi came with the house that stood by the railway line. So did the sofa on which he spent his nights. We had been left enough money for Wölfi's food till the end of the year. His owner would telegraph us from Hong Kong when he had found a place to live and we were to put his dog on a freighter to join him.

Wölfi was the second German shepherd dog in my life. I groomed him, talked with him, walked with him, played with him and shopped for him. I'd get on my bicycle and ride to the market each Saturday, to the corner of Route Say Zoong and Avenue Joffre. Wölfi's main food was, of course, rice and even the tiger in Jessfield Park got that. I'd seen it with my own eyes. Mami's artist friend Chen Chi had taken us there years ago when we were little. Rabe and I watched the animals being fed while Chen Chi sat on a park bench and made watercolour drawings of trees, paths and passing people. He did a drawing of the tiger and told us that he got soya bean curd mixed into his rice and the darker coloured lumps were curdled blood. It was curdled blood that I had now come to the market to buy for Wölfi.

The man at the stand cut squares out of the thickened curd and placed them on waxed paper into the pan of his balance. He slid the weight along the graduated beam, added another weight and brought it in close until the beam levelled and became still. He put the balance down on his stand and calculated the price on his abacus. He flicked the shiny black beads so that they clicked and clacked into place with unbelievable speed, then announced the price. His free hand signed the amount into the air and froze to await the wads of paper money that I had folded into multiples of one thousand yuan notes tied round with rubber bands.

I gave the change to a beggar who had his patch on the footpath up against a garden wall. The stumps of his legs overhung the wooden platform on which he sat. I held out the fifty yuan note to him and he lashed out at my hand, sending it flying into the gutter. He uttered a barrage of toothless sounds, then stood full height on his own two legs and brandished the platform at me.

I never went near him again. One day he was gone and didn't come back, but the outlines of his platform and of his back against the wall remained for a long time before indifference and the passing of seasons had erased their last traces from sight.

*

THE INSCRIPTIONS ON THE HEADSTONES in the old Jewish cemetery had frittered away and the stones themselves tottered above the hollows of graves that had long since caved in, the occasional bone sticking out above the fallen debris. I skimmed round them, running as if pursued. But Wölfi waited. From my hiding place I could make out the twin sentinels of his ears waiting for the sound of my whistle. The breathy sound of my storm-trooper's whistle from Daddi. It brought him bounding through the nettles and brambles, weaving among the headstones and clearing the graves, his wolf's brush flying, until he got me. He rose up and planted his paws on my shoulders and those craggy jaws laughed down into my face and lathered it with doggy breath and spittle.

Beyond the cemetery lay the open fields. Furled cabbages, maize and turnips made endless green frills across the silt plains. Wölfi, Rabe and I walked along rutted paths, stepping aside to let carts go by, piled high with produce. We skirted sewage ponds from which peasants fertilised their crops using four gallon tins that dangled from bamboo poles balanced on their shoulders. The tins broke through the crusted surface of the ponds and swung in the stinking air before their gleanings swilled around the bulbous stems. Whitewashed peasants'

227

cottages clustered together and persimmon trees hung their branches over roofs of cupped black tiles. Ancestral shrines looked on like miniatures of the homes of the living and burial mounds, the height of the cottages themselves, huddled together in family groups.

Creeks crossed the fields and ran out to the horizon between grassed embankments. They linked with other creeks, endlessly mapping the flat land. They joined the Soochow Creek, the Siccawei Creek, the Whangpoo River, the sea. They swelled and drained in unison and watermelons bloated in the slow water before being towed off to market on lighters. (Foreigners thought twice before buying watermelons from the market, but after their seeds had been roasted and salted and weighed by the street vendor, we cracked them between our teeth and spat the husks into the street as deftly as any Chinese.)

It happened to be a day of national celebration. Peasants abandoned their fields to watch parades of children with strings of paper flowers singing the joys of a blossoming People's Republic of China, which had been founded exactly two years earlier, on 1st October, 1949. They were followed by women beating drums slung to one side of their belted tunics. The women executed a rhythmic dance that took them three paces forward and two back, then forward again. Mami liked to joke that two forward and three back might have carried a more fitting symbolism. The marchers that made up the rest of the procession carried banners with political slogans and the ubiquitous portraits of Chairman Mao, Chou En Lai and Stalin and radiant peasant workers brandishing hoes.

The countryside had emptied. We led Wölfi through the

fields and came to a creek embankment. I snapped the lead off the dog's collar and let him run free, when I noticed four or five sheep coming over the brow. I wondered what they could be doing there. I had never seen a sheep before and nor had Wölfi, who was already shooting up the slope toward them. The sheep scattered. I yelled out to him. Then I blew my whistle and in the same instant three men appeared over the embankment. Their leader held a rifle. They were not uniformed, except for their army caps, but they had red armbands sewn to their sleeves. They were shouting, pointing at Wölfi. The dog came running to me. The leader stopped in front of me and spoke very fast in Chinese, indicating him with his rifle. Then he engaged the bolt and rammed shut the breech.

I threw my arms around Wölfi's neck, but the man shouted at me to get clear. He came closer and pointed the muzzle. I swung myself round between it and the dog and dug my hands into his fur. I heard Rabe telling me not to be stupid, but it only made me grip all the harder. The men were all talking at once and I couldn't make out what they were saying. Someone gave me a shove and I noticed the leader had lowered his rifle. He swung it at me to get up. Then he shouldered it and spun round. With a jerk of his head he commanded me to follow. I snapped the lead on Wölfi's collar and kept him close. We filed down a narrow path in the direction of an old ruin that I had once explored. Wölfi would remember. It had been a temple, probably burned down and never rebuilt. The porch was still standing but the main roof had fallen in, leaving the rear wall intact. It made a kind of open air courtyard and most of the debris had been taken away, the roof tiles to repair humbler roofs, the timbers to be made into charcoal fuel. The men stopped and debated the situation. To the right was a small room, the only one left standing, its plastered walls still showing the red ochre colour of Chinese temples. The door was barred and someone had written all over it in large red characters. A printed page of Chinese dangled from a nail. *Police*, said the leader and told us to sit down on the step. The other two men left, maybe to get someone else. We obeyed his command.

The leader leaned his rifle against the door post and then grabbed it again and placed it down among the weeds and squatted beside it. He removed his cap and lit a cigarette. He wanted to know our names and how old we were. Then he asked where we lived. He wrote it all down on a note pad. It looked unused. The pencil was new and sharpened to a point. I asked him his name and repeated it back to him. He smiled. Did we go to school? What was the dog's name? Did we have girlfriends? I showed him how Wölfi sat on command, lay down, stood. I got Wölfi to stay, but was afraid to go round the corner to hide.

We waited. The sun was high. The man with the gun wiped his head. Wölfi panted. There was no water. There was nothing more to say. I picked at the dry weeds. I noticed the man nodding off. I nudged Rabe. I thought, *Should we just run or grab his rifle first?* It only lasted a second or two and the man started, looked around. Too late. What a relief. He picked up his rifle and walked up and down. He was trying to make out it hadn't happened, but he could see we'd noticed. He had that guilty kind of look. Like a boy caught picking his nose. I thought that was a good thing.

One of his accomplices appeared in the distance, trudging through the fields. I saw him first and pointed. He held a bunch of papers. His leader studied them, then started filling out the forms. He copied down the registration number from the brass tag on Wölfi's collar. He copied down the other details from his pad. Then he gave it all back to the other man and sent him off. The third man must have gone home, I thought. The leader was probably the only one among them who could read and write.

His job was almost done. He tore a sheet of paper from his pad with a number written on it. He said to take it to the Great Western Road police station in the morning. He said a lot more that I couldn't understand, but his hands signed the message into the air as he spoke and it was perfectly clear and obvious—registration papers, certificate of rabies vaccination, that sort of thing. Then he picked up his rifle, drew back the bolt and pulled out the unspent bullet. He dropped it in his breast pocket and it made a clink. He probably had three of them, I thought. He would have to give them back or account for them to the authorities. He shook our hands and grinned. Then he slouched off. When he had gone some way, he stopped, shouldered his weapon, replaced the cap on his head and made an effort to look the part.

*

IN THE MORNING Rabe and I rode our bicycles to the Great Western Road police station with the prescribed documentation. We could see why it had taken the man so long on foot. He had had a route march, like the greatest of

231

China's heroes. There was, of course, a queue at the station. A silent one. This was a place you came to and didn't talk unless asked. You clutched your papers and listened to the repeated thump of the rubber stamp on the counter. You would get there soon enough.

A few days later we had a visit from Police Inspector Jinren. He looked more like an army officer in his belted jacket with the black leather holster. Amah showed him in and he formally introduced himself to Mami. He spoke perfect English. He carried papers bundled together with string. "I wish to report that the incident involving your two sons and the dog on Monday last at Hungjao has been referred to the Shanghai Western District Security Committee." He paused. "The incident has been viewed with grave concern, but after due deliberation it has been decided to take no further action in the matter. However," he paused again, "the Committee strongly recommends that your sons be re-educated."

Mami seemed to understand what this meant. She started saying something about the standard of education at the Shanghai British School and that it offered the Cambridge School Certificate syllabus, which Rabe had already completed and I was about to embark on. Inspector Jinren put up his hand and silenced her.

"We understand it may have been so," he said, "but education has moved on in China. Our schools do not look to the past. They prepare children for the future." He sat back in his chair. "Of course, we are aware that you have lodged an application to leave China together with your sons. This application will naturally have to be considered in the light of the Committee's recommendation."

"Amah, please make some tea for the inspector." Mami shifted into the role of hostess. "Thank you for your concern over the boys' education," she said. "There is nothing more important at this stage of their lives, is there? Do you have sons?"

Inspector Jinren would not be drawn in. Instead he said, "You will remember a certain Mr Siegel. He was often seen at your house."

"Onkel Siegel? He was an old family friend," Mami said. She looked puzzled.

"How old?"

"I met him before my children were even born."

"That is my point," the inspector said. "It has been noticed that your sons have a strong resemblance to Mr Siegel."

Amah pivoted through the swing door with the tea tray and Mami said, "Amah, the inspector thinks Onkel Siegel was the children's papa."

Amah laughed and spilled tea into the tray. A hint of a smile brushed Inspector Jinren's lips. Mami noticed it. She told us after he'd gone that she'd recognised him in that moment. He had been one of a party of three Kuomintang officials whom Daddi, then the German Vice-Consul, had invited to a dinner party at our house. Siegel might have been there, she said. It would not have been unusual. She remembered Daddi telling her that Inspector Jinren was from the secret police. He'd trained in Japan. "Watch out for him," Daddi had said. "He sees everything."

Seventeen years later, it appeared, he was putting his eyesight to good use for the Communists. Had he been serious about Onkel Siegel? Or was he just showing off?

Again he changed the subject.

"You get a good view of the trains from here," he said. The words crawled up my back like spiders. It was what I feared most. I had been the one who turned off the light as the train went past. Only a few nights ago. I had wanted to get a better look. We had all lined up in the window and watched wagon after wagon go by, all of them covered with canvas suggesting the hidden shapes of trucks, tanks and artillery. "War in Korea," Mami had said and in the same instant we were dazzled by a spotlight from the train. It made several passes across the window before it was turned off. We were too frightened to move. We left the house lights off and went to bed in the dark. I couldn't sleep.

Mami said, "When we first came here, the trains would keep us awake. Now we don't even notice them any more." She poured his tea. "So we really don't mind them at all," she said. I noticed that her smile came with some effort and I smiled, too, to help it along. But the inspector was busy writing. After a while he looked up and said, "I have a few more questions." He wanted to know the name of Mami's sister in Germany. Mami spelled it out. Then she had to spell out her address in Berlin. Then he took down the name of the professor Mami had worked under at the Tung-Shi university in Woosung. "You realise that was twenty-five years ago?" Mami said, but he paid no attention. Then he left.

A month later he was back. He asked Mami the same questions as if they were of great importance. Again he wrote everything down and left. Mami threw me a look and I followed him to the gate and opened it. Wölfi came bounding up and sniffed his boots. "Please keep him on a lead when you take him out for walks," he said and it felt as though my father were talking to me. "We have armed guards all over the countryside—and not just on national holidays." But Wölfi was already booked on the next ship to Hong Kong.

I made a drawing of a travelling crate and put all the measurements on it. It was high enough for Wölfi to stand and wide enough for him to lie down in. At one end it had a raised platform with circular cutouts that fitted his enamel eating bowl and the tin water bowl so they couldn't slide around or get knocked over. A carpenter made it exactly to my drawing. The bottom was plywood and the top and sides were wooden slats. An iron bolt held the door shut. I threw Wölfi's blanket into the crate and made him spend time in it to get him used to it.

The day before his embarkation, Teddy Heinrichssohn took a picture of Wölfi and me sitting on the terrace. At the end of the day we were still in the same place. It had begun to get very cold and I was shivering. The dog lay curled beside me, his wonderful big head against my thigh. I could feel his breath on my bare legs and see little wafts of it disappearing into the dark.

"I hate you," I said.

Wölfi's head pushed harder into me. "You think I love you, but I don't. I hate you. I've always hated you."

My hand raked his fur. My fingers dug deep. "That's why I had to beat you," I said. "Remember all the times in the garden when I beat you? You could never understand. I could never understand. But you always came back to me and I would beat you again until you squealed."

235

Wölfi stretched and thrust his paw into my lap, lay down flat. "I couldn't bear it when I made you squeal," I said. "I had to run away." I played with his gristly sentinel's ears that always stood up again, no matter how many times I folded them into themselves. Wölfi shook his head as though to free himself from a plague of flies. The flap and slap of his ears banished all remorse and washed the heavens clean. He looked up at me and replaced his head on my thigh. He made a growling sound deep inside his body that ran deep inside my own. I remained sitting that way, cradling his head, until I felt it had become too late ever to move again.

*

ONE CORNER OF THE CRATE rested on the footboard, whilst the rest of the crate obliquely overshot the sides of the pedicab and the top of my head. I called Wölfi up and he half stood, half sat with his front legs in my lap. The driver had to rise from his saddle to pedal his load over the hump of Columbia

Road and through into Bubbling Well. Then along Nanking Road, turning left along the Bund, up the gradient of the Garden Bridge, over the Soochow Creek, then freewheeling down the other side. He rang his bicycle bell to clear a path for his wide load as if it were privileged cargo. I caught sight of a shabby little freighter at the Hongkew wharf just around the bend of the Whangpoo River. Its funnel was running black smoke and a red flag hung from its stern. I called out and pointed to it.

Wölfi got restless and dragged his paws off my lap. His claws drew blood as they scored their way down my legs. I watched the dark globules swelling out of the frozen rills but felt nothing.

Two coolies trundled the crate toward a roped-off area where an official was checking the details of the consignments. I led Wölfi and told the pedicab driver to wait. He pointed to my bleeding legs and laughed merrily. People turned round to look and he entertained them with an account of our journey through his sugar-cane frittered teeth. Then he spat and a luggage trolley tracked through it and lifted it and left a row of wet patches on the littered floor as it went. I got my papers ready and Wölfi and I stood close and waited.

The official stamped the papers and then pasted them on the crate with rice paste. He folded the edges around the slats and told me to put Wölfi in. I snapped the lead off his collar and rammed the bolt shut. "You're going to your owner," I said. "You were never my dog. Just on loan." Then I pulled the bolt back again. I ran the storm-trooper's whistle over my head and tied it around Wölfi's neck. I rolled up his lead and tucked it into a corner of the crate.

I left him there and went back to my pedicab. I should have cried then, but my fingernails were drawing fresh blood from my thighs and every time I felt the tears coming, I dug them in a little deeper.

A week later a telegram came from Hong Kong:

WOELFI ARRIVED IN GOOD SHAPE STOP
HAVE REMITTED US $70 EXPENSES TO
YOUR A/C AT HSB STOP HUNDRED THANKS

The visible wounds on my legs were healing well and had already begun to shed the first of their hardened crusts.

Endgames

I sometimes wonder where we would have ended up if Rabe hadn't become a Christian. I thought we were Christians already, but he explained that it was different when you made a personal decision about it. Rabe made that decision in Shanghai at the age of fifteen and his friend Alan Knight guided him along the path.

From that time on, Rabe was never without his cards of Bible verses, which he learned by heart, citing chapter and verse. He graduated from the first series to the more advanced one on different coloured card. Then he moved on to the third series. Sometimes he got me to test him. "Don't butt in unless I ask you," he'd say. "OK." There was a spin-off for me. I was picking up Bible verses as fast as he was. I remembered them the way Rabe spoke them, in his voice, with his meaning.

> *When I was a child, I spoke as a child,*
> *I felt as a child, I thought as a child:*
> *Now that I am become a man, I have*
> *put away childish things.*
> *One Corinthians thirteen eleven.*

That card always followed a run of cards to do with love, so I shuffled the cards to make the test harder. I cut the pack. The face card came up: *1 Cor. 13:11.* I gave Rabe the reference. "What?" he said. "When I was a child..." So I shuffled the cards again and again it came up in the cut: *1 Cor. 13:11.* "I don't believe it," he said and rattled off the verse. When it happened a third time, we both laughed so much, we had to cancel the test.

In bed that night after lights-out, I said, "You know *Corinthians thirteen eleven?*"

"Yeah?"

"Is that what you have to do? Give away all Childish Things?"

"Put away."

"What?"

"Put away Childish Things. You put them all away," Rabe said, "when you become a man."

I thought about what I might put away. My little turtles in their enamel basin, perhaps. Hibernating they were, right then, tucked inside the cave I had built out of rocks and pargeted with mud. Then there were my books. Mostly about animals. "Are you still reading Zane Grey?" I said.

Rabe ignored the question. "It's not just things that are meant, but thoughts. Dreams, childish ways, habits, childish talk," Rabe said.

I slipped down into my bed and let the covers form an arch above me. I thought about my life. When people asked me what I wanted to be when I became a man, I always said, a forester. I saw myself in a cottage by the edge of the forest with a farmyard, horse and cart, axe, straw, goats, chickens and maybe a bear cub I'd rescued. Evenings by the log fire, my big dog curled up beside me, owls hooting in the trees. I'd be thinking about the girl I loved. The girl called Sajo, for instance, who talked to beaver and heard Nature whispering to her in the sound of a waterfall.

"There are some things I'm not giving up," I said. "Miss Penfold already knows I want to be a forester when I grow up and she's put it in her letter *To whom it may concern*. I'm doing a project on beaver dams at school and I've got to finish that. I suppose all of that falls under the banner of Childish Things?"

"You'll put them away when you're ready to become a man," Rabe said. "Now can you be quiet. I want to pray."

I wanted to scream.

*

THE MAN AT THE CHINA INLAND MISSION took me aside. "Let's find a quiet place to chat," he said. He opened the door and we went out onto the landing. "This'll do," he said. I crouched against the wall facing him. He crouched against the balustrade. I had to stand to let someone pass. He talked about the soul. "It is the part of us where we can be with Christ. It is what sets us apart from all other living things."

"From animals?"

"That's right. Jesus promises us a place in heaven—"

"I know," I broke in. "*I go and prepare a place for you. John 14:2.*" And then, "A place without animals?"

"A place with God," the man said.

"No animals?"

"Animals don't have a soul," he said.

241

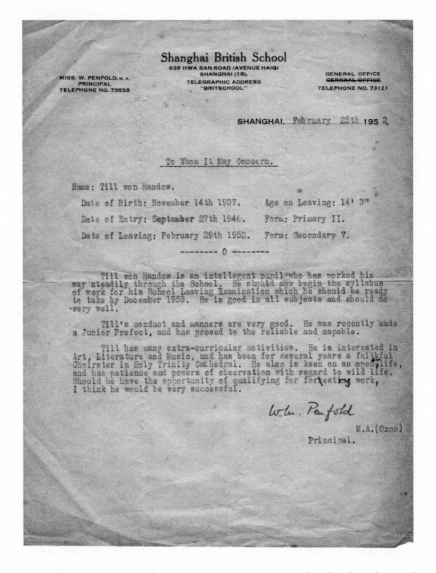

SHANGHAI, February 25th 195 2.

To Whom It May Concern.

Name: Till von Randow.

    Date of Birth: November 14th 1937.   Age on Leaving: 14' 3"

    Date of Entry: September 27th 1946.   Form; Primary II.

    Date of Leaving: February 29th 1952.   Form: Secondary V.

-------- 0 --------

    Till von Randow is an intellegent pupil who has worked his way steadily through the School. He should now begin the syllabus of work for his School Leaving Examination which he should be ready to take by December 1953. He is good in all subjects and should do very well.

    Till's conduct and manners are very good. He was recently made a Junior Prefect, and has proved to be reliable and capable.

    Till has many extra-curricular activities. He is interested in Art, Literature and Music, and has been for several years a faithful Choirster in Holy Trinity Cathedral. He also is keen on an open-life, and has patience and powers of observation with regard to wild life. Should he have the opportunity of qualifying for forkestry work, I think he would be very successful.

                      Wm. Penfold

                                M.A.(Oxon)
                      Principal.

"OK," I said and he asked me what animals I had and I said I just had some pet turtles but they were doing their winter sleep and he smiled and nodded as if to say, that's so cute, I wish I had some myself. I stood up and shook his hand and started down the stairs and he called out, "Aren't you staying for sing-song?" and I said, "Can't tonight." And then into the

Telegraphic Address
"SECLAB."

[Lab. Imm. 27.

In your reply please quote :

33/135/4789

DEPARTMENT OF LABOUR AND EMPLOYMENT
IMMIGRATION DIVISION

P.O. Box 310, TE ARO,
Wellington C. 2,
New Zealand.

AIR MAIL.   7th March, 1951.

Mrs. I.V. Randow,
885/1 Hungjao Road,
SHANGHAI,
CHINA.

Dear Madam,

    I have your letter of 5th February, addressed to the Comptroller of Customs, concerning your desire to emigrate to New Zealand, accompanied by your two sons.

    In reply, I forward a form of application for a permit to enter New Zealand, which should be completed and returned to this office accompanied by the specified certificates and photographs.

    Upon receipt of the application, careful consideration would be given to your desire to enter this country, but I wish to point out it is most unlikely that a permit would be granted to you.

                  Yours faithfully,

                  F. A. HOWELL
                  Director of Employment.

Enc.

empty street, "Can't ever, ever, ever again."

And yet. If Rabe hadn't become a Christian, where would we have ended up? Not in New Zealand, that's for sure. That notice from the Department of Labour and Employment (Immigration Division), which ended with the words, *I wish to point out it is most unlikely that a permit would be granted*

243

to you, would have been it. Only, Rabe had a friend called Alan Knight. And Alan's parents had served with the China Inland Mission in the interior and were now awaiting their chance to return to their own country, New Zealand. Alan had introduced Rabe to them, to their faith and to their church and when their time came they went and prepared a place for us in the land of milk and honey.

Had it not been for his decision for Christ, Rabe would never have spent a year in the King Country at the age of sixteen, milking forty Jersey cows morning and night for a Christian farming couple old enough to be his grandparents. Nor endured the church socials or the daily devotions and sing-alongs with Uncle Tom and the Sankey Singers on the radio or the milk-soft farm diet or having to admit to getting the loaf of *Reizenstein's* out of the rural delivery box each week from Mami. Who, for her part, would never have found herself in the company of returned missionaries celebrating the comfort of their homecoming with ease and milk and smiles and lots of sugar. Nor had to recount her own story in such company, with all its unfamiliar and disquieting content. Nor finally received this comfort in return: *Never mind, dear, God loves even the Germans.*

And the war widow who hosted us at the missionary home might never have bared her leg against my own under the table while she gave thanks for the gifts that we were about to receive. And those gifts might never have included her grown-up woman's tongue inside my mouth long before I had tasted my first kiss.

There are some things that come with the future that, had you known, you might never have gone there. That we did

244

go there shows that we couldn't have known and that we so wanted to go, we might have turned a blind eye anyway. And, quite simply, it showed that it had become possible for us to do so.

The Knights had gone and prepared places for us in New Zealand and the Department of Labour and Employment (Immigration Division) had written a second letter, this time advising that our accommodation in New Zealand had been secured and guaranteed by certain parties and that it had accordingly been decided to issue us with a permit to enter the country. The office of the International Committee of the Red Cross in Shanghai had provided us with documents *valid to reach country of destination only*, recognising that we had no valid passports. And the People's Republic of China, through its Public Security Bureau in Shanghai, after nine months' deliberation, had issued a visa authorising us to depart the country. Lastly, the Hong Kong Shanghai Bank had confirmed receipt of a remittance to Mami's account in Hong Kong from a Mr Henschel in the U.S.A. in settlement of an old debt. Or an old theft, to be exact. Mami must have trusted him with some funds, probably from her own divorce settlement. Now she had to settle for half. It was enough to pay our passage to New Zealand. The bank was awaiting Mami's instruction to make payment to Thomas Cook and Sons. The China Navigation Company's *MS Taiyuan* was due to sail from Hong Kong on 9th March, 1952.

*

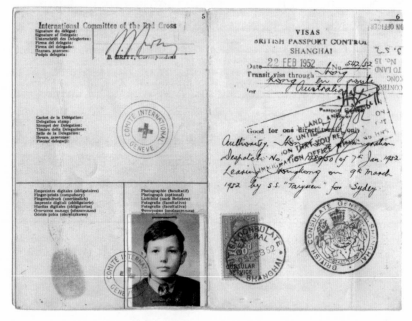

EE/75 (Revised)

PROVISIONAL CERTIFICATE OF NATIONALITY
CERTIFICAT PROVISOIRE DE NATIONALITÉ
VORLÄUFIGE NATIONALITÄTS-BESCHEINIGUNG

This is to certify that Ilse von RANDOW states that he (she) is a German national by virtue of* birth and that there is no reason to doubt his (her) statement.

This Certificate is valid only for the journey to the Western Zones of Germany, within 6 months from the date thereof, and must be surrendered to the Burgomaster in the place of destination immediately after issue of ration card, identity card, and residence permit.

It does not exempt the holder from compliance with any travel regulations in force in Germany or elsewhere or from obtaining a visa where necessary.

Il est certifié par le présent document que Ilse von RANDOW déclare qu'il/elle est de nationalité allemande par* naissance et qu'il n'y a pas de raison de mettre en doute sa déclaration.

Ce certificat n'est valable que pour un voyage à destination des Zones Occidentales d'Allemagne, pour une durée de 6 mois à partir de la date de délivrance, et doit être remis aux Maire du lieu de destination immédiatement après délivrance de la carte de rationnement, de la carte d'identité, et du permis de séjour.

Il n'exempte pas le titulaire des règles de circulation en vigueur en Allemagne ou ailleurs ni de l'obtention de visas nécessaires.

Hiermit wird bestätigt, daß Ilse von Randow *erklärt, daß er (sie) durch* geburt deutscher Staatsangehöriger ist und daß kein Grund vorliegt, seine (ihre) Angaben zu bezweifeln.*

Diese Bescheinigung ist nur gültig für die Reise in die Westzonen von Deutschland, innerhalb von 6 Monaten vom Ausstellungsdatum ab, und muß sofort nach Ausstellung der Lebensmittelkarte, Kennkarte und Aufenthaltsbewilligung dem Bürgermeister im Bestimmungsort abgegeben werden.

Es befreit den Inhaber nicht von den in Deutschland oder anderswo gültigen Reisevorschriften oder, wenn erforderlich, von der Erlangung eines Sichtvermerks.

Description
Signalement
Beschreibung

Profession *Beruf*	Kunstgewerblerin
Place and Date of Birth Lieu et date de naissance *Geburtsort und -datum*	Giessen/Hessen 15 Juni 1901
Height Taille *Größe*	178cm.
Colour of Eyes Couleur des yeux *Augenfarbe*	grey-Brown
Colour of Hair Cheveux *Haarfarbe*	dark Brown
Signature of Bearer Signature du Titulaire *Unterschrift des Inhabers*	J. v. Randow

Accompanied by the following minor children :
Accompagné par les enfants mineurs suivants :
Begleitet von den folgenden minderjährigen Kindern :

	Name Nom *Name*	Date of Birth Date de naissance *Geburtsdatum*	Sex Sexe *Geschlecht*
(i)	Rabe-Ruediger von Randow	14 April 1936	Male
(ii)	Tyll von Randow	14 November 1937	Male

Pour le Grand Général
Signed
Signé
Unterschrift   C. Ledan

Date
Le
Datum

Changhai, 9. 18 Avril 1950.

naissance", "Naturalisation", ou "Mariage".
"Geburt", "Einbürgerung" oder "Heirat".

Sichtvermerke auf der Rückseite

PSS/HQ/R1564*/200M/10-48

AFFAIRES ÉTRANGÈRES 500 FRANCS
AFFAIRES ÉTRANGÈRES 500 FRANCS
AFFAIRES ÉTRANGÈRES 50 FRANCS
AFFAIRES ÉTRANGÈRES 50 FRANCS
AFFAIRES ÉTRANGÈRES 50 FRANCS
AFFAIRES ÉTRANGÈRES 50 FRANCS
AFFAIRES ÉTRANGÈRES 50 FRANCS

"MAMI GONE OUT LONG TIME," Amah said. "She go see Hansi in Weihaiwei Road. Long time not come back." Rabe said, "Did Mami not telephone?" "No. I telephone Hansi, but no answer."

"She's gone to say goodbye," Rabe said. "The Heinemanns are leaving on Saturday, remember? I'll bet they're out celebrating, specially as we've just got our exit visa, too."

"It's Saturday today," I said. "The train went this morning."

Amah opened the front door and peered out. "Mami come now," she said. I met her at the back door. Mami put the bike away and pulled off her gloves. She removed her padded mouth mask and her breath made a white plume under the light bulb. "Is there no fire?" she said. "Fire gone out because no more coal," Amah said. "You please go put some water on the charcoal stove," Mami said. "Then we can have some tea."

Mami called us to the table. She waited for Amah to join us. Then she said, "They cancelled the exit visa without warning." She read our faces. "No, not ours," she said. "The Heinemanns'. This morning they came to the house and took Mr Heinemann away. Hansi wasn't at home. When she got back, she found Hannelore and Stephen and their amah alone in the house amongst the suitcases." Mami paused. She did that biting of her lip which I had come to know so well. "There has been no explanation and no charge," she said, "and Hansi can't even find out where they've taken him." Mami and Amah looked at each other in silence. Not mistress and servant. Just two women who understood the experience of loss.

"You're the same age as Hannelore," Mami said to Rabe. "When she was a three-year-old girl, the Nazis closed down her father's bookshop in Berlin. They said his books threatened the interests of the Reich. They managed to escape to Shanghai where he opened a new bookshop. Four years later the Japanese boarded it up and threw the family into the Hongkew ghetto. When the Americans freed them, Heinemann again set up a bookshop, the Western Arts Gallery, in Weihaiwei Road. You've been there many times. Then the Communists came and said foreign literature was against the interests of the People and closed it down." Mami took a breath and said, "On top of all that, the morning of their departure they come and take him away. That man never had a political thought in his life."

"Why did Daddi go to prison?" Rabe said. The question didn't seem to surprise Mami. "Daddi's job at the consulate put him in charge of Jewish re-settlement in Shanghai," she said. "But I've never heard anyone speak badly of him in that connection. After the war he was held by the Americans for something completely different, but the charges were never substantiated and he was acquitted."

"Of what?"

"The busiest time of his life." Mami laughed. "Between Hitler's suicide and Hiroshima he was officially out of a job, but a bunch of them kept the consulate alive. The Americans said later he was involved in some kind of political work. But he managed to squeeze in our divorce and marry Alix before the war ended and they put him in Kiangwan camp. By the time the Americans caught up with him, Didi was already being born."

"I go make tea," Amah said and went out.

*

249

IT WAS JOAN RADIK WHO WALTZED INTO THE CLASSROOM on the first day of term. "As you can all see," she said, "Mr Radik and I are going to have a baby." She looked round the class, all seven of us. And me. We smiled back. We *could* all see.

"Now, Mazda, what would you like to be working on this term? I know you told me, but I'm afraid I've forgotten."

Mazda Haas stood up. Tall, splendid. "I would like to continue working on my old project."

"Which was?" said Mrs Radik. "I'm sorry, which is?"

"Catholic minorities in Dutch Indonesia." There was a low murmur from the other girls. Who *was* this newcomer?

"And have you enough material to work from?" Mrs Radik said.

"I have..." Mazda began, "I still have some books from my old school library. I did not have a chance to give them back."

Mazda blushed. Mrs Radik came up to her and we thought she was going to put an arm around her, but she stopped herself. "If there's anything I can do to help, I'll try my best," she said. "That I promise you. And that goes for all of you, specially those of you who have come to us from other schools that have had to close. How about you, Cleopatra?"

Cleopatra Aluhna ran a hand through her hair and tilted her head to reply. Then she remembered that Mazda had stood up and she did the same, only we noticed the undulation of her body as she did so. She said, "I also am wanting to continue my project, which is called The Shoe."

"*The Shoe*?" Mrs Radik gave her a big smile and looked down at her own flat suedes. But Cleopatra had stepped forward and planted her foot on the desk in front, with her

250

heel barely missing the inkwell. We all noticed her short skirt and she said, "Ladies' shoes, fashion for the fifties." The other girls applauded. I shot a glance at York Lutz and saw that he was smiling. A shy smile. Then we both started clapping, too.

"What would you like to work on, York?" Mrs Radik's voice was very respectful.

The girls' heads turned to look at him. He stood slightly bowed and a strand of his Brylcreamed hair fell across his brow. "Lufthansa flights over China," he said. "In the twenties and thirties."

"And you have some sources you can work on?"

"My father flew the route. He flew Junkers F13s. He told me about it. I even have technical information. My father is dead. All the sources I need have come from him." He nodded his head once and sat.

It took a moment for everyone to start breathing normally again.

"Antonina?"

"Well," said Antonina Kolnichenko, "I started working on project about babies. I think maybe you can help."

We all laughed. "You may be able to give *me* some advice," Mrs Radik said. Then she turned to me. "Still doing beaver dams, Till?" she said.

"Yes."

"And, Natalie, you've got your project about your old Russian school in Mukden? And Monika, you know what you're doing and I imagine you want to get on with that."

The girls nodded.

"I'd almost missed you, Eurydice, hiding back there." Joan Radik said. She had to lean sideways to see her. "Is there

251

anything you would like to work on?"

The girl's mouth lifted two little folds into her cheeks. "I am not sure. I have not thought about it."

"*Eurydice*, that is such a beautiful name," said Mrs Radik. "And so unusual. Can you tell me about it?"

The girl's forehead made puckers above her eyebrows. She studied something on her sleeve, taking her time. She picked it up with her fingertips and blew it away. "My mother," she said. "She choose my name...choosed?"

"Chose."

"My mother chose my name." The smile returned.

"You play the violin, don't you?" Mrs Radik said.

Eurydice nodded her head and her cheek flushed. She covered it with her hand.

"Perhaps you could do something with that," Mrs Radik said. "Do you come from a musical family?"

"I am sorry?"

"Does anyone else in your family play music? Your mother perhaps?"

"No."

"Maybe we can talk about that together another time. What d'you think?"

"Can I write it in French?" Eurydice held back a giggle. She caught me doing the same. Then she let it out and blushed. Again she covered her cheek with her hand.

"Well, that's a thought," said Mrs Radik. "Of course, you went to Sacré Cœur, didn't you? On the other hand, why don't we get together and write it in English? I would love that."

"I think, maybe yes," Eurydice said, meeting the teacher's eyes for the first time. "Thank you."

Joan Radik picked up a manila folder and leafed through it. "Curriculum studies," she said. "Mr Radik will take you for most of those. Now, we have Trigonometry, Algebra (your favourite quadratic equations, exponential functions and so on), what else? Oh yes, French, History, Hygiene and Physiology. The last two with Miss Penfold. Miss Schofield will take you for Latin as before, I beg your pardon, I mean Mrs Wong. I'll still take you for English and we can look forward to more readings from Till out of *The Song of Hiawatha* while he is still with us."

Someone clapped and everyone joined in. I had a feeling it had been Eurydice who started it, but she was looking out of the window when I turned my head to see.

*

"WE MUSTN'T FORGET TO RELICENSE THE BICYCLES this Saturday," Mami said.

"Oh, no, do we have to? We'll be gone in a couple of months."

"And what will you do until then without your bikes? Anyway, don't count your chickens."

The relicensing place was in Siccawei, a short ride from home. "Oh look, there's Teddy," Rabe said. His red Schwinn stood out although it was some fifty bikes ahead of us on the creek embankment. Teddy Heinrichssohn was staying at the Hungjao house with us and sometimes he let me ride his Schwinn to school. It had balloon tyres and wide handlebars, like antlers. Very different from my Hercules roadster with its handlebars the size of ordinary coat hangers.

Teddy had been to the American school and remembered us, although he was much older. He must have been over twenty now and he went into town every day to work. I once saw him get out of the pedicab and lift up the seat to get his weekly pay where he'd stowed it for the ride home. It was all in cash notes, folded and tied in stacks and there were three stacks eighteen inches long. "That's inflation for you," he joked as he passed me, cradling them in his arms. "I've already spent the other half," he added. "This pile of paper will be worthless by the weekend."

I held my old licence plate in my hand. The enamel had cracked and the metal under it had rusted where it had got bent. That must've happened when I crashed my bike. The screws were so rusty, I had to break them off. I hoped they would give me new screws. I looked at the bikes of the people who'd already got their new licences but I couldn't see if they had new screws. The new plates were white on purple and you had to mount them between the fork and the front mudguard stay, facing right. When Teddy passed us still waiting in the queue, he grinned and waved. On *his* mudguard was a new licence plate in *red on white* and it was double-sided and had a red border around it and he had mounted it centrally on top of the guard like a fin.

Teddy Heinrichssohn was impressive. He was always right, he always got his way (he was fluent in Chinese) and he shot from the hip, like Tom Mix. Once I was practising the piano and Mami said to him, "Do you think Till plays well? He's got rhythm, don't you think?" "Rhythm is the thing he hasn't got, sadly," Teddy replied, "but there isn't too much wrong with his ear." Just as well, I thought, because I was composing

254

a piano piece for Api Brenner entitled *Abschied*, by way of goodbye. Api got me to play it for him at his farewell party. It put tears in his eyes.

We got our new licence plates. I *did* get new screws *and* a new shiny-black mounting bracket, because the old one was broken. *Wait till Teddy sees this!*

"I have a surprise for you," Mami said. "The weaver has a brother-in-law who dyes indigo cloth. Come. They're expecting us." We followed.

Sheets of material hung above our heads, some plain, some patterned with chrysanthemums, phoenixes and dragons. They were drying on bamboo poles that criss-crossed the street. "Siccawei is the only place in Shanghai where indigo dyeing is done," she said. "The only place in China. In the world, probably." She was checking the house numbers on the southern bank of the Siccawei stream. She stopped and knocked. A girl opened the door and bowed and then a woman appeared and the women bowed to each other and then the weaver came out with his brother-in-law and introduced him to us and his sister and the girl stood aside. The owner of the establishment welcomed us into the warm inky haze that filled the interior of the factory and we all bowed and he showed us to a table and the women served us tea. None of them wore indigo, but synthetic prints. Except the weaver, I noticed, whose trousers, overlapped at the front and tied with a band, were a well-washed, faded indigo.

As were those of the workers who turned the cloth in the rows of steaming vats of indigo dye and lifted it into cooler vats and finally hung it up to drain. On large tables, others had stretched new lengths of the raw fabric and placed stencils and smeared a paste into the pattern of the stencil. When the paste had solidified, they reversed the cloth and repeated the process on the other side, matching the pattern exactly. It was the weaver who took me aside and showed me what it looked like before it was put into the vat. Just an intricate pattern of whitish grout on unbleached cloth. Then he showed me a finished piece, from which the last of the grout was being scraped, revealing a brilliant white pattern on the deep indigo background. Mami bought several pieces, allowing Rabe and me to choose our own and mine had big chrysanthemum blossoms and his had bamboo leaves.

Mami wanted to be back home in time to wave to the Wenzels as their train went by the house. Rabe and I took our last tram ride to the YMCA. As though by design, we got on the red tram. *Mao's tram* we knew it as, the others being green. He (Mao) was closing down the Y and we were going to have our last swim. Only the week after, the British Country Club was having its swan song. The kids from our school were a mere handful, mainly juniors. Rabe took Helga Biedermann and I tagged along. After the speeches, we had a look round the familiar corridors and came to the indoor swimming pool, in which all three of us had learnt to swim. It lay there like a stranded hull, empty but for a rusty puddle at the deep end. The lane markings on the bottom slanted into it.

Everyone seemed to have gone home, so we went out into the garden. The willows were bare and the sugar cane brown amongst sticks and tall weeds in the unkempt corner of the grounds. Here we ran, tagging each other, Rabe, Helga and me breaking off dry canes and using them as swords, throwing them like spears. Mine hit Helga and I ran. I could hear her closing behind me. Then I tripped and fell, turned over on my back just as she came down on me, pinning my arms to the ground, breathing wildly into my face, her weight warm into my body, laughing, heaving. *Don't go,* I thought, *don't go yet, don't go, ever.* Helga stood. It was over. "Let's go," Rabe said.

The dusk came down as we walked back across the grounds and a single light shone in the Country Club. We headed towards it. No one spoke, as if we had just spent the sadness of yet another ending and had nothing left to say.

An uneventful journey

We waited for the curtains to thaw. Day after day they clung icily to the washing line under a bleak sky. It had been Mami's idea to wash them before packing them up in trunks for New Zealand. As if that place were a land too pure for Shanghai's dust.

Two days, now, to the consignment's deadline. "I've got to see the man at Butterfield and Swire's," Mami said. "He knows me. I will ask him if he can extend it till Monday. D'you want to come?"

The tram took us all the way down Avenue Joffre into the

heart of the city. We found the office, but there was no one there. The door stood ajar. There were dust covers on the desks. Mami didn't waste her breath. "Let's go," she said.

Back down in the street Mami quickened her pace and we turned a corner into the Bund. It was wide and grey and deserted. We crossed over to the promenade on the river embankment. Nothing grew in the gardens and the trees looked wintry and forgotten. Mami turned up her jacket collar and led the way to a steaming noodle stall. She pointed to a rusty little coaster in the Whangpoo River. "That'll be the one," she said. Then she added, "I hope so, because it's the only ship out there." We slurped our noodles. "This was once the busiest port in the world," she said. "There could be twenty foreign ships anchored out there or tied up in the docks. Now you couldn't even get one up the river, because the dredges are all lying idle."

We watched a tugboat towing a barge upstream. It was empty. Tied up below us was a mat of sampans and house boats. A woman was scouring out a kong[1] over the side. Mami looked past them. "See the Floating Restaurant?" she said. "That's where Diestel took me for lunch to celebrate our last commission. The one the weaver just finished. We had Peking duck. It was very good. We'd nearly finished when Diestel pointed up-river at a low-flying plane dropping bombs. As we watched the bursts of water coming closer, he said, *If one of those gets us, I won't have to pay for the Peking duck!* By the time we stopped laughing, the waves were rocking the restaurant and we could feel the floorboards shift beneath our feet."

"What would've been the point of that?"

1 A lidded wooden barrel used as the family chamber pot.

"God knows, a little provocation from Chiang, a postcard to say we're still here."

"Look, there's Mao's red tram," I said, pointing. "Let's catch it home."

"Anything for a bit of colour," Mami said.

"Catch-as-catch-can!"

"What does that mean?"

"You never know. It could soon be the last tram still running," I said.

*

THE FROSTS WENT ON and Amah stayed up all night with the charcoal iron, raising curtains of steam out of the sodden pile. The weaver worked long hours, too, weaving remnants of wool into rugs for our journey. Mami had bawled him out that morning. She'd caught him going through a photo album among piles of books waiting to be packed. The album dated from 1935, the year my parents married, and it featured honeymoon photographs of Mami and Daddi naked on beaches and rocky promontories under a rolling sky.

Rabe and I stood by for the moment when the rugs were cut free from the forward roller and we could take the loom apart and pack it into the crate. Then we encoded all the connections for re-assembly, bagging the screws and wooden pegs, the spools and shuttles separately wrapped and bedded into nooks and crannies with still enough room for a few silk scrolls and a skein of jute.

Mami wrote down everything we packed. Later, we typed up the inventory for the Chinese Customs on her Hermes

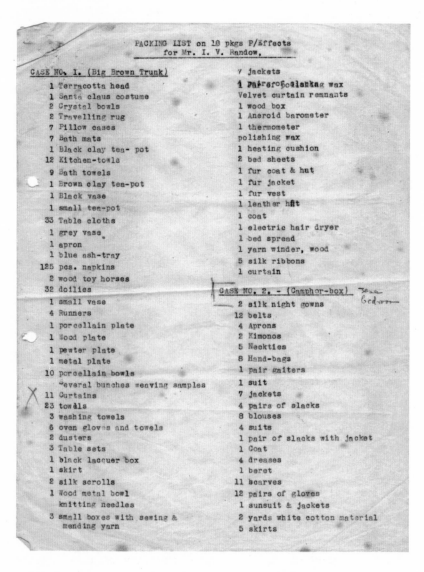

```
            PACKING LIST on 19 pkgs P/Effects
                 for Mr. I. V. Randow,

CASE NO. 1. (Big Brown Trunk)        7 Jackets
                                     1 Pairs of blankag wax
   1 Terracotta head                 Velvet curtain remnants
   1 Santa claus costume             1 wood box
   2 Crystal bowls                   1 Aneroid barometer
   2 Travelling rug                  1 thermometer
   7 Pillow cases                    polishing wax
   7 Bath mats                       1 heating cushion
   1 Black clay tea- pot             2 bed sheets
  12 Kitchen-towls                   1 fur coat & hat
   9 Bath towels                     1 fur jacket
   1 Brown clay tea-pot              1 fur vest
   1 Black vase                      1 leather hat
   1 small tea-pot                   1 coat
  33 Table cloths                    1 electric hair dryer
   1 grey vase                       1 bed spread
   1 apron                           1 yarn winder, wood
   1 blue ash-tray                   5 silk ribbons
 125 pcs. napkins                    1 curtain
   2 wood toy horses
  32 doilies                    CASE NO. 2. - (Camphor-box)
   1 small vase                      2 silk night gowns
   4 Runners                        12 belts
   1 porcellain plate                4 Aprons
   1 Wood plate                      2 Kimonos
   1 pewter plate                    5 Neckties
   1 metal plate                     8 Hand-bags
  10 porcellain bowls                1 pair gaiters
     Several bunches weaving samples 1 suit
  11 Curtains                        7 Jackets
  23 towels                          4 pairs of slacks
   3 washing towels                  8 blouses
   6 oven gloves and towels          4 suits
   2 dusters                         1 pair of slacks with jacket
   3 Table sets                      1 Coat
   1 black lacquer box               4 dresses
   1 skirt                           1 beret
   2 silk scrolls                   11 scarves
   1 Wood metal bowl                12 pairs of gloves
     knitting needles                1 sunsuit & jackets
   3 small boxes with sewing &       2 yards white cotton material
     mending yarn                    5 skirts
```

typewriter. It got packed last. We had to list every single item. The lists ran to fourteen two-column typed pages. "I've put the curtains down to go in the big brown trunk," she said, "but we won't pack them until the removal truck is here."

The weaver gathered up the warp ends and bagged them. I wrote down a four-figure number and gave it to him. He

CASE NO. 5 - Cont.

J.V.Eichendorff, Life of a Playboy
B.Henneberg, Attempt to reconstruct the early classic constellations
R.Henseling, Astronomical Booklet-1940.
Michelangelo, His Life and Work
1 Volume, Spitzweg,Schwind, Waldmueller, Feuerbach, Richter,Oberlaender
T.V.Scheffer,Legends of the Stars
2 Dictionaries, engl.-german and vice versa
S.Hensel, The Family Mendelssohn (2 vol)
Dr.K.Ploetz, History
O.P.Trautmann, Bridge of Singers
H.S.Chamberlain, Foundations of 19th-Century (2 vol.)
L.Schmidt, Masters of Musik in 19th-Century
1 Rubbing
2 knives
3 small spoons
4 big spoons
3 forks
6 knife blades
15 shopsticks
4 knife seats (glass)
1 curtain

CASE NO. 6 - (Yellow Camphor-Box)
2 Suit cases
1 personal paper file
1 file with paternal letters
1 file with maternal letters
1 file with fraternal letters
1 file of own letters
1 file with friend's letters; poems & Literatur
1 file with drawings
1 file with notes on weaving
9 diaries
1 polymeter with directions
1 broache with moonstone
1 stationery box
3 negative albums

Various personal photo and Negative albums
1 Sewing basket
buttons, Yarns and sewing-utensils
bandages & borax
2 rubber syringes
3 bath towels
4 bath mats
7 quilt cases
9 bed sheets
14 table cloths
66 napkins
10 doilies
2 bed spreads
9 quilt covers
10 pillow cases
20 silk ribbons for fastening
8 scrolls
4 table legs
1 carpet
1 leather writing folder
journals of German art
1 empty oil can
1 morning gown
Shakespears (5 vol.)
Goethe, Wilhelm meister
H.Eulenberg, Silhouettes
"   "   New Pictures
J.Huizinga, utumn of the middle-Age
E.G.Wilson, Have we lived before
1 Tea warmer & cover
1 bread knife

CASE NO. 7 - (Big-Box)
1 detached swedish loom and other apparatus therefor
4 Scrolls
1 home-made star map
5 rubbings
1 bunch of jute

grinned and fingered the combination lock barrel and then rode away on my bike. His brother-in-law had written up a bill of sale for eighty thousand yuan and I'd written a receipt. The weaver and I went to the licensing place together and exchanged documents and got them stamped. The subterfuge had been Mami's idea. "After thousands of years running on gifts, bribes and gratuities, the new China has declared even the humble cumshaw corrupt," she said. "So I wouldn't want the weaver to get into trouble for accepting the gift of a bike."

*

I TOOK MY BOOKS FROM THE SHELVES one by one and stacked them in two piles on the floor. One to pack up, the other to leave, or, rather, to *put away*, like childish things. Out went Albert Payson Terhune's collies. So did Sajo and her Beaver People. Then I retrieved her from the pile and put her in the pile to pack. I hesitated over Ernest Thompson Seton's stories of wild animals. Leafed through one of the books. His pen and wash illustrations, his margin doodles. Then I closed it and put it with all the others that would not be packed. Sixty years later, I have managed to replace some of the books.

Amah came into the room with an armful of clothes and put them down on Rabe's bed. They gave off the faint smell of a hot iron. Then she sat on the edge of my bed and folded them and made two piles. When she got up to put them away in the tallboy I said, "Just leave them on my bed. I have to sort out what to pack." She hesitated, stood, holding the little stack of clothes as if they contained something fragile. She didn't look at me, but I noticed that her cheeks had drained away from under her eyes, leaving them staring. She didn't move. I scrambled onto my feet and left the room. I ran into Mami sorting through the linen on the landing. She unfolded and held up a table cloth. Slightly frayed and with a faded red spatter of candle wax. "Shall we pack it?" Mami said. "No," I said.

264

Trunks filled the sitting-room. Mami stencilled numbers on them in blue oil paint. Teddy Heinrichssohn looked on. "No room for error," he grinned. "Mismatch the lists and there's no telling what may befall."

"We won't believe this when we get there," Mami said.

"When's that?"

"In April."

"Don't count your chickens," Teddy said.

"My turtles," I said. "I have to let them go."

"It's spring," Mami said. "They'll be waking up. They'll be hungry. It's a good time to set them free." But only one turtle had survived its winter sleep. The other three were no more than just the carapace and the shield and nothing in between.

"I'm coming with you," Mami said. "And bring your sketch-book. It's going to be our last ride into the Hungjao countryside."

I borrowed Teddy's Schwinn. We put Honeymunch down on the muddy banks of a creek and Sweetiepie's shell beside him. Billy and Bonny's we tossed in the water. They floated.

The tip of Honeymunch's head peeked out from under his shell. "We should have brought some food for him," I said.

"I brought a banana," Mami said. "But you eat half. He'll never get through it."

I couldn't eat it. I thought maybe I should do a drawing of him, but something in my throat was tightening and my vision was blurring. I got the Schwinn and rode away. A little way on I got off again and did a drawing of a shrine among some grave mounds. Just a pencil drawing. "It's very good," Mami said.

*

265

AMAH MET US AT THE GATE. "Policeman here," she said. "Same man last time."

Inspector Jinren introduced himself, adding, "You will remember me."

"I hope you haven't been waiting—" Mami said.

"Not at all," he cut in. "I should apologise for calling unannounced. I see your travel arrangements are under way." The inspector indicated the trunks.

"They're going tomorrow," Mami said. "Won't you sit down?" She pulled up the weaver's stool.

"Ah, you have this book, too." Inspector Jinren had picked up *Chinaflug* from the top of a pile. On the front cover was a photograph of a Junkers F13 flying over endless folds of mountains somewhere in China. "Very good aeroplane, that one, F13," he said, tapping his finger on the image. Then he leafed through *Modern Flight*, taking his time over diagrams of a plane performing a dive, a roll, a skid. "Who is the aviator in the family, hm? You?" he grinned at me, showing gold teeth. Then he undid the red tape on his folder. He turned over a few pages. "Ah yes," he said, "I see you have a railway booking on the third of March. That's in just over two weeks. Congratulations." Mami waited. He turned over a few more pages. "What I've come about," he said, "is to check the address you gave me for your sister in Berlin. And if you could spell her name again, please." "I'll just get my address book," Mami said, and he closed his folder as she passed. Funny, I thought. Even I know Tante Lotte's address by heart.

Then it struck me. Mami's other sister, Tante Eva, had just fled from East Berlin. Was he fishing for her new address in the West? The inspector's question must have rattled Mami

266

and she had given herself a moment to think. It was rattling me, too. But she came back smiling, address book in hand. "How could I have forgotten my sister Lotte's address? Here it is." And she spelt the name for him as he'd asked.

Inspector Jinren said, "Thank you," and wrote it down on a new sheet. He stood and held out his hand. Mami took it and he gave a very slight bow. "I wish you an uneventful journey," he said and left.

"Uneventful journey, my foot! Thinks he's God," Teddy Heinrichssohn said. "I couldn't help overhearing. You look washed out."

"It was a tricky moment," Mami said.

"It's all tricks with him, the old Jap. Goes by the book, no imagination," Teddy said. "He won't last."

The luggage went next day, curtains and all. The unwanted shoes, books, clothes went on Monday.

> *Mai dung-shi*
> *Alla dung-shi mai!*

The man who bought scrap. Amah did the bargaining. The man filled his baskets and said he'd come back for the books. I was there for that. "How much for the paper?" I said. I tried to push up the price, saying they were good books. "Good books are heavy," he said. I understood that much Chinese. "But they bring the same as newspaper." He stuck to his price. The bamboo pole drooped across his shoulders and the baskets bottomed out on the street at every step. The breeze riffled the pages of the book on top. I just caught the pen-and-wash drawing of Lobo, King of Currumpaw, before it fell shut again.

ON THE MORNING OF THE THIRD OF MARCH, nineteen hundred and fifty-two, a taxi came up the lane. It passed the gate, did a three-point turn at the tee and then pulled up. We carried out the three leather suitcases. Mami sat in front, Rabe behind her and I next to him on the far side. The taxi smelt of old leather and gasoline. A '46 Chevrolet. It shook when the engine started. The carburettor made a hissing sound. Amah came up to Rabe's door as he was about to close it. She stretched her hand across to me, cupped open like a beggar's. An aged hand, brown, showing work. I hadn't held that hand for years. "North Railway Station," Mami said.

It was a hard ride. The gearbox ground under the floor. A seat spring worked its way into my bum. The potholes didn't help. "It's Amah's birthday," I said as we pulled in at the station. "She'll be waving to us from the garden," Mami said. "Lucky we're on the right," Rabe said, taking the window seat of the sleeper. "We'll be able to see." It took no time. "We're almost there," he said and already the familiar houses were clustering against the railway line up ahead.

The shock of the brakes threw me off my seat and the

squeal of steel on steel peaked until the wheels locked and we skimmed along on the rails and rammed the couplings in front and behind losing speed by bumps until we came to a standstill with our house and garden directly outside the window.

No one was home. People came running along the path from the level crossing. Rabe pulled down the window and looked up front, but Mami looked straight down on the rails and saw it. She grabbed the latches and pulled the window back up. "You'll keep it shut," she said. Then she pressed her back into the backrest and shut her eyes. I didn't shut mine, but I could picture the sliced flesh.

"What did you see?" Rabe said.

"Someone. I couldn't tell."

I am back in the taxi. I am holding Amah's hand. I'm afraid to look at her. Then, for a split second, I do. She is framed in the taxi's open door, leaning in. Her eyes melt into mine as if that's where she lives. It only lasts a split second. It stays for life. Her streaming face of pain. And then her empty hand.

Two women wearing white armbands with a red cross carried something away on a covered stretcher. The path emptied. A whistle blew. The house and garden slid out of sight, gathering speed.

The train must have stopped again. "Welcome back," I heard Mami say.

"Where did you go?"

"Nowhere," she said. "You've been asleep."

"Where are we?"

"Hangchow. I could use some of those Quickies." Then she added, "So could you. Your forehead is burning."

"*Quickies*, I remember!" I sat up. Images of my dream reassembled themselves into a sequence and I told the story.

"We were at the checkpoint in Shum Chun. A border guard was handing out Quickies. Suddenly, I realised you and Rabe weren't there. You must have gone ahead. I tried to find you, but Inspector Jinren appeared and told me to follow him. He said he knew where you were. We kept on having to cross railway lines and we were getting further and further away from the checkpoint.

"Then we came to a train standing in a shunting yard, no platform or anything. Inspector Jinren told me to climb on. It was one of those old wooden trains, green, with slatted benches. I went in and out of the row of carriages looking for you, but there was only the occasional Chinese sitting and waiting among piles of empty baskets. I noticed that the train had started to move, so I asked where it was going, but none of them seemed to know, or they just looked at me blankly.

"Then I was back in Hungjao, at our house, calling for Amah through empty rooms. Teddy Heinrichssohn appeared. I asked him about Amah. He said she went up country to stay with Bao-jin. That she'd been gone a couple of months."

By now we had left Hangchow behind and were heading

south. "You should write your dream down," Mami said, but no one had any paper, so I just had to remember it. What Teddy Heinrichssohn said puzzled me, because we'd only been gone a few days, but then that was often the way with dreams.

Mami pointed out hills, villages, old temples. "It's the country of your childhood," she said. "You may never see it again." Rabe and I concurred without conviction. "When I look at pictures of New Zealand," I said, "especially the beaches, I get the feeling that's the country where I belong." Mami remained silent. My words continued to sound in my ears as if they needed something more to finish off what was still inside. After a while she went on. "I have lived here for twenty-five years," she said. "Since I was twenty-six years old, in fact. Half my life. I married here, had two sons, nearly had a daughter. Not everything went as I might have wished. But I have loved this country."

"Did she have a name?" I said.

"I wanted to call her Biggi."

"Biggi?"

"It's short for Brigitte."

"Biggi," I said again, trying to hold on to the sound, or just the feeling, unsure where I'd heard it before, but it had already vanished.

I tried to visualise the girl at the age she would now have been, here with us in the train, the darkened landscape wheeling past outside.

Girls fill the playing field. Yellow summer frocks and so many arms and legs flying. I am back. I am back, but I don't recognise anyone and no one seems to notice me. A girl walks past but doesn't turn around. I notice the arched nape of the

271

back of her knees. It has a bluish tinge. I think it might have been Ann. I go up to my classroom. Everyone's there. It's all the same as before, except that my desk has been taken away, leaving an empty space. Eurydice is the only one who sees me. She is trying to tell me something, but I can't hear her. Her hands fold and unfold in the air. She frowns a little. I try to speak to her, but can't make a sound.

When I awoke, Mami and Rabe were fast asleep. I didn't feel like going back to sleep, so I lay there thinking about my dream. The country of my childhood went flying past in the speed of its rails, but I was beginning to doubt for the first time whether I would really be leaving it behind.

Take-off

Shum Chun Junction was nothing like my dream. It seemed to be there more for the pigs, chickens and vegetables heading for Hong Kong, than for the people. The checkpoint went without a hitch, they didn't even open our suitcases. Some twenty yards ahead across a narrow bridge, the flag of Hong Kong and the Union Jack waved lazily side by side above the British border post. To the left, the British train waited on the platform. "Don't turn round now," Mami said. "Just keep walking." We had to carry our suitcases all the way to the other side. I could hear Mami's breathing behind me. And then the British Customs officer greeted us and asked a few questions. "Splendid," he said. "You are now in the British Crown Colony of Hong Kong. My congratulations." He waved his arm. "Porter!"

"Welcome," said the railway guard and shook our hands. "It's champagne on the house, if you'd like to follow me to the dining car." Mami was cautious. "Shouldn't we wait till we've left the station?" she said. "If any Communist tries anything on now," he replied, "they'll have the whole of the British Empire to contend with."

I stayed put in my seat. Mami came back with a large

bottle of fizzy water. Just for me. She put the back of her hand against my brow. The train pulled out of Shum Chun. "Only twenty-two miles to Hong Kong," the guard said. "Would you like me to tilt the boy's seat back?"

We went in and out of tunnels. I must have gone to sleep. The next thing I remembered was getting into bed. The cool sheets. The curtained room. Ships' whistles. The buzz of Hong Kong in the streets below.

*

SOMEONE BROUGHT IN *KELLOGGS CORNFLAKES* for my breakfast. With white sugar and a silver jug with milk and the water droplets still clinging to it. A dish of sliced peaches. The kind that come out of a tin, with thick sweet syrup. Toast, butter and jam. In little packets with pictures of the fruit. Then Rabe came in, smelling of harbour salt breezes. He held up a postcard of a ship. "*MS Taiyuan*," he said. "I got it for you." "Our ship? Wow!" It had a black hull and a brilliant white superstructure with a tall black funnel. "Mami says it's a fake," Rabe said. "What?" "The funnel." "Why? It wouldn't look like a ship without a funnel," I said and Rabe said, "Because a motor ship doesn't need a funnel. Steamships had them because they burned coal and made lots of smoke. Modern ships really only need an exhaust pipe like a truck or a diesel locomotive." "That would look stupid," I said. "So what's in the funnel?" "Nothing much." Rabe shrugged his shoulders. "Just a ladder up the side so you can get up and paint it, I suppose."

"Thanks for the postcard. I like it a lot. In spite of the funnel," I said.

"Mami's just such an aesthete," Rabe said.

"A what?"

"An aesthete. It's people that talk about art. Like Misha. I think Mami got it from Misha," Rabe said.

"I think she was like that long before she knew Misha. You remember the house in Columbia Circle? Those wooden beams on the ceiling?"

"No."

"In the sitting room. Right downstairs. Can't you remember? Mami always said those beams were a fake. She said they were just thin boards with nothing inside."

"I can't believe you remember that," Rabe said.

"Of course I do. I remember because Mami called me a fake too. She used to say I was faking when I cried. It made me so mad."

"I remember her saying Daddi was faking when he laughed," Rabe said.

I thought about that. "She always said I was like Daddi. You weren't. You were OK."

"Oh forget it, can't you?" Rabe said. "In a couple of days we'll be on that ship and all the rest will be history."

"I can't wait," I said.

But Mami's footsteps were coming up the stairs and she appeared at the door holding an atlas and a pad of paper. "For you to write your dreams," she said.

The cover read: 125 LEAVES QUARTO WHITE UNRULED. The sheets were bound at the top like a sketch pad. I felt a rush of pride that she'd got me paper without lines. "Dreams don't need lines," she said, as if reading my thoughts.

Mami puffed up the pillows behind me and put the atlas on my knees. It was big and flat. "You'll need that," she said. "I got it out of the library downstairs."

"Thank you."

Mami put a thermometer in my mouth. "I wanted to buy one, but they're all in Fahrenheit. Impossible to read. So I borrowed this one from a German lady downstairs." She paused for the mercury to climb. "Thirty-seven-six. You'll be staying in bed another couple of days."

The people downstairs sent up a get-well card. I remember the jingle that was printed inside.

> *Here's hoping you will come on down*
> *As soon as you are able*
> *Just slip into your dressing gown*
> *And join the folks at table.*

I really liked getting that card, but I don't think I ever managed to get downstairs for a meal.

*

I STARTED WRITING DOWN MY DREAMS from the train journey. Naturally, I had my Sheaffer fountain pen with me. The one Bill Richardson's wife had given me. Sylvia. Years ago. I was never without it. But it had run out of ink, just as I was getting started. Then a miracle happened. In one of the compartments of a bureau across the room, among things like note paper, envelopes, a hole punch, a little cardboard box (the outline of a paper clip in blue on the flap), I spotted what looked like a bottle of ink. I pushed the atlas and paper pad aside and got out of bed. The label on the bottle read: SHEAFFER'S *Skrip* BLUE-BLACK FOUNTAIN PEN INK. The bottle was clear glass and it had a little reservoir inside, just below the neck. What you did was turn it over before you opened it and the reservoir would fill up with ink. Only Sheaffer's had that. It meant you could dip the nib into the reservoir and not get ink all over the barrel of your pen.

The words began to flow. But I must have been quite sick, because I kept on falling asleep and having really vivid dreams. Each time I woke up, I would find my last words trailing off down the page, becoming illegible, and the open pen bleeding blue-black ink all over the sheets. I would have to scrap the page and start a new one. I tried to piece all my dreams together, but it was hard to remember them properly. I know I was flying an aeroplane. I remembered the take-off. It was like when Bill Richardson took us up in the C-46. That was the plane he flew over the Hump. Only it wasn't as big as a C-46. It certainly wasn't a B-24 Consolidated Liberator. Those were the days. It was probably a Junkers F13, the plane York Lutz's father flew. I remembered that someone was sitting beside me in the plane. I thought he was supposed to be the pilot, but he

277

turned out to be a priest. He was telling me something very important, but I couldn't hold it together. Yeh-ching was there somewhere in my dream, and Teddy Heinrichssohn too. At one stage I was riding his Schwinn. And the guy who grabbed the handlebars of my bike the day I tried to find Yeh-ching, he was there, too. At some time Teddy Heinrichssohn was playing mah-jong with Inspector Jinren.

I couldn't make sense of it, so I made up a story using all the bits of dreams and stringing them together. I really enjoyed doing that, but by the middle of the next day, I got tired of the whole thing and started resenting Mami and Rabe taking the ferry across to Victoria and the funicular up to the Peak without me and the day after that I got out of bed and went with him to find Elizabeth Berge at the Peninsular Hotel.

She wasn't there. "Elizabeth has gone to the cinema with her friend. I've no idea when she'll be back." Mrs Berge held the door ajar while she spoke. Then she slowly shut it.

*

THE *TAIYUAN* CLEARED THE VICTORIA DOCKS under the blinking eyes of the Peak. She swung south, keeping it close on her port side under a heavy sky, and then broke away. China dipped quickly out of sight as we headed into the first of the ocean's darkening swells. We sat, Mami, Rabe and I, below a painted landscape in the empty lounge bar. Our cabins were way down below. Mami had to share hers with three unwell women. Rabe and I with two unwell men. "It's better up here," she said. "It doesn't roll so much and you don't have that smell." The Chief Officer, four stripes on his cuffs, crossed the lounge bar on his sea legs and frowned. Then he nodded as if acquitting someone of some lesser crime and left. I think we stayed there all night.

"Nice painting," I said. It was, too. It ran the length of the wall. It was done in a real Chinese style, with mountains and a river and overhanging trees and rocks and a little man in a wayside tea place. "Tasteless," Mami said. I thought she was going to say, *A fake.* Anyway, I needed to be sick. "Go out," she said.

The door slammed shut behind me and the wind strafed my hair. A long way down, waves surged and broke against the hull. I clung to a stanchion thick with salt and paint and leant over the rail, but the sea rose and lit up with sea spray and flung itself in my face. I'm sure the ship shuddered then and held its breath, while the scuppers drained and the black ocean slid past just below my feet. But once again the side of the ship began to lift and, as it did so, I left behind everything that was still inside me and that I had not already put away.

If only. The truth is, after another day or two of heavy seas and misery, bits started coming back. "Pity we missed Elizabeth," Rabe said. He could have been reading my thoughts. The dining tables were unstrapped and people began to fill the room. Waiters in white criss-crossed the floor with trays. Through the windows the sea was blue. The Chief Officer stopped to greet us. "I'm happy to say you're looking a great deal healthier this morning," he said and indicated a table with three free places. "I'm Chief Officer Watson." We introduced ourselves. Rabe and I bowed. "Andrew to you," he said and shook our hands. Andrew and I were to exchange letters for many years to come.

Someone was travelling with a daughter. A young girl, about thirteen. The age Elizabeth would have been, had I caught up with her. When I did, six years later (and we got married), she wasn't a young girl any more and I had missed those years. I still miss them. As for the girl on the ship, we never exchanged a word until we disembarked in Sydney. I didn't even know her name. It didn't matter. "Bye," I said. The wire braces glinted on her teeth. "Bye," she replied.

The Union Steamship Company's *Monowai* was laid up with engine trouble and we had to wait for a replacement ship to come in. She was called *MV Matua*. She was dark and cramped and the Tasman kicked her for five days and the *Kornies* were disappointing after *Kelloggs Cornflakes*. Rangitoto brooded on the left as we rounded the North Head and saw Auckland trim and tidy like a street map with Norfolk pines and church steeples and grassy hummocks on the skyline. The museum looked out over a bib of green. A Sunderland flying boat left a white mark on the water where it lifted into the air. Mami gave Rabe a five pound note and waved him goodbye as he headed off for the King Country farm in Sandy Gordon's car. "It may not go very far," the old Shanghai scout master said. "I mean the five pounds." "It's all I've got for him," Mami said. "I'll make it do," said Sandy. He spent four of them on a pair of work boots for Rabe.

*

THE MANNEQUINS IN THE WINDOWS of Milne and Choice on Queen Street wore bunny masks with ears. Mami turned round and rolled her eyes. "It's Easter," I said before she could come up with a remark to embarrass the Knights. "Whitcomb and Tombs on the left," Mr Knight said. "The Number One bookshop." Mami didn't even turn her head. "Smith and Caughey's on the corner," he went on, missed the Civic with its giant billboard of movie stars kissing. Then, "The Town Hall," he said and pointed upward. I had to crane my neck to see the top of the tower out of the rear window.

"And what is the temple?" Mami asked. "It looks very grandiose." "The Baptist Tabernacle," said Mr Knight. "It's our church," added Mrs Knight. "And that's George Court's over there," said Mr Knight, but we couldn't see it, because a tram with the destination KARANGAHAPE RD. via Town Hall had come to a standstill on the intersection. It wasn't an easy name to pronounce. I got as far as CAR-HANGER APE. The tram listed on the hill while its pole sparked off the web of cables that tossed above our heads. "Should've come past Farmers," Mrs Knight said. "That's where we shop." No one responded. We watched the tram conductor wrestle with the line until he had bent the pole into submission and climbed aboard. *The car-hanger ape,* I thought to myself. Tarzan of the Auckland tramways. It had begun to rain.

"Maples' on the left," said Mr Knight, inclining his head to where entire lounge suites competed with each other in autumn leaves. "Good idea, those loose covers," said Mrs Knight. "Grafton Bridge," said Mr Knight.

"Auckland Hospital, Domain and Museum," he went on and I said, "Oh, can we please drive in there?" and he said, "Another time perhaps." Then he wound down his window and put his arm out as if saluting someone. The rain came in through the window. The car stopped. Mr Knight pointed up ahead. "Auckland Grammar." But my attention was already swamped by the yeasty musk that flowed in through the window. "What's that smell?" I said, sniffing the air, leaning forward. Mr Knight wound the window up and the car turned left down the hill. *Lion Brewery*, I read. "Can't take you anywhere," Mami said to me that night.

*

SCHOOL WAS ALL BOYS. I had never seen so many boys. I found it hard to tell them apart in their blue uniforms. I got lost every time we changed classrooms. We changed classrooms five times a day. My uniform was approximated out of the clothes I had or could scrape together. Mami gave me her blue silk blouse. It buttoned to the wrong side. I coated Robert Oates' brown suede shoes with black Nugget. At least I must have been easy to find.

"Where're ya from?" they would ask. I came to dread that question. "China." A look of puzzlement. I learned to break in. "No, I'm not Chinese, I lived in China. I have come here from China."

"If you're not Chinese, why were you living in China?"

"Lots of people live in China that aren't Chinese," I would say. "At least, lots used to. Under the Communist Regime they're having to leave."

Pause.

"What does your father do?"

"Well, he was a diplomat. He worked in a consulate—an embassy—that's right. But he left long ago, just after the war. He had to go back to Germany."

"What did he have to go there for?"

"It's his country. Our country. Germany."

"You're Krauts!"

"What?" I hadn't heard the expression before.

"Jerries."

"Yes."

"You're kidding me. You're a Kraut? How come a Kraut talks like a Pom?"

"I went to a British school."

"I thought you said you lived in China."

"A British school in China."

Pause.

"So, what are you? Where were you born?"

"In Japan."

"You're a Nip. You speak Japanese?"

"If you're born in a stable, that doesn't mean you're a horse."

"What does it mean?"

I wanted to say, think of Jesus, but didn't.

"D'you play football?"

"Yes. I play full back or goalie."

"There's no goalie in football. You mean soccer. No one plays soccer," and a free laugh on me all round.

It wasn't as bad as all that. No one tried to beat me up. I just stopped bringing wholemeal sandwiches to school. Then I stopped bringing any kind of lunch to school. A third former called Marsden noticed and offered me his last sandwich.

"I'm not hungry, thanks," I said.

"Keep it for later," he said and dropped it back in its brown paper bag. "You will be."

He twirled the bag by the corners between his hands. Then he held it out to me. "There you go," he said. I noticed it had grown ears.

"What's your name?" Marsden said.

"Till."

He depressed a pair of invisible tabs and as the imaginary drawer sprang open he rang out a high-pitched *ding!* and slammed it shut again.

"See ya later," he said.

We sat in the basement of the building between walls of glazed brick and watched the rain make rings across the yard. Boys tossed limp crusts to the sparrows. Apple cores browned and orange peel withered under slatted seats. Lunchwrap plugged the gaps between the slats. A teacher thrust a broom into my hand. It was at least three feet wide. His arm made a wide sweep. "Go f'yer life!" he said. I hadn't understood. "Pardon, sir?" It dawned on me that I had been put on cleaning-up duties. I stepped backwards onto a luncheon sausage sandwich and extruded the sliced flesh. I retched but didn't throw up. There was nothing in my stomach.

He was our English teacher. He also took us for Social Studies. I learned about ayes and noes and where the Speaker sat in the House and how many sat on the Legislative Council. It was new to me. In English we had to do a book review. I hadn't read a book since we left Shanghai, nor some time before that. I hadn't set foot in the school library. My own books were still in storage somewhere. The ones I kept. I could remember *The Adventures of Sajo and her Beaver People*. Enough to write a review. I followed the format for writing book reviews exactly as prescribed by the teacher. I worked at it all weekend. After class on Monday I dropped my work on his desk as I passed. "Book review," I said. "Oh, are they due today?" he said. "Book reviews, you jokers, come on. Hand them in." Those still in earshot chorused *Oh sir...!* and he said, "OK, if you haven't finished, make it next Monday without fail." He held up my review for me to take back. When I hesitated, he said, "Go on, take it, or it'll only get lost."

A couple of weeks later he called out our names and marks and we came up front to receive our reviews. He had difficulty with my name and I can't remember my mark. Just the comment at the end: *A remarkably juvenile choice of reading material.*

For my next book review I tried the school library. The school's dux, also head prefect with a silver badge the size of a half crown, was librarian. He showed me where to find Alexander William Kinglake. I leafed through *The War of the Crimea* in eight volumes and went for his travelogue entitled *Eothen* instead. I found the excerpt about the Sphinx that had appeared in one of our textbooks:

> *Comely the creature is, but the comeliness is not of this world...*

I took out *Eothen*. It looked pretty dry all in all, but if I were ever to become a man, I thought, this would be as good a place as any to begin. And so I put away Grey Owl and Sajo and all the beaver dams as the first of my Childish Things.

Land of milk and honey

The man at the careers advisor's office in Newmarket came back with a handful of periodicals on forestry. "Have a flick through these," he said, "while I look out some info on tertiary courses. Massey Agricultural College is probably the place for you. Palmerston North. D'you know where that is?" "Yes sir, I've even been there. You get in at 4:19 a.m. My thumbprint is on the aliens' register at the Palmerston North police. We stayed with Miss Campbell. She's the librarian at Massey. She took us there for a visit." "Well there you go," the man said and went out. Had there been a broom handy, I could have swept up my spatter of words off the lino and put them in the bin.

The first periodical I picked up was about experiments using a variety of compounds for the eradication of a beetle that infested the roots of pine trees. Another concerned automation in planting seedlings. A third was about logging tallies, transportation, export markets, that sort of thing. Then some material on investments, plantation life cycles, the costs of various chemicals for the preservative treatment of timber against decay and wood-boring insects. There were photographs of straddle cranes, forklift trucks, moisture meters and endless tables of figures. Interspersed amongst these were photographs of men in white laboratory gowns who all looked like my science master at school. The message had become clear. I walked out of the careers advisor's office with an embarrassed thank you and a new path.

Perhaps not quite new. Neil Guyan, my classmate, reminded me fifty years later that 'Streak' Nicholls, our maths teacher, had stopped by my desk and squinted at the geometric figures I was constructing with ruler and compasses. They must have looked a bit like the Kremlin or St Mark's with all those ogee arches and domes, because he boomed out: "Quadratic equations? I think not! Have you ever thought of becoming an architect?"

Yes sir, I had replied.

*

WITH MY CAREER CHANGE, I had put away the second of my Childish Things. The forest cottage and the rescued bear cub faded in the excitement of architecture. It had become overdue. I had already mapped all my favourite houses on my way to school and on the wooded streets under Mt Eden. Their straight lines, dark stained weatherboards and grids of windows in crisp white frames had me in thrall. I drew plans of houses on squared paper. I constructed cardboard models of them. I stood them in the sun and studied the play of light and shade on them.

The Goethe Society held meetings at the student cafeteria of the university. Professor Jock Asher spoke on the German romantic poets. Someone read poems by Karl Wolfskehl, who had lived in New Zealand. Once, we were all invited to the house of the Czech architect, Henry Kulka. It was a Sunday and the Austrian conductor, Georg Tintner, was introducing Bruckner's eighth symphony. We listened to the whole work on long-playing records. But it was Henry Kulka's house that quietly spoke to me. *Clarity*, it said. And *Good fit*. I was too awed to speak to the architect himself.

When we got back to the missionary home, they asked if we'd been to church. Mami said, if you listened to serious music, it was like being in church. The next Sunday, we were being mustered at breakfast to join everyone at a special service. One of our fellow guests at the missionary home was to be the speaker. Mami said she was sorry, but we were already going to church. "Come," she said to me, "or we'll be late."

We took the tram to Karangahape Road and found the Unitarian Church around the corner in Ponsonby Road. Mami must have been told about it by one of her new intellectual friends. There were no crosses or anything. The man spoke about ordinary people like us. The present time, he said, was full of ordinary people taking things apart and studying their differences. *This* is the opposite of *that*, they say. It's the way we're taught. We split the atom, we divide countries, we build walls. Maybe there's another way of looking at things, he said. One that unifies everything. He even mentioned Einstein and his search for a unified field.

That evening we were bundled into a car and driven in silence (but for the odd attempt to break it with niceties) to a church already packed and waiting only for us to fill it up. Our seats had been reserved close to the front. The speaker was,

289

indeed, the man from our table, doing double duty. He never once took his eyes off us. "I was asked the other day what I knew about the Unitarian Church," he said out of the blue and followed it up with a deadly warning: "The Devil himself lurks just within its doors. He invites you to eternal damnation." He was still glowering at us when Mami whispered in my ear: "How can he know we have been there?" I gave no reply.

The man stood by the door and shook everyone's hand as we went out. "Just a little squeeze and I'll know you are telling me you're ready to be saved," he had said. My hand went as limp as a rag.

*

THE WEEKEND SUPPLEMENTS of the NZ Herald were filled with pictures of debutantes. They looked a bit like bridesmaids. It was years before I discovered their place in the world. The captions said they were *coming out*. Mami couldn't help. "Have they spent the winter in mothballs?" she said.

As spring arrived, so did the daffodils on the slopes of Mt Hobson and they, too, made the papers. But it was the centre spread of new-born lambs that had me climbing to the summit to see them in the flesh. All the metaphors of birth and innocence descended on them with their long tails and jumpy legs. It was disconcerting, though, to find their mothers chewing on the blood-smeared afterbirth, even when I'd remembered Rabe telling me in a letter from the King Country that he'd seen cows doing it.

The summer holidays brought Rabe up to Auckland and we took our first ferry ride to Waiheke Island. The Fibrolite bach[1] at Arran Bay was ours for a week. It stood above the beach, clinging to the slope. The row of bunk rooms and the kitchen opened off a wooden verandah that ran the length of the building and bleached in the morning sun. A metal pipe carried rainwater from the eaves gutter into a corrugated iron tank. The water from the brass tap over the sink delivered a dance of mosquito larvae into your glass.

Rabe and I shared a bunk room. I grabbed the top bunk. We talked well into the night. He told me he always had to get up really early to milk the cows, because the hedgehogs would snuggle up to them while they lay sleeping and drink all their milk. I believed him. I told him about the films I had gone to see with Mami. Rabe hadn't seen a film all the time he was on the farm. So I told him in detail everything about my favourite film, *The Sound Barrier*. Ralph Richardson was the main actor and I had already seen him in *Outcast of the Islands* and *The Fallen Idol*. I really liked the way he cocked an eyebrow to emphasise what he was saying. I practised that for hours in front of the mirror, but didn't tell Rabe.

What I told him was all about supersonic flight. About Hurricane fighters running into the sound barrier and going out of control. I told him how Ralph Richardson explains what happens when a plane accelerates up to the speed of sound. It's like catching up with the ripple your plane is making in the air. Only at that speed it's quite a big ripple, more like a wave, so that when you fly into it, you get tossed around.

"What you have to understand is that the speed of airborne sound is 768 miles an hour," Rabe said calmly. "If you're flying below that speed, your sound will run ahead of you. If

1 New Zealand holiday cottage

you fly above it, you will leave your sound behind. Never try flying *at* the speed of sound."

"Why not?" I said, my flying rug whipped out from under my feet.

"You get shaken to bits."

The sea lapped lazily onto the coarse sand, making a slapping sound, followed by the tinkling of shells as it pulled back. A clinker dinghy bobbed close to the shore and two girls in bright summer cottons sent it turning in circles with their flailing oars. Their laughter skimmed over the water to where Rabe and I swam. We headed out into the bay, calling to each other, knowing we would be heard from the shore. We staged swimming races. We dived like dolphins and stayed under as long as our breath would allow. And then we floated on our backs and paddled up to the beach and the girls laughed and shrieked as their dinghy rocked. But we never came near them and we never once spoke to them.

"I've been thinking about those ripples of sound," I said. "We make ripples in the water, too. What say we make ripples all the time just by being alive? They'd be all around us and we wouldn't even know they were there. They could be running ahead of us, carrying our stories to places where nothing's happened yet and they'd be waiting for us to catch up with them and bump into them. It would be like flying into the sound barrier."

"And so?" Rabe said.

"You get tossed around."

"Go to sleep."

Before the week was over or the sun and sea could have their fill of me, I packed a small bag and caught the dawn ferry to Auckland to answer the roll call on my first day back at school. I stood alone in the ferry's bows and, as we cleared the headland, the northerly caught us on the starboard side and the salt spray stung my eyes. I was thinking about the girls in the bay and their laughter still echoed in my ears. I wondered in what part of the world Elizabeth now lived. She was about the age of those girls.

The city hove into view and a Sunderland in Mechanics' Bay tuned its engines in readiness for take-off. I wanted to watch it, but we had begun to turn and were making ready to tie up at the wharf. When at last I merged with the straggle of boys closing in on the school gate, it struck me that the laughter of girls was something I hadn't heard for a long time.

*

GRACE, THE WAR WIDOW at the missionary home, greeted me when I got in after school. She had filled the cake tins with ginger squares, coconut squares and lemon squares and she opened them for me in succession. I was hungry from my early start and Grace watched me as I savoured the sweet rewards of her labours. She poured me a tall glass of milk and touched my hand as she slid it across the wooden kitchen counter.

After dark that night, I stood at the window in the dining room (the tables already set for breakfast), and looked out over the harbour where late ferries passed with their tiny rows of windows all lit up inside. I thought about Mami and Rabe still at Arran Bay. They'd probably be sitting together at the kitchen table in the Fibrolite bach, playing Nine Men's Morris by the light of a kerosene lamp. It had been good to see Rabe and I thought how much Mami would be enjoying his company after his long absence down on the farm. I thought about the year that had passed since we left Shanghai. Everything was so different now. It was mostly good, but I felt very much alone. Was that different? Maybe not. I watched the Rangitoto lighthouse sweep its beam over the rugged reef and out across the channel. It winked its red eye at me every time it passed my window. I tried to catch it by winking back at the very same instant and sometimes our eyes met. Then I felt we'd made contact. I supposed it was lonely, too.

I passed Grace on my way up to bed. She had just finished clearing up in the kitchen. "I'm having a Milo," she said. "Would you like one?" Again she touched my hand as she passed me the cup. She beckoned me to follow her into her bedroom. She showed me a photograph of her fiancé in his pilot's jump suit, standing on the wing of a fighter plane. He never returned from the war. She told me how they'd met. They were my age. When I said good night, I had the feeling she didn't want me to go.

*

IN MAY, 1953, EDMUND HILLARY climbed Mt Everest. In June, Queen Elizabeth was crowned. The papers ran supplements with full page pictures of the magnificence of these events. The country spruced itself up for the Royal Visit. There would be bunting and pohutukawa blossom and thousands of flags to wave. God smiled on the land.

They arrived on the morning of Wednesday, the 23rd December, 1953. We heard the gun salute from the North Head. The next night, Christmas Eve, the northbound express plunged into the Whangaehu River at Tangiwai. The bridge had been washed away. A hundred and fifty-one people died. On Christmas Day, we tuned in to hear the Queen's speech, but it was Prime Minister Sid Holland's broadcast on the Tangiwai disaster that stole the thunder. When the papers came out again after the long weekend, they carried pictorial supplements of tumbled carriages and rescue workers and the Queen and Duke of Edinburgh at the Boxing Day races.

*

I WAS NOW SIXTEEN YEARS OLD and about to enter the sixth form at school. I spent most of my time alone. I walked the slopes of Mt Hobson among indifferent sheep. I suffered from unexplained headaches. I caught myself grinding my teeth in my sleep. I had nightmares. There were two kinds. In one, I was hiding from soldiers in padded uniforms. They were all around, hunting for me, rifles at the ready. One of them had Mami's face. I always woke the instant the barrel was lifted to my chest. I never told her. In the other, I watched with horror as an airliner stalled in flight. It tilted until it seemed to be standing on its wing tip. Then it began to fall. I never saw the crash. I called it my holocaust dream.

Grace's affections had intensified. She would appear at the corner of passageways, take my hands and pull me to her with her elbows, so that my hands pressed into her waist. She would tell me that I was very special to her. She had never felt this way before. She stood tall, leaning into me. She lifted her face and let her eyelids rest easily on her smiling eyes, like a movie star. I tried to smile back, but only felt the untruth. Her mohair cardigan swelled against my chest. I would have to remove the hairs from my jersey before I went upstairs. Now her knee pressed into my legs. I felt her tongue pushing through my closed lips. Then I broke. My head snapped sideways, first this way, then that. Still she held me. I said, "Someone's coming!" I looked at my wrist watch. I said, "It's late, I've got homework," and pulled free.

"You won't give an inch, will you?" Grace said. Her voice was thick and choked. She had let go of my hands. I stood back and looked into her eyes, now bloodshot, bulging, wetting over. Her jaw was set hard, the corners of her mouth turned down. Her tongue flicked out like a reptile's to catch a tear. *Not even an inch.* The words struck like knives.

"Sorry," I said.

*

RABE WAS NOW LIVING WITH US at the missionary home. We would go to the movies together. We saw all the Ealing Studio comedies featuring Alec Guinness. Our favourite was *The Lavender Hill Mob*. We saw him again as the reconnaissance pilot in *Malta Story*. This film was *not* a comedy. In a scene near the end, Alec Guinness flies a Spitfire on a solo mission and five Messerschmitts get him from behind. There is no blood or anything. The mirror shatters. His eyes half close. We see his hands losing their grip on the controls. The plane spirals into the sea. His girlfriend listens to the silence on the speakers after his last words, *This is where it gets tricky.* Then she removes the token with his flight number from the operations room table.

It was an evening screening at the St James in Queen St. We had left enough time for a milk shake before it started. There was a sudden roar of motorcycles. Utterly black but for the chrome studs on their petrol tanks and jackets, the apocalyptic riders thundered through the gap between the kerb and the trams. They came to a stop with a final burst from their engines just outside the milk bar and hauled the motorbikes up on their stands. Leather to leather, they jostled each other as they went inside. We were left standing paralysed on the footpath, looking at the backs of their rock-and-roll haircuts and tight trousers. When they came out again, they were sipping milk shakes from metal containers through twin straws. Their girl friends remained sitting cross-legged on the pillion seats, smoking cigarettes. The dark make-up around their eyes made them look as if they had neither eaten nor slept for weeks. The milk-bar cowboys hit the news the following day and embedded a new dread in the public mind: *delinquency*. We didn't have our milk shakes.

On the 22nd June, 1954, a body was discovered in Victoria Park in Christchurch. The following day, Pauline Parker and Juliet Hulme were charged with murder. They were *schoolgirls*.

The murdered victim was Pauline's mother. The prosecutor called the girls *incurably evil*. The newspapers published the details of the murder, the brick in the stocking, the girls' personal histories, the chorus of outraged voices from the righteous and the process of the trials, until the evil had become a fact of life, of living people and of New Zealand, our Land of Milk and Honey. And as that bright vision of the land darkened in the shadow of crime, I, too, put it away as the third of my Childish Things.

As if to leave us in no doubt about that shadow, in September of the same year came the Mazengarb Report. We heard about it obliquely, the way we'd heard about the Kinsey reports. Only Mazengarb's was about juvenile delinquents and the juvenile delinquents weren't in America, but right here in New Zealand.

Mr Russell took us for English in our sixth form. We had spent the winter term dissecting *Hamlet*. However, since Mr Russell had steered well clear of the more Freudian aspects of the story (we weren't *that* naïve, after all), he had failed to lift the great work off the page. I did, briefly, revive my passion for the doomed Ophelia who, I believed, could have been Hamlet's half-sister (her mother never gets a mention in the play), but, needless to say, I didn't raise the matter. I thought what a pity it was that Ann Murray never played the part. It was a surprising thought, coming out of the blue, with all the innocence of our affections in the vanished Shanghai days.

In the spring term, Mr Russell instructed the class on how to write an essay. That done, we learnt about journalistic writing. We had to produce our own creations in both genres for marking. Finally, we tackled the précis. It was a double

298

period at the end of the day on a Friday in September. Mr Russell set us an assignment to write a précis of a newspaper editorial. He said, "You will take the editorial in tomorrow morning's Herald as the matter for your précis and none of us can have any idea as to what it will be about, so you can look forward to a surprise. You will hand them in to me first thing on Monday. Good day."

The form representative collected the assignments and placed them in the tray in Mr Russell's office as instructed. We had to wait until the following Friday for our marks. We were keen to get them back, because it hadn't been an easy assignment. The editorial had concerned itself with the findings of the Mazengarb Report. The study had revealed, among other staggering revelations, that one in four boys and girls of our age had already had *carnal knowledge*. I had to look it up in the Oxford Dictionary. We duly recorded this finding in our précis.

On Friday, Mr Russell made no mention of the assignments until the final bell had rung. Then he said, "As to your homework, it concerns me greatly that any student of your purported intelligence should be willing to lower himself to a discussion on the level of filth your work discloses. Needless to say, I have destroyed it."

*

IN THE WINTER OF MY LAST YEAR AT SCHOOL I took part in the production of *The Merchant of Venice*. It was directed by the superlatively dramatic Mr McSkimming, as a combined production with Auckland Girls' Grammar School. The

299

previous year's play had been *Julius Caesar*. Two of my classmates were in it. They had never stopped talking about it or hearing each other's lines. I only listened. I must have missed the announcement or simply lacked the courage to put myself forward for a part. Or both. Privately, I understudied all the principal roles and knew them by heart. Those towering roles: Brutus, Cassius, Mark Antony and others. I could have died for a chance to declaim that last heroic couplet of Octavius Caesar's:

> *So, call the field to rest; and let's away,*
> *To part the glories of this happy day.*

My turn came with *The Merchant of Venice*. The play had already been cast, but the Prince of Arragon had pulled out. I auditioned for his part and got it. We rehearsed twice a week after school. I could hardly wait for that last bell. It felt like glorious summer.

In the early weeks of rehearsal, one of the boys in the cast would stand in for Portia, Nerissa or Jessica and read their parts. However, the day came when the three of them appeared in the flesh, chaperoned by a formidable woman, who turned out to be their drama teacher. We rehearsed the casket scenes and collapsed with laughter on my line:

> *What's here? The portrait of a blinking idiot...*

It took a major effort of will after that not to laugh every time I had to say it. We rehearsed the courtroom scene and the moonlight scene. The girls played their parts like seasoned

300

actors. We felt our performances lift. We shaped them. We played off each other, looked each other in the eye and held the special moments in the palms of our hands. At the end of rehearsals, we said thank you and good night. We had become a workforce of our own and we worked toward a common goal. And we were content. All the way home I felt a new firmness in my stride.

Grace kept my dinner warm on top of a simmering pot. "You're later than normal," she said. "I suppose you had to see those girls home. I wouldn't let you if I were your mother." There was that clenched jaw again. I wanted to take my dinner upstairs, but she stopped me. "There's pudding," she said.

Our rehearsals intensified. The art department under Mr Crippen put the finishing touches on the stage set and moved it into His Majesty's Theatre. At the technical rehearsal, we heard the school orchestra playing the incidental music to *The Merchant of Venice* for the first time, with Mr Hopkins conducting. The Doge's March was to haunt me for a long while after. We got into our costumes for the dress rehearsal and they glued on my moustache and beard with spirit glue. Girls in fairy dresses practised their dance moves for the moonlight scene. Cameras flashed. I lost all track of time. And then we ran the entire play. It was midnight when we finished. Someone's parents must have run me home.

Next day I stayed in bed, smothered my chest in wintergreen oil and rubbed Vicks into my throat. I was sure I was getting a fever. The door opened and Grace came in. She stopped by my bed. "I know you don't want me, but I never thought you would treat me like this," she said. Her voice had changed. There was no feeling in it at all. "I waited up for you and I haven't slept all night."

I tried to say something, but didn't make a sound. Grace sat on my bed and leant over me, pinning down my arms. Her face hung above mine and the veins stood out on her forehead. A cross dangled from her necklace. Her cheeks were unbelievably flushed and their flesh hung down swollen and damp. She stared at me for a long time and burned that image of herself into my memory forever. Then she pulled back and said, "You have ruined my life. The sooner I put an end to it, the better." She got up to go. "What's left of it," she said. With whatever force I could muster, I rasped: *"Please, I'm sorry. I don't know what you want!"*

*

WHEN MAMI CAME HOME, I didn't wait to hear about her day. I sat her down beside me. She was still wearing her coat. "You're shivering," she said. She took it off and put it round me. "Mami, listen," I began, but she hadn't finished. "You've got a performance tomorrow night and you'll need to get well," she said. Her coat was warm. "Please listen to me," I said again.

I told her the whole story about Grace from when it all started, eighteen months back. "Help me," I said as I got to the end, my voice a hoarse whisper. "I don't know what to do."

Mami didn't react as badly as I thought. She remained silent for a while when I'd finished. Then, "Funny," she said. "Rabe has been telling me that Grace is desperately in love with *him.*"

A clean slate

All this time a house was being built on the far side of town. It was to be our new home and we planned to move in by the end of the year. Every Sunday, we took the tram to the city and then the bus (two hours in all) to check on progress. We celebrated the day the roof went on. We signed our names in the whiting on the newly glazed windows. We collected off-cuts of weatherboards to make a letterbox.

The house stood lightly on wooden jack studs amid a group of young pines. We had pleaded with the builders not to cut them down. "You'll regret it," they said. "They'll grow so big, they'll be a danger to you. And your gutters will fill with needles." We paid no attention. "They will be our Christmas trees," we said. "Living Christmas trees under the night sky." "Watch your presents," they said. "It rains at Christmas."

Coarse grass covered the slopes of the quarter-acre section and gorse clustered around the drain where the slopes converged. We bought a scythe and took it with us on the tram, holding its twisted handle in the air. We felt cadaverous, like the Old Reaper, but no one turned to look. Gradually, we brought in the land. Rabe kept the blade sharp with a carborundum file and soon a pyre rose up, ready for Guy Fawkes night. We were

303

making a difference. And it felt good.

The house was barely ready when we moved in. We waxed the newly sanded floors, painted the walls and soaked the ship-lapped weatherboards in a mixture of creosote and Stockholm tar. We bought extra fine paintbrushes to paint the windows. They stretched in a long grid along the north side of the house and welcomed the sun into the rooms. This was the architecture of my dreams. A new life was beginning and I couldn't wait.

*

THE TRUCK ARRIVED WITH ALL OUR TRUNKS. Shanghai spilled out of them into the house—books, pictures, Chinese scroll paintings, vases, ornaments; bed linen, table linen, bath towels; shoes, clothes; Mami's silk scarves; the family silver. Stuff we hadn't seen for three years. We checked off every item against the packing lists. Nothing had broken. Nothing had gone astray, except for some photographs Mami had taken twenty years earlier. The corner mounts still marked the blank spaces above captions reading *Beggar* or *Homeless family*. The Communists would not have wanted them to be shown abroad. "You can't say they weren't thorough," Mami said. "Good thing I had no gold bars to smuggle out."

We reassembled Mami's weaving loom and immediately hanks of yarn were spooled and threaded and stretched into a warp. The familiar *click-clack* of the flying shuttle returned. What remained of the living space had to wrap itself around the loom. Mami's bookcases had already taken up an entire wall, crammed full with the faded spines of German classics.

I was happy to see *Chinaflug* again, with the F13 flying over endless folds of mountains. The book seemed smaller than I remembered.

We unfolded the curtains Amah had stayed up all night to iron. "Look, how nice," Mami said, pushing her nose into a fold of the cloth. "No dust." They fitted the windows of our new living room as though made for them. They didn't even need taking up.

Four large Chinese chests consumed the remaining wall space. We were left with a pile of things we didn't know where to put and so we packed them back into the chests. Then we spread the Mongolian saddle rugs over them to make seats. The room had seemed a lot bigger when it was empty and free to breathe.

All the things we unpacked carried memories. The train journey. Amah's face in the door of the taxi on the last day. Crossing the border at Shum Chun. Mami talking about Biggi. I still regretted not getting to see Elizabeth in Hong Kong. I remembered spending most of my time there in bed. I wondered what happened to the story I wrote. It wasn't really finished. Maybe I would finish it some day. I was bound to run into it again some time, somewhere out there, waiting for me. But not now. Things were just beginning and I was wiping my slate *clean*. I didn't want anything getting in the way.

Finally, my own books came out of their boxes. I sat on my bed. I held each one in my hand the way I might have held my own hand—could I have reached it—my boyish hand of three years ago. I opened *The Adventures of Sajo and her Beaver People* by Grey Owl, that *remarkably juvenile choice of reading material,* as my teacher had called it. I read:

305

And Sajo stood there very still, like a many-coloured little statue, in her gay tartan dress and pretty moccasins, her head-shawl fallen back and her glossy black braids shining in the glow of the setting sun.

Then I put it up on the shelf.

*

IT IS MY BIRTHDAY. I'm turning seventeen. The book that is open on my lap is called *Built in USA: Post-war Architecture.* Published in 1952 for the Museum of Modern Art, it hones the cutting edge of the new. The names of the architects are all unknown to me, but will become part of my own language. A language of new forms to accommodate a new humanity. The forms are abstract. They are made up of lines and planes and slabs. They enclose space, or they throw it wide open. They embrace the landscape and they make their mark on cities. They are unencumbered by tradition and they will generate a humanity that can boast the same. My book is open on the page showing the Farnsworth House by Mies van der Rohe (1950). It is a simple rectangle, whichever way you look at it. The rectangle is held above the ground on eight steel posts. There are no walls. Only glass. You can see the trees through it. Standing free inside the rectangle is another rectangle. This one is made of solid walls. That's it. Far beyond abstraction, the house has arrived at its author's ultimate aesthetic: *Almost nothing.*

MY HEADACHES HAVE VANISHED. So have my nightmares. So has Grace. I go to sleep every night imagining myself at the controls of an aeroplane about to take off. I accelerate along the runway and then the ground falls away and I leave it behind. The last thing I feel is the lift under my wings.

My Dream Story

finished at last after bumping into it again 60 years later

Aeroplanes also land, don't they?

I returned to the house of my childhood. We'd only been gone a few days and it was all as we'd left it. Yet the rooms seemed emptier, as if there should have been a memory clinging to the walls, a little warmth of family. I pushed the kitchen door and it swung twice and came to rest. It let through the smell of places long closed up. I didn't go in. I was listening to the clacking of mah-jong tiles upstairs. I found Teddy Heinrichssohn sitting across the table from Inspector Jinren. The other two chairs were empty. Yet the wall of tiles had been broken out and tiles dealt to four players. "You are just in time," Inspector Jinren said. "You are the South Wind.

It is your turn to play." "Who is the North Wind?" I said.
"The undisclosed player," said the inspector. I noticed he was
wearing a dog-collar under his uniform. "You will find out
everything in good time," he said.

Teddy Heinrichssohn had stood up and was peering down
into the street. "Hide," he said. He swept the mah-jong
tiles into a bag while the inspector and I hid. Teddy pushed
something heavy against the wardrobe door. If anything
happens to him, I thought, we're stuck. I could hear footsteps
coming up the stair. Official voices speaking Chinese. Teddy's
answering them in Chinese. Then they all left. It got stuffy in
the wardrobe. The inspector crouched down. He clicked his
lighter. "You light that, I'll scream for help," I said.

I must have passed out in the bottom of the wardrobe.
When I heard Teddy's voice in a rush of fresh air, it was like
the moment I was born. I had to take hold of myself or I
would have cried like a baby. The inspector lit his cigarette.
"I've brought you noodles," Teddy said. "In the morning
you're taking my Schwinn. Bit conspicuous perhaps, but
could get you out of a tight spot. I'll give you the papers, of
course. That thing's like a holy cow to the Chinks. I can say
that. I'm half Chink. You say it, I'll never let you forget it."
He thrust something at me. "Take this rucksack," he said.
"There's a map in there and food and things. Your destination
is Changsha. My Mom and Dad will look after you there. Oh,
and I've filled the water bags on the bike. That water's worth
more than your life." I ate my noodles. I missed Mami. I had
no idea what was going on.

Sleep, Teddy said.

When he woke me, it felt like five minutes later. *Eat*, he

said. More noodles. "Your trouble is, you don't exist," Teddy Heinrichssohn began. "Your mother and brother got out and are in Hong Kong. She's got your Red Cross passport. Your exit visa is in that passport."

"We got separated at Shum Chun. Inspector Jinren turned up and said he could help me. But instead, he put me on a train back here," I said.

"That's right. He needs you. The Commos are down on him and he needs to get out. You're his only chance."

"How come?"

"There's a plane waiting for you at Kunming. It's going to take the two of you out of China. There were supposed to be three of you, but the inspector bungled it. You are flying to India."

"Over the Hump?"

"That's right. Just like the Flying Tigers."

I said, "I don't understand."

"You will," Teddy said.

"Where's Jinren?"

"He's gone. I can't tell you any more. You will meet again in Kunming. If anyone approaches you, say *I'm going to see my teacher of Chinese calligraphy.* Their password will be *Welcome the swallows in Kunming.* Have a safe trip." With that Teddy gave me a push start and my Schwinn sped me down the lane and away.

It took me a whole month to get to Changsha. When I did, it was on foot, dragging my straw sandals in the dust. My trousers were folded across in front and tied with string. I wore a faded indigo tunic with the padding hanging out and a cotton cap with the flaps buttoned up to reveal my shaven

313

head. Somewhere in the countryside I had passed through, a deaf and dumb slit-eyed Chinese boy was riding around on an American bicycle and wearing European clothes. I hoped he hadn't been picked up and put away.

"Where are you headed, young boy?" said a voice behind me. I spun around. A man in the clean cottons of a household servant had appeared out of nowhere. "I'm going to see my teacher of Chinese calligraphy," I said. "Welcome the swallows in Kunming," said the man.

I hadn't expected to see the ambassador from Pei-tai-ho come striding off the verandah. "My, how you've grown," he said and clasped my hand in both of his. "And changed!" The ambassador snatched the cap off my head and laughed. "You certainly look the part," he said. "But your feet are sore. You will rest for two days and move on. You will not need to walk. The donkeys are ready for you."

"Donkeys?"

"Oh yes," he beamed. "You will travel with a guide. His name is Garn. He will protect you from the bandits. He even says he knows you."

"Garn?" I remembered the man on the mountain. Tien Mu Shan. Five years ago. His grey eyes, soft features.

"Your mother very strong lady," Garn said when we'd waved goodbye to the ambassador and started climbing the path up the mountainside. "She beat me. She beat me."

"She didn't beat you, Garn. She shouted at you," I said.

"She shouted at me. She shouted at me," Garn said.

I wondered how we were going to get on over the long journey that lay ahead. "She made a mistake, Garn. She thought you wanted to kidnap me," I said.

"Kidnap you. Kidnap you," Garn said. I thought it best not to react.

"Abbot man want you. He send me for kidnap you. You be his *special boy*."

"Where are you taking me, Garn?" I said.

"To abbot man. To abbot man. Up in mountain."

My donkey and I turned on the narrow track and went hurtling down the mountainside. At a fork we stopped and looked back. I knew he wouldn't be following me. From before. I remembered a saying Yeh-ching had once taught me: *When you come to a fork in the road, take it.* I did.

Kunming was much further than I thought. And empty. Just an old man standing under a tree on the lake shore. You couldn't see the far side of the lake. I rode up and said, "I'm going to see my teacher of Chinese calligraphy." He didn't even turn round. I loosened the reins and patted my donkey on the flank. "You've got thin," I said. A few paces down the road I looked over my shoulder. The old man had raised an arm and was pointing along the shoreline. There was nothing there but some boys flying kites. The tree above him was bare although it was spring. I wondered if there'd be any swallows to welcome in Kunming.

We made for a line of long low roofs some way off. Kites swooped and dipped around us as we passed. I had to duck my head when a kite with a forked tail came out of a low dive. The boys jeered and laughed from the lake side.

The fence was high. It bristled with barbed wire. Between walls of corrugated iron I could see the runway. What had been the runway. On the far side, a mast, with what had been a wind sock. A broken door hung out over the path in front of me. Rows of windows marked the bays where beds had stood. Each of the four panes of each window made a jagged opening. Starlings darted in and out. A door to a small room had a card holder with the card still in it. I brushed it with my finger and it fell in flakes to the floor. I knew it had once read:

CAPT. MILNE
14th Air Force

My donkey chewed on grasses by a roadside ditch. I envied him. Food. A starling screeched at me. Another dive-bombed me, dropping limed excrement into my lap. Ugly birds, I thought. Only then it struck me. Those kites with the forked tails! How could I have missed it? They were larger-than-life aerodynamic bamboo-and-rice-paper looping Kunming swallows!

So I welcomed them.

A boy led my donkey by the reins and three of them jostled me along a path to a compound. They pushed me up to a door. A card in the card holder read:

YEH-CHING
Master Calligrapher

Someone was playing an organ inside. I could feel the pedal note through my feet. The sound almost blew me over when Yeh-ching opened the door. His eyes twinkled at me through thick lenses. Then he cupped a hand to my ear. "That is Father Anselm playing," he said. "Please do come in."

Father Anselm had pulled out all the stops for the last

chord. "Bach," I said. "Buxtehude, actually," said the Father. I immediately recognised him as Inspector Jinren. "Good disguise, Inspector," I said, covering my shock. "That's not the half of it," said Yeh-ching, "as you will see. Only you must call him Father."

I could smell food. "We have already eaten," Yeh-ching said. "Sit down." He brought in the rice pot and lifted the lid through billowing steam. "You will have time to talk on the plane. Tonight is new moon. You leave after dark."

We met at a gate on the far side of the aerodrome. Father Anselm clicked his lighter and held it up to a poster. It looked new, but was already losing its grip on the crumbling plaster of the wall. Two armed guards had a man pinned down with their bayonets. The man's face was that of Inspector Jinren. He wore a Japanese combat hat with the emblem of the sun. "What does it say?" I asked. "*Imperialist Japanese Collaborator – Traitor of the People*," the Father said.

"Your plane is waiting for you." It was Yeh-ching's voice. He thrust a box into my hands. "Take it. It's your memory box. Remember?" I didn't at first, but I took it from him. It was wooden. Light. I felt the rusted handle and my fingers traced the raw patch on top. "Ah, yes," I said. "Thanks." I remembered scraping Minnie Mouse off the lid. I wondered if it still had some of my pens and pencils inside. It seemed a lot smaller. Yeh-ching laid his hand on mine. "Just stow it inside the tail of the plane," he said. "One day you can open it. Not now." He was peering at me through his thick lenses and I watched his face soften into a smile that took me right back into his room with the electricity meters on the wall and the writing things on the table. "Now go," he said. "I'm off to

317

light the runway for your take-off. There is only one safe lane."

The Junkers F13 stood outside an open hangar, its dark nose looming above our heads. "Mind the propeller," I said. I ducked under the wing and knocked my head against something. "Auxiliary fuel tanks," the Father said, giving the cylinder a dull-sounding pat. "What a good idea!" He helped me onto the wing and I gave him a hand up in turn. A light came on in the cockpit as I opened the door. No sign of a pilot.

"Are you flying this thing?" I asked the Father. "No, you are," he said. I stared at him. "You're the aviator. You've read the books," he said. "Climb in."

The F13 taxied toward the first of Yeh-ching's markers. "I think I can manage the take-off," I said, "but I can't vouch for the other end." "Don't worry," said the Father, crossing himself. "Aeroplanes also land." He gave me a shrewd look out of the corner of his flying goggles. "Don't they?" he said. I brought the F13 round and revved the engine and we accelerated into the darkness between twin rows of Chinese paper lanterns, each with a hand-painted character for good luck, long life and prosperity. When the tail lifted and the juddering and jarring of the undercarriage fell away, a solitary lantern remained swinging below us before it vanished right under our nose. Then we banked, circled. I had seen the hills that morning. The lanterns looked like jewels from the air.

"Where are we going?" I asked.

"Dibrugarh," said the Father.

"Where the hell's that?"

Tsk tsk tsk. The Father shook his head. "Assam, the Brahmaputra River, gateway to the Hump, the 14th? You surprise me."

318

"How far?"

"About 500 miles as the crow flies, heading west."

"How high are the mountains?"

Father Anselm studied the map on his lap. "Up to 17,000 feet."

"We're at 8,000 going up," I said. "Oxygen all round."

"Can't be right. It's too quick," said the Father.

"Not really. Lake Kunming is 6,000 feet above sea level before you start." I put on my mask and felt the rush of fresh air. "Yeh-ching has seen to everything," I said. "Is it his plane?"

"Mine," said Father Anselm. "I inherited it. From my uncle. On my mother's side. The Japanese branch of the family. Supreme Commander of the Imperial Army he was. He got it as a buy off from the German ambassador. Some claim over a five year old boy."

"Sounds like he did well," I said. "What happened to the boy?"

Father Anselm gave me a shrewd sideways glance. "The commander never flew in it, poor devil. Now it's your turn." He gave me a wide grin, showing gold teeth. "Divine justice."

"Almost 10,000 feet," I said. We had left the cloud layer below, cool and silent. A line of peaks pierced it, pale on the horizon far ahead. "We should try to run those mountains out to the south," I said. "We'll never get over them. Give me a course."

"Try 18 south. That'll bring them down to 12,000 feet. Once we've crossed the Mekong, we can get back on course."

"Will we feel the splash?" I said.

The Father ignored me. "It's taking us well out of our way," he said and switched off the cabin light. The instrument cluster vied with the busy stars outside. The F13 thrummed to its six-in-line cylinders and stretched its wings far out on the unimaginable air. The world had never looked so clear before.

"What was that about collaborating with the Japs?" I asked.

"That? Well of course I did. So did your dad. In the last months of the Pacific war. Did you think we could run with the Generalissimo? That's a good one, *pacific* war!"

"You knew my father, didn't you?"

"Yes."

"You came to the house."

"Yes."

"You've seen a thing or two."

"A thing or two more than your dad. Or your mum, come to that."

"What d'you mean?"

Father Anselm fell silent. Then, "I could use a cigarette," he said. "Don't worry. I've given them up." He grinned again.

"We're two hours in," I said. "That should be around 180 miles. Altitude 12,000 feet. We should just about clear those mountains at that."

"I'd take her up a bit more," the Father said. "They're famous for their downdraughts."

We levelled out at 13,000 feet and bumped our way across the range. Neither of us spoke. When it was over, I noticed that the Father had nodded off. "You going to tell me what you meant by your remark?"

"Where was I?" the Father said with a start. "Oh yes, fasten your seatbelt."

"I can't hear you."

He fumbled with his mask and switched the sound back on. "Better?"

"Don't do that again," I said. "Tell me what you meant."

"You know that story about your sister? The little girl that died at birth?"

"Yes?"

"Well she didn't. Oh yes, she was born with a heart problem. A transposition, they said. They took her from your mum to assess her while they kept her on oxygen support. It was another baby in the cardiac unit that died. There had been a mix-up, you see. They operated on your sister and she survived."

"What are you saying? How can you know that?"

"From her mother," he said. "The mother who'd lost her own baby, that is. Eurasian lady. Married to a rich Portuguese. Catholic."

The fuel gauge said a quarter full. Air speed 100mph. Altitude 14,000. "Downdraughts my foot." I throttled back and let the plane settle. My ears popped. "You better be kidding," I said.

"I'm not," said the Father. "Your sister grew up in Shanghai in that family. And the Eurasian woman was the only one who knew it was not her child."

"So how did you find out?"

"She told me, like I said. Before the baby girl was baptised, she came to confession and told me the whole story. I absolved her before God."

"You shouldn't have told me," I said.

"Perhaps not," said Father Anselm. "But I baptised the baby girl in my church and I have carried a debt to my conscience and to God ever since."

"What was she named?" I said.

"Eurydice." He let the name hover, waiting for a foothold. "I think the two of you have met."

"The girl from Sacré Cœur?"

"Yes. I taught her violin."

"And you took the boys' choir at Ste Jeanne d'Arc," I said.

"How do you know that?"

"I almost went to that school myself."

"Pity you didn't," he said.

I let the plane drift. The propeller made a swishing sound. A white disc, spinning without bite.

"*Eurydice,*" I said. "Her mother gave her that name, didn't she? Her new mother."

"From the land of the dead. *He* liked to call her *Biggi*. Don't know where he got that from," he said.

It hit home. I pulled out the throttle, lifted the nose and banked steeply.

"What in heaven's name are you doing?" said the Father.

"Going back."

"You can't."

"I'm going back."

"Don't be stupid. We're over the Hump. Look at the fuel. You'll never make it back to Kunming."

"There's the auxiliary tanks."

"OK. Cut them in. See how much they give you. Then work it out for yourself."

"You did that on purpose, didn't you. You waited till we'd passed the point of no return. You bastard."

"Turn round," said the Father. "Even if we make it back, *they'll* be waiting for us. In broad daylight."

"No."

I started climbing to clear the ranges we'd already crossed. Father Anselm sat with his hands folded in his lap. He had slackened off his oxygen mask again. The fuel gauge now showed just under half full. The mountains made a jagged black line across the eastern sky. I continued to climb. As I followed the altimeter through its graduations, I made a wish that this would turn out to be only a dream. Then I took a deep breath and throttled right back and put the plane into a stall. Father Anselm jumped. The altimeter unwound dizzily as we fell. When I ran out of breath, I pushed the stick forward. The nose came down, the propeller wound up and we banked once again, not as steeply this time, and began a wide circle to the north. I straightened out at last and settled on a nor'westerly course. "Get that mask on and talk to me, damn you," I said.

"I had it all worked out." He was back in the world of the living. "Eurydice was supposed to be with us on this flight. Oh yes, it wasn't just for you and me."

"She was the North Wind," I said.

"Yes."

"What happened?"

"I don't know. They nearly got me."

"They?"

"You were there," he said. He turned his head and looked at me. "Sadly," he added, "she didn't turn up."

"I can't believe," I said. "I can't believe we got that close."

"I'm sure that goes for the two of you," the Father said.

"The two of me?" I asked.

"Why not?"

The stars faded and the indigo washed from the sky. Father Anselm held out a photograph. "That was taken at the baptism," he said. "That's me." It showed him holding an infant and leaning over a woman whose arms had reached out to receive it. It was wrapped in a straw mat and only its tiny head showed. It had a dark crown of hair.

*

THE WORLD OUTSIDE whitened as if flushed with snow. My hand fumbled for the sun shield in the overhead pocket and clamped it over my goggles. Far out ahead the shadow of the F13 undulated over the blinding blanket of cloud.

"Are we going to make it?" I asked the Father, but he had fallen asleep again and I decided this time not to wake him.

As the sun climbed into the sky behind me, it teased tumuli of vapour out of the cloud. I watched the plane's shadow ride over them and I thought about the stories of my life and how they'd run ahead of me without me even knowing and how I kept bumping into them when I least expected it.

I wondered where I was. I should go down and have a look,

I thought. Yet it was perfect up here in the clear air and the sun, with my shadow spreading its wings straight and steady on the clouds, leading the way. I could have stayed forever.

The engine stuttered, revived, hummed again, as sweet as ever. Then it gasped. The propeller blades materialised out of nowhere, batting at each other round and round in a crazy circle, until they tired, out of breath, rocked just one more time and stood still. Silence. The plane's shadow came in closer under me and its arms spread wider. I flew into a spire of cloud and out again into the sunshine and the shadow was there, huge (was the plane really that big?), and then we closed.

It grew dim. The plane fell, recovered with a bump and shuddered. Something enormous lifted it up again and turned it over and buffeted it and buffeted it until all dimension, all direction, all opposites broke down in turmoil. And the rain began to splatter against the windshield.

Endnotes

Index to the endnotes

Place names. I have named places as they were named when my stories took place. They are listed in the left hand column below. In the right hand column are their present day equivalents. English and French street names now have Chinese names. And Chinese names have been re-written in *pinyin*. This is the revised form of representing Chinese words in the Latin alphabet. Once mastered, it renders a more faithful encoding of the Chinese pronunciation. *Pinyin* is in current use.

The Bund	*Zhongshan Donglu*
Amherst Avenue/Fahwha Lu	*Xinghua Lu*
Tunsin Road	*Wuyi Lu*
Columbia Road	*Panyu Lu*
Avenue Joffre	*Huai Hai Zhonglu (Zhong=east)*
Rockhill Avenue	*Huai Hai Xilu (Xi=west)*
Great Western Road	*Yan'an Xilu*
Bubbling Well Road	*Nanjing Xilu*
Nanking Road	*Nanjing Donglu*
Avenue Haig	*Huashan Lu*
Route Ferguson	*Wukang Lu*
Route Say Zoong	*Changshu Lu*
Whangpoo River	*Huangpu*
Soochow	*Suzhou*
Hongkew	*Hongkou*
Siccawei	*Xujiahui*
Hungjao	*Hongqiao*
Fahwha	*Fahua*
Lungwha	*Longhua*
Woosung	*Wusong*

Tung-Shi University	*Tongji* University
Jessfield Park	*Zhongshan* Park
Kiukiang	*Jiujiang*
Nanking	*Nanjing*
Tsinan	*Jinan*
Yellow River	*Huang He*
Tientsin	*Tianjin*
Chinwangtao	*Qinhuangdao*
Pei-tai-ho	*Beidaihe*
Hangchow	*Hangzhou*
Szechuan	*Sichuang*
Tien Mu Shan	*Tianmushan*
Peking	*Beijing*
Shum Chun	*Shenzen*

My reason for using the old names has been to preserve the language of us foreigners at the time, which carried with it the attitude that we really only had to make the Chinese world we inhabited manageable for our own purposes. Not to honour it for its own sake. And the Chinese world accommodated us. Streets like Avenue Haig and Avenue Joffre became part of mainstream Shanghai place talk, even if the Chinese tongue despoiled them of any obvious connection to the names of their illustrious WWI English and French namesakes.

Personal names. I have given persons the names by which I remember them, barring the odd one, which I have changed for the usual reasons. Chinese names appear in the form in which they were known at the time. The more recent *pinyin* rendering of Chiang-Kai-shek, *Jiang Jieshi*, would probably

332

be less recognisable to most readers. His political party, the Kuomintang, is now written *Guomindang* and Mao Tse-tung has become *Mao Zedong*. As for myself, I appear as *Till*, which is the old spelling, now written as *Tyl*. This was a conscious choice, because *Till* has remained unshielded and open-ended.

The foreigners in Shanghai. I have been asked by friends who have read the manuscript of this book what all those foreigners were doing in Shanghai. Since I had grown up as one of them, they were simply how the world was made. As were streetlights, trams and running water. As was the fact that none of these existed in the Chinese quarters of Shanghai. So a look into the origins of foreign settlement will do no harm.

As recently as a hundred and seventy years ago (ca.1840), Shanghai was a walled city on the banks of the Whangpoo River, roughly oval in plan, just over a mile long and just under a mile wide. Outside the walls were villages and fields criss-crossed by creeks.

Foreign countries had been carrying on trade with China for centuries and Chinese commodities such as silk, tea and porcelain were prized abroad. In the nineteenth century the British began to put pressure on the Chinese for increased trade, but were hard put to offer them anything they really wanted in return. China kept its gates shut and its ports closed. Only the port of Canton allowed foreign ships in.

Then the British hit on opium and very soon the balance of trade turned in their favour. Opium addiction became widespread throughout China. The Chinese government responded by declaring opium illegal and the trade went underground. However, it did not abate. A showdown came when the Chinese Customs confiscated a shipment of opium and Britain retaliated with its navy. Heavy battles ensued, in which the superiority of British fire power became decisive. British warships pushed up the Yangtze River to Nanking, China's southern capital, and forced a treaty legitimising foreign trade through five Chinese ports including Shanghai. Further terms of the treaty provided for settlement rights, the establishment of foreign consulates, the cession of Hong Kong to Britain, the control of Customs by the British and the payment of millions of dollars to Britain by way of compensation for the confiscated opium and war costs. That was 1842, the Treaty of Nanking. By way of note, New Zealand's Treaty of Waitangi was signed two years before, in 1840.

It wasn't long before the British were settling an area beyond the walls of the old city of Shanghai fronting the Whangpoo River. That frontage was later to be known as The Bund. Not long after, the Americans followed suit downstream in Hongkew. The French negotiated a Concession of their own and their muddy shore came to be known as the French Bund. The *foreigners* had moved in. They reserved anchorages for themselves on the river, built wharves, warehouses and all the infrastructure of trade, except the French, who built monasteries. Shipping offices, banks and insurances proliferated. Clubs, apartments, schools, churches and missions followed, as did hospitals to treat the victims of malaria, polluted water sources and untreated sewage. National ensigns fluttered over the consulates and commerce thrived and the British got to build the Customs House.

Within a decade the foreign settlements had doubled in size and before long the still bigger International Settlement was founded, amalgamating the British and American sectors alongside the equally expanded French Concession. By the end of the century the foreign settlement covered an area over fifty times the size of the old walled city of Shanghai and completely swallowed it up. And it was all about trade.

Shanghai had become the gateway for foreigners to suck up China's vast resources and spew them out again as manufactured goods on the export market. Those resources weren't only the raw materials such as cotton and silk, but an unlimited supply of cheap labour that surged into the city eager for work. The growth of industry called for transport networks, roads, railways and bridges all over China and the foreign powers were quick to finance huge loans to the Chinese government to pay for them. Business opportunities opened up for overseas professionals in construction and engineering and for overseas manufacturers to provide the machinery to run the electricity companies and the waterworks and everything a modern city needed. The ensuing wealth fell to the foreigners.

This is why they were there.

For further reading on foreign settlement in Shanghai I can recommend *Building Shanghai, the Story of China's Gateway* by Edward Denison and Guang Yu Ren, published in Great Britain 2006 by Wiley-Academy.

The Japanese occupation. They'd always squabbled over territory. China, the giant endowed with the blessings and burdens of an ancient civilisation, and Japan, the young upstart of the islands. Yet up until the time of the Treaty of Nanking in 1842, neither had actually won any ground. Things began to change as the foreigners exacted their concessions from the

335

Chinese imperial government in the wake of the treaty. Japan was not to be outdone. The Land of the Rising Sun took Korea under its shadow, then Taiwan (renaming it Formosa) and then Manchuria (renaming it Manchukuo).

By the early twentieth century the Japanese military had become a powerful force; so much so that they often acted independently of the Tokyo regime. They were also well equipped to conduct modern warfare on the European model. The Chinese weren't. Their empire had been so weakened by the decline of the Manchu Dynasty and the self-interest of the provincial warlords (each with his own army), that Chinese resistance to foreign pressure was failing on every front. This suited the Japanese who, by the nineteen-thirties, had their garrisons stationed all over northern China.

And then in 1937 an exchange of shots between Chinese and Japanese soldiers stationed at the famous Marco Polo Bridge resulted in the battle over Peking. Neither side had declared war. But Peking fell. Meanwhile both sides had begun stationing troops in and around Shanghai and again a shooting

incident lit the fuse that resulted in three months of vicious fighting. And again no one had declared war. Shanghai fell to the Japanese in November of the same year.

In August 1937 at the start of the fighting in Shanghai, my family had been on holiday in Japan. My father was recalled to his diplomatic post at the consulate in Shanghai, while my mother, together with my older brother and our amah, remained behind in the relative safety of Japan. This is how I came to be born in Kobe in November 1937. But by December the fires had burned down and we were able to take a steamer to Shanghai, where my father met us on the Bund. Shanghai was under Japanese control. The rape of Nanking was still to come in time for Christmas.

The Japanese occupation lasted until August 1945, when the Americans put an end to the Pacific War at Hiroshima.

For further reading on the topic I recommend *When Tigers Fight, The Story of the Sino-Japanese War, 1937-1945,* by Dick Wilson, first published 1982 by The Viking Press and reprinted by Penguin Books in 1983.

Following is a copy of a (presumably) handwritten letter by an eye witness of the Japanese attack on Shanghai in 1937. I don't know his name or whom he was writing to. But he mentions Mr. Oates, who features in this book (p.207). Mr. Oates was managing director of Paton and Baldwins woollen mills in Hongkew at the time of the attack.

I am writing this letter as I thought you might like to hear some first-hand news from someone out here.

Although trouble had been hanging around for quite a long time we never expected it breaking out to the extent that it has done round Shanghai, and even after the fighting had started and the Japanese Officer and driver had been killed on the settlement road in Shanghai first hand information was hard to get. However, on the 12th. August word came through that anything may happen in the Chapie and the Woosung district, which is only a short distance from our Mills, so it was decided to evacuate the women and children to an Hotel in Shanghai for a few days, to see which way things went. On Friday, the 13th. of August, at 4 p.m. guns started booming, some of them within a few hundred yards of the Mill, and fires could be seen quite easily from the Mill top. Although the hands had been gradually dwindling away all the week, going to places where they thought they would be safe, we managed to keep all the Mill running. When this firing started, although the hands turned up, we had a hard job to get them to start work. They wanted their wages so they could get away, and it was only by promising to pay on Saturday morning that we could get them to start. The wages clerks had to work all night to fix this up. On the Saturday morning 250 wages had been paid and all the foreign had been called together to fix up shifts as watchmen etc., with a view to stopping looting or stealing by the chinese. This had all been arranged and everything was running smoothly but there were still a few more wages and the men were all in conversation at 10 a.m. when over came some chinese planes and we actually saw them release their bombs over the mill and the explosions were ear splitting, and with rattle of machine guns and anti air craft it was like being on a battle field, and Mr. Oates gave orders for every man to get away into Shanghai. Some who had their own cars went in them; the others were sent down in the Mill bus. When the excitement of this had blown over, there was Mr. Oates, Mr. Kenyon, Mr. Creasy and myself left in the warehouse bottom floor, along with some chinese who were still to pay a little later. Dickinson came in; he had been packing. The chinese were eventually paid and were sent part way down the road in the Mill truck and van, accompanied by Sgt. Lawman (I might say this man helped wonderfully). When all the chinese had been cleared, Mr. Oates told Dickinson to get down to Shanghai; Creasy who was waiting for a cable was to follow him down. The reason Creasy was at the Mill was because he had brought some food down, as Mr. Oates, Mr. Kenyon and myself intended to stay as long as possible. When Creasy tried to get back to Shanghai in the Firms - , he found it impossible, so he was sent down on the Power Co's. launch, and by all accounts he had a very hectic time going down the river, as he was going down at the time of the second air raid and he says there were bullets and shrapnel flying in all directions. The experience of the second air raid decided us that the three who were going to stay at the Mill should evacuate. We were over at the Power Co. and had been having a cup of tea and had started back to

338

the Mill when eleven planes came over and started bobing.   We had
to run as fast as we could go for the Warehouse, as the bombs were
dropping quite near, and machine guns were rattling away.   We quite
expected any of us getting some shrapnel or a bullet which may be
flying about stray, and if raiding was going to keep on all night
we felt certain that the Chinese troops would go through ~~xxxxxxx~~
near the Mill, so we cleared out to Shanghai.   You will no doubt
have read in the paper at home of the havoc of loss of life this
second bombing raid caused in Nanking Rd; also in this rai' one
bomb just missed by ten yards the American Flag Ship Augusta, which
had only tied up to her buoys ten minutes before, lucky it dropped
in the river;   another one killed six people close by the Augusta;
others caused several fires, the biggest at the A.P. Co. by dropping a
bomb amongst their tanks.   After filling the mill van with
luggage that had been left behind by the men in their scramble to get
away, we took the van to the Police Station with a view of getting it
up to Shanghai later.   We took the Mill car and Mr. Konyons car and
made a dash for Shanghai and after a hectic ride reached the Hotel at
8.30.   On the Sunday morning some people began to realise they had
no clothes only what they stood up in and started to moan about it,
so Mr. Oates asked a chap called Claxton and myself if we would go
with him and get some that were in the van and we said we would.
When we got to the Police Station we could not start the van, but
as it turned out, it was lucky as Mr. Oates and myself had left our
cars at the Mill, so I got mine.   Claxton and Mr. Oates had Konyons
so we got everything away that was in the van and we set off for a
hectic drive to the Hotel, and to beat another air raid which was going
on at the time;   someone took a pot shot at Mr. Oates and missed.
We had to drive through debris and all kinds of things to get back,
and how pleased we were to do so.   As things were getting very hot
with the continual shelling, Mr. Oates decided to evacuate the women
and children to Hong Kong on the first boat if possible, as they could
get no sleep, and the children, although they stood it well, were
terrified and had faces like this paper.   He got them on the first
ship and they went on board the British Battleship, the Falmouth,
and even though both parties had promised there should be no firing,
some chinese planes came over and had to be driven off by anti air craft
guns while the evacuation was going on.   This was on Tuesday,
August 17th.   Mr. Oates next decided that as none of us here had had
a holiday for three years, he would send us to Hong Kong for a week or
so in order that we could have a rest in readiness for cleaning up when
it was safe to return.   We left Shanghai on the 20th., and arrived
here on Aug. 23rd.   When we came down the river we could see   that no
big stuff had touched the Mill, although th Japanese had taken it
over on Monday, August. 16th, and had taken the U ion Jacks down, so we
are hoping that the luck we have had so far will hold out.   Although
we have read in the papers to-day that the Chinese have taken over a
foreign worsted mill in that district, and we think it must be ours,
but we hope that this is not true, otherwise we are afraid that

everything we have will have gone.   Mrs. Oates left here
for home on the Patroclus, so she will be able to give you some .
verbal details of what has happened.   All the rest left here
are quite well, except Mrs. Booth.   She is in Hospital
resting after her ordeal.   She had only come out of Hospital
in Shanghai two days before this lot started.

              I hope you will accept this letter as data which
I thought you might be interested in.

The Amah. If you had grown up in China in the thirties and forties, as I did, you would have grown up in the care of an amah. She would have been a Chinese woman from upcountry, probably with grown-up children of her own, and she would have spoken pidgin English. Our amah had come to us from another German family and spoke German as well.

I have never heard of a school for amahs, yet they all seemed to know the ways of a foreign household, foreign hygiene and social standards. And to any foreign mother of children, her amah would quickly become indispensable. In the home, because she saw to all their domestic needs, and outside it, because she guarded their foreignness against encounters with her own countrymen and their children.

Our amah had come to us before my elder brother was born and stayed with us until the day we left Shanghai for good. We were adolescent then and her role in our lives had reduced to mending our socks and mosquito nets, washing and ironing and sweeping our room. But in the household at large, it had increased to that of a fully fledged domestic and more. Amah did all the shopping and cooking and housekeeping and brought tea. She also kept unwelcome visitors from the door.

It wasn't necessarily the case with all families, but in ours (specially to us boys) Amah was as close as it gets.

Amherst Avenue. (pp.46,199,331) Ever since the publication of J.G.Ballard's novel *Empire of the Sun* in 1984 and its incarnation in film by Steven Spielberg a few years later, the name *Amherst Avenue* has popped a flag whenever we read of British residential opulence and decadence in Shanghai during the thirties and forties. It celebrates the name of Lord Amherst, who had brought an embassy to the Emperor of China from King George III in 1816 and who had had to return home profitless and complaining of the recalcitrance of the Chinese court and the insults that had been heaped upon him and other dignitaries of his mission.

Notwithstanding this ignominy, in 1930 Amherst Avenue pushed the western boundaries of the International Settlement up to the railway line to spearhead the extra-settlement area west of Shanghai and satisfy the tastes of foreigners in search of upmarket accommodation in a variety of styles from Tudor to Edwardian, from Spanish bungalow to Bauhaus.

The Ballards lived at 31 Amherst Avenue, a minute's walk from 131 Columbia Circle *q.v.* where we lived. As far as I know, our families never met. J.G.Ballard was seven years older than me, we were Germans, there was a war, the Ballards were interned by the Japanese and after the war the young JG was sent to boarding school in England. For all that, when he writes about his Shanghai years (I am currently reading his *Miracles of Life*), it is the parallels that move me. Sadly he died.

Hellmuth von Ruckteschell. (pp.34,165) This man's career as a German naval officer is well documented. Whether commanding a U-boat in WWI or an armed merchant raider in WWII, he comes across as a lone hunter and a deadly foe. A man at war who takes no chances with the enemy, but dispatches him in the night. He takes survivors on board, but not at the risk of his own crew or the safety of his ship. His aggressive U-boat tactics had earned him the rancour of the Royal Navy, and his subsequent notoriety as a raider—with more than twenty enemy ships at the bottom of the Atlantic—left him friendless, but for the Germans who decorated him with the Knight's Cross with Oak Leaves.

After WWII he was tried for war crimes by the British Admiralty and found guilty on three charges essentially concerning failure to provide for the safety of survivors. He was sentenced to ten years' imprisonment. One of the charges

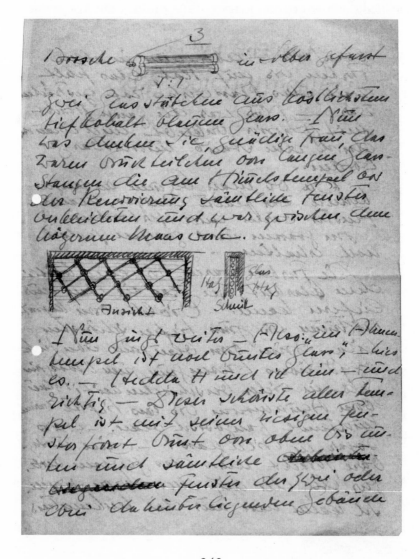

was later dropped and the remaining ones have been debated ever since. His sentence was commuted to seven years and then, on grounds of ill health, he was to be released after just one year in prison. But he died.

Hellmuth von Ruckteschell's active service ended in 1943, when he put his ship into the port of Kobe, Japan, and came ashore. He was in poor health and spent some time in hospital. In the following summer he was in Pei-tai-ho, a holiday resort in the north of China, as guest of the German ambassador. My family happened to be there at the time and we became friends. He then spent some months in Peking and took pleasure in visiting the temples of the Forbidden City. He came to visit us in Shanghai. When the war ended he was tracked down by the Allies and repatriated on the American troop ship *Marine Robin* to face the charges brought against him.

We never saw him again, but quite recently I came across two letters from him to my mother, written in Peking (one is dated December 1944, the other of imprecise date because the first page is missing). My mother must have folded them away between pages 142 and 143 of Juliet Bredon's *Peking* where they still were when I found them. A passage in the text of the book had been underlined in pencil and *Hellmuth* written in the margin. The following text is a transcription of part of one of the letters, freely translated by myself. I include it because of the enjoyable and rather less publicised aspect of the man that it reveals.

> Then I discovered something I'd already known intuitively and that turned out by a strange coincidence to be correct. While enduring a long bed rest last year at the Wilhelm residence, which is an original Chinese residence complete with paper windows, I set to wondering about those windows and why the owners hadn't used glass in them instead. It must have been a possibility, I thought, given the skills of Chinese craftsmen with a great variety of materials including coloured glazes. They could have transformed the sunlight into glancing colours.

My host scoffed at my ideas. I put it to sinologists and art experts and old China hands. They all demurred. Even old Fischer, who gave me a pitying smile and only talked about blue curtains, which he said could cast a particular light into the room. Glass? No.

One day, while visiting Hedda Hammer [the photographer better known as Hedda Morrison], I came upon a brooch consisting of two glass rods set side by side in a silver mounting. It was quite small and the glass was a deep cobalt blue. Now, Madam, what think you? They were fragments of much longer glass rods from old windows out of the Temple of Heaven prior to its reconstruction [after the fire]. In the original, these rods would have been arranged like reeds in a window blind and held between inner and outer faces of wooden latticework. [Here follow sketches showing the arrangement.]

The story goes on. 'There are still some coloured glass windows in the Ancestral Temple,' said Hedda Hammer. So off we went to see and – true to her word – this most beautiful of all the temples had coloured glass ranging from top to bottom across its entire vast facade. Glass in all colours other than red (the wooden latticework was painted red). Only the whole glorious display had been pasted over with paper and on the outside the dust was so thick, you couldn't see it.

The colours had a delicate clarity, as only glass can deliver. Violet from *caput mortuum* to a deep beautiful lilac. Green from blue-green through zinc oxide through meadow green to moss green. Yellow in all its hues. Blue from aquamarine through into a deep and warmly glowing French blue. Even white milk glass. Indescribable magnificence unfurled before that exalted throne...

Isn't that a remarkable discovery? I think there could be many more things to discover if one only kept one's eyes

345

open. Things even the 'learned' sinologists don't know
because they search in books.

Yes, it would be wonderful if you were here and we could
spend time looking around. Only one needs to know the
language and my brain is too stupid and too old for that.

I have many fond memories of the times we spent together.
Only the very fondest, in fact – that's the truth.

Give my love to your boys.

Your devoted

Hellmuth von Ruckteschell

I have found excellent biographical information on the
Internet under *Hellmuth von Ruckteschell* and *Hilfskreuzer
(Auxiliary Cruiser / Raider) – Michel.*

Holy Trinity Cathedral. (pp.126,167) This red brick and
stone early Gothic style church was designed by architect
George Gilbert Scott in England in the upper 1860s. It has
a spire sitting on a square tower, recently restored, since the
Communists had earlier removed it. They had also hung a
ceiling the length of the nave and constructed a tiered floor
to suit the cathedral's new function as a place for official
gatherings. All this has now been taken away and the church
restored.

The cathedral naturally hosted a choir, with the trebles
recruited from the Cathedral Boys' School, which shared its
grounds. J.G.Ballard talks about it in his book *Miracles of Life.*
After WWII it was the Shanghai British School that filled the
lower choir stalls, augmenting their number with girls. The
photo shows the choir in 1948.

The photo also shows two persons not mentioned in this
book, but very much at the heart of the British community

Top row centre is Dean Trivett.
Bottom row centre is Dolly Eynstone. On her right, Diana
Newcomb. On her left, Peter Newcomb.
Between and above Dolly and Diana, Vera Eynstone.
Behind Peter and to his left, myself.
On my left, my brother Rabe.

in Shanghai. They are Billy Hawkings in the back row (one
in from the right of photo) and his wife Mavis Hawkings
in the middle row (one in from the left of photo with head
inclined). They lived at *The Limit*, their house and garden at the
furthest western outpost of Shanghai. There they witnessed
the Japanese armed offensive and twelve years later the
Communist one as Shanghai was in turn taken. Noel Barber
in *The Fall of Shanghai* covers their story in depth.

The Bund. Shanghai's stately frontage to the Whangpoo River (west bank) has been, from the time of foreign settlement, the city's monument to investment and commerce. Following the river's curving flank, it features a wide road and a landscaped promenade that stretches along the river embankment for the best part of a mile, ending in the public gardens where the Soochow Creek flows into the Whangpoo. The Bund boasts all the major banks, insurance companies, shipping company offices, newspapers, clubs and hotels. It has also been Shanghai's political showcase, parading the consulates of all the foreign countries that once had a stake in Shanghai's trade and in the ships that lay at anchor in the stream. Not to mention the warships, Japanese, British and American naval strengths that took turns to signal power and unrest, nor the sandbag emplacements or the columns of soldiers that have marched in waves along the Bund under their different colours.

Despite the changes and the spate of rebuilding that Shanghai has been subject to, the Bund itself has remained largely unchanged, except in name—it is now called Zhongshan Donglu. But the promenade is still referred to as the Bund.

The Heinemanns. (pp.209,248) The Communist authorities held Heinz Heinemann for more than a year after his arrest in Shanghai in 1951 and still no charge had been laid. When they released him, it was at short notice and without explanation. In a letter to my mother, his wife wrote that he was so wasted, she hardly recognised him. She added that, to her, he was nevertheless the handsomest man she'd ever seen. In March 1953 the Heinemanns sailed out of Shanghai headed for Canada, where they settled and once again created treasure houses of books. Stephen Heinemann visited me a few years ago (we hadn't seen each other for some 55 years) and presented me a copy of Hannelore Heinemann Headley's book *Blond China Doll - A Shanghai Interlude 1939-1953*, in which his sister tells her story. That is, her family's story, beginning with their exodus from Berlin. Hannelore died in June 2013.

Emma Bormann. (p.48) A frequent visitor to our home, this remarkable printmaker with a love of Oriental themes enriched the artistic endeavours of our childhood years. She got us to do lino cuts and to paint with a strong sense of colour and, like her own work, a strong expression. Emma Borman has exhibited in many countries, including Germany, Japan and the United States of America. Her work is represented in the Metropolitan Museum, New York, among other significant museums internationally. She died in California in 1974.

Chen Chi. (p.226) I can remember him from when I was five or six years old, this kind and joyful man who painted in watercolours and taught my mother the deft strokes and transparent colours that characterised his own work. As a child I loved looking at the book he gave her, published in 1942 in Chinese and French, featuring sixteen of his watercolours. I still do. In 1975 he wrote to my mother from New York and, not long after, his book *China from the Sketchbooks of Chen Chi* arrived in the post. His work has been widely exhibited in the USA and in 1999 it was commemorated by the opening of the CHEN CHI ART MUSEUM in Shanghai. He died in 2005.

Ilse von Randow. New Zealand will remember my mother as the weaver who put the art of weaving on the map of New Zealand as a fine art and not just an occupational therapy. Her biography by Douglas Lloyd-Jenkins is in the New Zealand Dictionary of Biography and his essay entitled *The Textiles of Ilse von Randow* first appeared in conjunction with a retrospective exhibition of her work in the Auckland Museum in 1998.

It was her engagement with the rapidly awakening art scene in New Zealand in the early fifties that got my mother her foothold in this country. Her creative work took off and her two weaving looms were never idle. The larger of the two was the one made for her by Studio Seagull in Shanghai, which we had dismantled (pp.261) for the voyage to NZ in 1952. It is now owned by the Auckland Museum. The curtains for the Auckland City Art Gallery were woven on it. Since the loom was only three feet wide, they were woven in sections and the eight drops sewn together side by side. The curtains hung in the portal between the City Gallery and the Mackelvie Gallery until the seventies, when they were taken down for building works and never put up again. The curtains are in the possession of the Auckland Museum.

Ilse von Randow taught alongside other artists at a number of summer schools, the first of which I recall taking place at the Auckland City Art Gallery in 1954, put together by the new director Eric Westbrook. Jan Michels, Nelson Thompson, Colin McCahon, Louise Henderson and Len Castle were among the tutors. The Society of Arts ran them every year after that. Years later, Catherine Mitchell organised summer schools for the arts on Waiheke Island and Ilse taught at these. She also had a number of private students, whom she taught weaving and spinning. Zena Abbot was among the first and she later made a name for herself as a weaver in her own right. A circle of artist friends began to gather around my mother. Many I can remember as young women making their first serious foray into the arts. My mother's role in taking them under her wing struck me as mutually fulfilling.

Largely through Zena, who knew some of the young architects in town (her husband was a builder), we got a house built in Terry Street, Blockhouse Bay, with Zena building right next door. Both houses were designed by Bill Wilson of the Group Architects, who had little truck with stale ideas or the dull weight of convention. The houses breathed. My mother engaged the Returned Servicemen's Re-establishment League to make chairs of Rimu with jute webbing to modern Swedish designs. They were light in colour and light to lift in and out of the French doors. Soon her woven hangings appeared on the walls of the house. My mother had stepped forward into a new age (below R). She was fifty-two at the time. Twenty years earlier the newly married Ilse von Randow had taken a photograph of her sitting room in Tunsin Road (below L). She sent it to her father, Professor Bruno Henneberg, in Giessen, Germany, with the caption *Our House.*

It was barely two and a half years since our arrival in New Zealand. Rabe and I lived in the Blockhouse Bay house with our mother for some years and helped to repay the 3% City Council loan from our holiday earnings, mine, stacking timber at Ronald Neil's yard in Portage Road or dragging bricks at Amalgamated Brick and Tile in New Lynn and his, working in a light engineering workshop owned by a German acquaintance. When Elgar, Ilse's ex-husband, our father, was once again posted in the German diplomatic service abroad, his monthly financial remittances were a considerable boost to our slender economy.

Soon Ilse was working from home. I built an extension to the house to accommodate her weaving looms. It was my first architectural assignment. The Art Gallery curtains were woven there.

My mother never remarried. There had been overtures from a couple of German gentlemen, which she turned down. When I asked her about it, she said, *I have my two sons. What do I want with some kind of a strange man in the house?* But, in truth, she preferred the English cut. She was secretly in love on at least two occasions, once later in her sixties. English gentlemen. And there it remained.

She had her Old World friends in Auckland. Among them were Eugen and Sofie Maier, for whom Henry Kulka had designed a house, and Ilse had woven the curtains. Sofie's sister, Berta Zimmermann, was a regular guest at our house, turning up on a Vespa scooter at the end of a day's work as itinerant nurse. She lived in the downstairs apartment of Bob Goodman's house near the Rose Gardens. The Reizensteins lived in Pah Road and there Ernst hosted a string quartet and my mother joined them. A bit like Shanghai days. Ernst Reizenstein played first violin. He also had an impressive library, not just German, but rich in Pacific culture, and I remember him showing me rare prints of Maori subjects in pre-settlement days with European Romantic features and poise. Of course, he made Reizenstein's bread, no longer exclusively for expatriate Germans.

By 1966 many of the people in my mother's life had either moved on or left the country or died and she was beginning to feel estranged from New Zealand and New Zealanders. She was drawn instead towards Europe. She settled in England.

Not Germany. Again she avoided the country of her birth and chose to live in a strange land. She championed Edward Heath for his pro-Europe stance and looked forward to the flowering of a new unity. She bought a cottage on Mersea Island, Essex, in the estuary of the River Colne, and lived there for twenty-two years. She connected with the Sunday painters at Colchester and made the *Minories* her artistic centre. English landscapes, seascapes, still lives and life drawings filled her days and she was content.

For the best part of that time, her family were nearby. My brother Rabe in Germany and myself in London doing my OE. Both married with children. My mother was a terrific grandmother, as the grandchildren will all aver, giving the epithet their own distinctive hues. But as times changed, she again started to feel estranged.

She was getting older and her sons' families had dissolved and bits of them disappeared to New Zealand. Besides, Margaret Thatcher had come into office and displeased her very much. My mother was ninety when she decided to leave England and return to New Zealand. Her old country remembered her. The Museum's retrospective of her work coincided with the opening of two new galleries at level one in the body of the building. The other gallery hosted work by sculptor John Edgar. I reassembled the old Studio Seagull loom, which had been in the ownership of the late Lady Turner, and it stood in centre place.

The Art Gallery curtains came out of their boxes and were hung again (only for the exhibition). My mother's woven wall hangings were borrowed back from their owners from all over the world and displayed. Her notebooks and working samples

were on show. There were many black-and-white photos of my mother from days gone by.

And among the many people who came to the opening, I remember the late and dear Len Castle kneeling in front of my mother's wheelchair (she was 97 at this time), holding her hands in his. Were they both remembering their joint exhibition some forty-four years earlier at the Art Gallery's Wertheim Room, when Eric Westbrook had just become the new director and everyone was still young?

Ilse von Randow died later that year, in 1998. Rhondda Greig spoke at her funeral. She said Ilse had been an inspiration to many young aspiring artists like herself, just emerging from art school in the New Zealand of the nineteen-fifties and sixties. She had given them the belief, Rhondda said, that to move out into the world as an artist and as a woman with only Art for a livelihood offered not just a fulfilling vocation, but a sustainable one.

Elgar von Randow. The Internet gives an outline biography of my father's life. I was eight when he left Shanghai and I was to see him again when I was twenty-four. He came to New Zealand in 1961 with his fourth wife, Franzi. They stayed at my mother's house. I was married at the time and had a child. I didn't know how to behave towards my father or even how to address him, so I kept him distant. I never spoke to him alone. I was surprised by my mother's friendliness toward him, given that she had always spoken about him in derisory language.

Later I lived in London and visited him in Hamburg, where he lived in retirement with Franzi. I got to know him a little more and once or twice we even talked together about personal things. He invited me to his home with my little son Daniel and insisted against both our wills that the boy stay with him and Franzi whilst I travelled around Germany visiting old relations. On one visit he took me out to a strip tease club and to see Andy Warhol's film *Flesh* in German. I think my father wanted to see me grow into a man on equal terms with himself. Something he realised he'd missed out on. I was thirty-five at the time.

For all that, I had begun to like him. When I became aware of this, it surprised me. But the thing that was more important to me was the realisation that *he* had actually begun to like *me.*

When he died, I inherited a file containing all our correspondence over twenty years. His letters to me were there in draught form; he wrote everything out in clean copy in his distinct and very tidy hand. In a letter I had written to him from London in 1975 in an equally tidy hand, I said (translated):

It makes me really happy that we have now had the chance
to clear away all the shadows and cobwebs between us.
One finds one has, so to speak, arrived.

Rabe von Randow. We left my brother Rabe on 5ᵗʰ April, 1952,
having barely set foot on Princes Wharf (p.280), whence
Sandy Gordon sped him away in his car. After cruising around
for a couple of weeks, Sandy delivered him to the people who
had a dairy farm, where Rabe worked as a farm help for a year.

Rabe went on to have a distinguished academic career as a
mathematician, qualifying first at Auckland University College
and going on to post-grad studies in Germany, where he gained
his doctorate. Following academic posts in Tuscon, Dunedin
and Durham, Rabe was appointed professor at the University
of Bonn. His published work is listed on the Internet. He lives
in Germany.

I asked him what he would like me to include concerning
himself in these endnotes. He wrote to me with reminiscences
concerning our friends and neighbours in Shanghai during our
childhood years. Many of these have made an appearance in
the pages of this book. He went on:

> Secondly and more importantly, there is one big point that
> I feel should be included, because of us as a family, not just
> me, although I am principally involved. The sequence goes
> as follows. SBS Scout and Wolf Cub outing to Lungwha
> airfield, essays called for, mine won first prize, Rotary
> dinner with Mr. A.H.Gordon, Chief Scout in Shanghai,
> trip to Nanking in 1948, my trip essay in newspapers. This
> formed my connection with Mr. Gordon who soon after
> left for New Zealand. When we thought about where to go
> (Canada Heinemanns, Australia nobody except Bobby and

his Mum who couldn't help), NZ came to mind and there we had a sponsor! His help was of cardinal importance, he went to Wellington for us. And I stayed with him after our arrival to make things easier for Mami. I would like you to incorporate that as a tribute to him who changed our lives so decisively.

A.H.Gordon (Silver Wolf). (p.280) Also known as Sandy Gordon, he had lived in China for thirty years by the time he left for New Zealand in 1951. He was Commissioner of Scouts and Rabe was in his troupe, which had always been connected with the Shanghai British School and the Holy Trinity Cathedral. I can remember the outing to Lungwha Aerodrome as a wolf cub. We were shown into the hangars and I can still see Rabe inspecting the engines of planes that had had their cowls removed for maintenance. He was excited when he read the manufacturers' name *Pratt & Whitney* on the side of an engine. Even more so when he came across *Curtiss-Wright* on another. He was familiar with the makes of engines from his study of *Popular Mechanics* magazines. In his written essay on the outing Rabe must have amazed his assessors and Mr. Gordon in particular with his keen observation. Rabe was twelve at the time. The essay was published in the North China Daily News. The trip to Nanking and back in a C-47 was his prize. And the dinner. He had made his mark with the old scout.

As Rabe points out in his passage above, Sandy Gordon had a cardinal role in getting us to New Zealand. This is not explicit in the pages of my book, because of the Knights' more dominant role in my personal recollections. I hope this note sets the record straight.

Hubertus Court. (p.220) Laszlo Hudec, the architect of Hubertus Court, designed over 50 Shanghai buildings. This apartment building now operates as a hotel. As a child I loved its modern lines, which are smooth and rounded and horizontal. There was an image of a springing stag sandblasted into the glass above the entrance doors. This probably depicts the stag that magically appeared to Saint Hubertus (AD 656-727) and advised him on the ethics of hunting and the dignity of animals. Whatever the case, I loved it. Hudec also did the German Evangelical Church (p.39), which the Communists later demolished to make space for a major hotel. His work ranges from houses such as his own villa in Columbia Road to the famous Park Hotel on Nanking Road and has become well researched in recent years as the Internet coverage shows.

131 Columbia Circle. Hudec also designed the estate known as Columbia Circle (1930) and most likely No.131 Columbia Circle, the house we grew up in (below R). It resembles his own villa (below L) from the half-timbered gable down to the fake beams in the ground floor reception rooms! Both houses were rented to German consular personnel from the late thirties or early forties.

The tenancies of the houses changed with the end of the war. Hudec's villa in Columbia Road has now been restored and turned into a memorial museum of his work. As to the Columbia Circle house, we were able to remain there after my father left, occupying attic rooms only, for some years, whilst the body of the house became home to American servicemen and later to Russian and Italian families. I never really knew who owned the house, but it will have passed into the ownership of the People's Republic at some stage. I don't know if it still stands.

Shirley Grey Brewer. (p.198 et seqq.) Shirley completed her schooling in Canada and has held a post at Sanford University for many years. She published a book of poems entitled *Thistledown* and a biography entitled *The Rabbit in the Moon.* Both deal to a large degree with her life as a girl in Shanghai.

Shum Chun. (pp.270,273) The Shum Chun (or Sham Chun) River south of Canton was designated as the southern boundary of China in 1847, when Hong Kong became a British Colony. About the turn of the century, the British constructed a railway between Hong Kong and Canton. They called it East Rail. A rail bridge was constructed across the river at a small fishing village called Lo Wu. It became the checkpoint between China and the British Territory of Hong Kong. In 1949 the Communists closed the border and no passenger trains were permitted to cross the bridge. From this time until the cession of Hong Kong (1997) the southern leg of East Rail terminated at Lo Wu on the south bank of the river. Its northern leg stopped on the north bank, where the small village of Shum Chun became China's border crossing station, pouring produce and merchandise into Hong Kong. People had to cross the Shum Chun River bridge on foot. It was heavily patrolled. To foreigners leaving China it acquired a legendary ring. Shum Chun grew rapidly in its new role. It is now called Shenzen and has become a major city.

Chain pumps. (p.22) The type of chain pump described in the text of this book is known as the square pallet chain pump. Other types used buckets and other variations to lift the water

to the higher level. They have been used in various places around the world (even Egypt) and go back at least as far as the Han dynasty (1st century A.D.) in China. Joseph Needham recorded chain pumps in his 17 volume work *Science and Civilisation in Ancient China*. There are also detailed drawings of chain pumps in a much earlier (1637) Chinese encyclopedia, which can be found on the Internet. I don't know if chain pumps are still used in China today.

Junkers F13. (pp.251,266,318) I have never flown in one of these aircraft nor even seen one. I always held them to be legendary for their design and for the way they reached out into the most far-flung places on earth. Lufthansa and Eurasia flew F13s into China across the remote mountains of the interior. F13s broke records for distance and for height. F13s brought the mail into China.

The author of *Chinaflug,* the German airman Wulf Diether Graf zu Castell, describes what it was like to fly at high altitudes in one of these planes, in which the pilot and co-pilot sat in an open cockpit. My F13 must have had an enclosed cockpit or I would have frozen to death. But then it *was* only a dream.

The Exit Visa. Had you been, as we were, among the few who were still in Shanghai in 1952, you would have had only one ambition: to get out.

You would have seen to all the usual things like passports

and travel bookings and procured (praise be!) a permit to enter your new country. In our case, New Zealand. You would have seen to the disposal of property, shipped off your household belongings and packed your bags. Finally, you'd have said goodbye to your friends, whom you hoped to see again, and taken leave of your servants if you still had any (in our case, our amah), whom you knew you'd never see again. And with all that behind you, you might have been free to go, but for the exit visa, without which you wouldn't get very far.

Following your friends' advice, you would have applied for your exit visa a year in advance. It gave the authorities time to enquire into your past activities and to question you about them and to let you wait. And this you did in silence, though you were pure as silk. If you were unlucky, a single loose thread or a tip-off from nowhere could see you accused of an offence against the People's Republic of China and your exit visa would be blocked. And if you were lucky and came to grasp the coveted document in your hand, you might weep for joy and share your tears with your friends, but to the rest of the world you would still say nothing. Not until you had crossed the border and set foot in your new country, and then not a soul would understand what you were trying to say.

I was fourteen when we got our exit visa and left China. I think they must have kept the visa at the checkpoint; I can't remember what it looked like. Anyway, it had done its dash and permitted us to walk across a bridge and out of the country. It took less than a minute. Yet it has taken more than fifty years for me to realise that the visa had also given me permission to exit the incomplete world of my adolescence.

Some years ago I re-entered that world and opened it up

to the light. When I did, I found it as I had left it, fresh and raw and adrift with unfinished stories. In writing them down, I have also written my own exit visa and with it I hope to leave them behind.

The Farnsworth House. (p.306) When I was young, we often visited friends in the Hungjao countryside on the western outskirts of Shanghai. A friend of my mother's called Momber had a bungalow there and it was one of my favourite places, because he kept a houseboat in the garden in a specially made shelter (below R). It had an elevated floor and a roof and no walls. Herr Momber always allowed us to play in his houseboat.

Did the Farnsworth house (above L) remind me of that shelter?

Notes to the illustrations

Photo Juras Shanghai.

right and centre. *Photo kindly lent by Rosamond Stewart of Bethells Beach, whose family were in Shanghai at the time.*

338   Eye witness letter of the Japanese attack on Shanghai in 1937.

342   Two pages out of a letter from Hellmuth von Ruckteschell to my mother (ca.1944). The sketches show details of glass rods in the windows of temples in Peking. Written in fountain pen on onion skin airmail paper (two sided).

347   The choir in 1948 on the steps of the Holy Trinity Cathedral cloisters.

351   The house in Terry Street, Blockhouse Bay, designed by Group Architects (1954). On the deck from L-R: Rabe, Ilse, Frieda Bilger, myself (17) mirroring her stance. Frieda (21) was a frequent visitor at the house. She called my mother 'Momma'. *Photo by Tony Pausma.*

352   My mother's house (L) in Tunsin Rd, Shanghai (1935) and (R) in Terry St, Blockhouse Bay, Auckland (1955)

355   The author assembling the weaving loom at the Auckland Museum (1998). It had been built for Ilse von Randow by Studio Seagull in Shanghai ca.1948. It is now in the possession of the Museum. *Photo by Tania Walters, curatorial team, Auckland Museum.*

359   Laszlo Hudec's villa in Columbia Road (L) and our house in Columbia Circle (R). Here Hudec's villa is the venue of a family Thanksgiving event hosted by the then resident German ambassador.

361   Chinese chain pump operated by a buffalo (ca.1933).

362   Chinese postage stamp featuring a Junkers F13 mail plane above the Great Wall of China.

364   Farnsworth House—Mies van der Rohe (L). Momber's boat shelter, Hungjao (R).

Images, texts etc, wherever no source is given, are from the author's own collection.